THE SET OF THE SAILS

Born in Melbourne in 1903, Alan Villiers went to sea in a square rigged ship, the barque *Rothesay Bay*, shortly after the end of World War I, intending to follow a career in the Merchant Navy. Service in another barque, two four-masted barques and the schooner *Hawk* followed. In 1923 he joined the pioneer modern pelagic whaling expedition into the Ross Sea from Sandefjord, Norway. This led to a request from an American publisher to write a book on that little-known subject, and this began his writing career. Returning to Cape Horn Sail in the four-masted barque *Herzogin Cecilie* for her race with the Swedish *Beatrice* from South Australia to Falmouth in 1928, he worked as A.B. in the Finnish ship and wrote a book called *Falmouth for Orders* in watches below. In 1934 he bought the old Danish school-ship, then named *Georg Stage*, renamed it the *Joseph Conrad*, and sailed it 57,000 miles round the world. He has since sailed from Arabia, with the Portuguese fishermen to Greenland waters, with the Maldivians, always recording. He sailed the new *Mayflower* to America in 1957, and the film ships for Peter Ustinov's *Billy Budd* and George Roy Hill's *Hawaii*, among others. He lives now in Oxford and has a punt on the Cherwell. His books include *By Way of Cape Horn*, *The Way of a Ship*, *The War with Cape Horn*, and *Cruise of the 'Conrad'*.

THE SET OF THE SAILS

The Adventures of a Cape Horn Seaman

ALAN VILLIERS

PAN BOOKS LTD : LONDON

First published 1949 by Hodder & Stoughton Ltd.
This edition published 1955 by Pan Books Ltd,
33 Tothill Street, London, SW1.

ISBN 0 330 02990 8

2nd Printing 1956
3rd (Re-set) Printing 1973

Printed in Great Britain by
Richard Clay (The Chaucer Press), Ltd, Bungay, Suffolk

CONTENTS

LIST OF ILLUSTRATIONS

(*between pages* 80 *and* 81)

A weather-side view of the *Parma*
The *Beatrice*
Working on the high yards of the *Grace Harwar*
The *Herzogin Cecilie* from the fore-top

(*between pages* 192 *and* 193)

Making fast the mainsail of the *Parma*
A maindeck view of the *Parma* near Cape Horn
Looking along the leeside of the *Grace Harwar*
A lower topsail being changed on the *Parma*
The *Parma* under all sail
A typical Kuwait *boom*

MAPS

CHAPTER ONE

EARLY DAYS

THE equinoctial gales howled about the little weather-board house and roared through the riggings of the square-rigged ships at the bottom of our street, on the night when I was born. It was September 23rd, 1903. My parents lived at North Melbourne, close by the depot there of the Melbourne and Metropolitan Tramways Board for which my father worked. He was a gripman on the cable trams, and he worked long shifts. The prospect of financing a second son in our small household could not have been a pleasant one, on his small pay. But in the course of the next few years two more sons were born, and two daughters. We were happy enough, I remember, despite financial stringency, which was a state my mother took in her stride and to which my father must have been well accustomed. He was thirty-one years old when I was born, and had been making his own way in the world since he was fourteen. He had spent ten or twelve years pioneering in the Australian bush before he came to the Melbourne trams. My mother was an Irish-Australian from the Clan Hayes, of Ballarat, in Victoria. Her father had sailed out to Melbourne in a small brig from Limerick, in the gold-rush days, and though there was nothing to show that he had ever gathered much gold, he had brought up a family of fourteen stout-hearted and strong-limbed young Australians.

My father's father had died before I was born. His fate was seldom mentioned. All I knew of him was that his name was Frank Villiers, and that he was English by origin and Australian by adoption. From a few things which I overheard, I gathered that the choice of Australia as his domicile might not have been his own. He was well connected in England; he might have been one of those Englishmen whose families sent them to the colonies to be out of the way. The only grounds I ever heard suggested for this banishment were that he had married an actress on the London stage, who travelled with him to Melbourne, and there bore him seven children. There was not even a photograph of this lady in our house. There was some mystery about her, and several of the children. My father's father lost his life in a sailing-ship bound for England, while still a comparatively young man, and his widow, when she heard the news, promptly left for California with her youngest children. As far as I know, nothing more was heard of her, or of our grandfather. I gathered that he was on his way to England to claim some estate when he lost his life, but when I knew that he was a passenger and not a sailor, my childish regard for one who had been dead so long faded to almost nothing.

I remember little of the house where I was born, for we moved very soon to another, farther from the tramway sheds. The house that I remember most clearly is the two-storeyed place on Spencer Street where several of my Ballarat aunts and uncles lived. From the balcony of this house we could see the shipping in the Yarra River and the Spencer Street Docks very clearly. It was exciting to have access to a house with a balcony in Melbourne, where most of the smaller homes were single-storey cottages or bungalows. A house from which you could clearly see what went on aboard great ships seemed wonderful. In the Melbourne of the early 1900s the deep-sea sailing-ship was still a vessel of importance. The square-rigged Cape Horner still competed, more or less successfully, with the low-powered steamer for the long-haul bulk trades, such as wheat and wool from Melbourne to Europe, lumber from the Pacific Slope to build Australian homes, and Baltic boards to floor them. Almost always then, there were a score or more big sailing-ships secured in Yarra berths and in the docks at Williamstown and Port Melbourne. All these were in sight from the house on Spencer Street, and my earliest memories are of gazing at them for hours, before I could walk very much, with wonder and admiration. There were many uncles whose delight it was to take me walks round the docks to see the ships. I don't remember that we ever looked much at steamers, except as necessary and movable parts of the general water-front background. My uncles at Spencer Street were big men whose business was gold. They were prospectors, whose comings and goings were mysterious and eventful. I remember them as tall, browned, bearded men, who used to arrive aboard large ships, come from somewhere out of the blue. Sometimes they came all smiles and prosperous, and would empty little bags of gold-dust and nuggets on the table; more often they returned after years of wandering, feverish and needing rest. They did most of their prospecting in West and North-west Australia and round the New Guinea islands.

I don't remember that they ever told me much about their prospecting adventures, for their life seemed commonplace to them and they rarely spoke of it. But they loved sailing-ships. I was three years old when I first wandered round the Melbourne wharves with them, and stared with wonder at the lovely lines of the *Lochs* and *Glens* and *Shire* ships which then abounded, or aloft at the high riggings, where the west wind sang and the brown-backed sailors scampered at their work. This love of ships and delight in water-front walks were features of Australian life in my boyhood, and there was nothing unusual in the sight of a very small boy trudging along beside some very large uncles in the shadow of a full-rigged ship.

My father also was interested in ships, though it was his custom to regard a trip round the docks as a lesson in visual geography for us. He was much more interested in camping trips round the bay, when he cooked us damper in the ashes, or to the nearby Dandenong hills and along the banks of the Plenty River. I remember my father driving his trams, taking us walks round different parts of Melbourne (always with some purpose, to broaden our minds), and at home writing. He wrote poetry and political articles. His poetry was about the bush and the strivings of man; the articles were to point the way towards a better world, for he was a pioneer in the Australian Labour movement and wrote extensively for its journals. He must have been a man of terrific energy, mental and physical: he did not seem to know what rest meant. Above all, it was his ambition that we children should have a better chance than he had, and he sacrificed his own interests towards this end. I recall his horror when he realized that I should probably go to sea. His attitude towards dock visits changed after that, and I began to organize my own trips there. That was easy enough, for to go right round the berths from our home in Collett Street near the Flemington racecourse, and back again, was a walk of only four or five miles. It was a walk I often made. I kept a secret book in which I drew all the sailing-ships I saw, as accurately as I could present them, and kept a list of their names.

It was my hobby and my delight to make friends aboard the sailing-ships in the docks. Timidly, I went aboard – first, the tiny brigantines and schooners lying in the picturesque Little Dock, at the foot of Spencer Street (long since filled in to make way for an ugly bridge), and then, gathering courage, the great Cape Horners through whose great riggings the west wind roared. I liked Norwegian ships best, as they were the friendliest. My younger brother Frank and I made staunch friends among these. One day we brought Christian Christiansen, able seaman in the barque *Hippen*, home to Sunday dinner, and my parents, though possibly astonished, made him very welcome. After that I saw a good deal of Mr Christiansen and the pretty barque. I secretly renamed myself Christian Christiansen, for this seemed to me a seamanlike and fine-flowing name, far more suitable and adventurous than my own. I tried to get a job in the *Hippen*. I was eleven then, and I knew from Marryat's books and the lives of Cook, Flinders, Bligh and Nelson that that was the right age to go to sea.

Christian Christiansen put in a word for me with the mate of the *Hippen*, a huge man with a pair of enormous walrus *mustachios*. There was nothing strange to him in the idea of a boy of eleven going off to sea, for he had done just that himself, from his home in Grimstad. He was good enough to say that he would gladly have me, but the shipping master would not allow me to be signed on. There was an Australian law against the employment of boys under the age of fourteen: how could this difficulty be overcome?

By hiding aboard, I suggested, and coming up when the barque was outside and it was too late for the shipping master – whoever he was – to do anything about it.

'No, no, sonny,' said the mate. 'That won't do. Only criminals and foolish people hide in ships.'

'But Mr Christiansen could help me. I could be in the forecastle,' I chirped hopefully. 'It wouldn't really be hiding. You could know I was there.'

The big mate laughed. He pointed out, however, that at the time there was a dreadful war in Europe, towards which the *Hippen* was then bound. She might not arrive. And if she did arrive, how could I get back to Melbourne? I could easily find myself in the position of being either stranded in a port many thousands of miles from home or compelled to follow the sea as a mere means of livelihood. The Norwegian mate gave me some excellent advice which I have never forgotten.

'Don't be *forced* to stay at sea, sonny,' he said, 'just because you commit yourself before you know what you are doing. If you came here with us, or in any other of these deep-water ships' – he swept a critical eye round the berths where many lay – you'd have to stay, or be stranded. It is better to sail in your own ships first, out of your own port, so you can know whether you wish to stay. The sea needs the best men,' he went on, 'and not just those forced into its service. Give yourself a chance. Get a voyage in a Tasmanian schooner or in the trade to New Zealand; then you know you'll be home again, and when you come you'll know just what being in a sailing-ship is like. It's easy to imagine that it's more adventurous and exciting than it really is. The sea is a dreadful place. Men aren't fish, and ships can founder.'

'But Mr Christiansen said you went to sea yourself when you were ten, sir!' I said, taken aback.

'Yes, I did. And I'm still a mate. And I don't know my own children. Mind you, I don't regret going in ships. But I like to see a young fellow do things with his eyes open.' He gave me a shrewd glance. 'I didn't read books, you know,' he went on. 'I went to sea because I had to, and when I'd gone I had to stay. Don't let the books fool you, my boy. There's no sailor writing them.'

So the *Hippen* sailed, after many days, without me. It was as well I did not try to run away in her, for she never came in again – neither she, nor three other Norsemen and a French four-master which sailed with her.

One of the other sailing-ships which went out with the *Hippen* was a Norwegian full-rigged ship named *Asmund*, another favourite of mine. She lay in the Victoria Docks a long time. She was a big ship with white masts and yards, and the captain had his family aboard. This included a small girl, perhaps five years old. She was always playing on the poop when I came near the ship. Her incredible fairness and seemingly angelic disposition – I never knew her well, for I spoke no Norwegian and she no English – bewitched me. All the small boys and girls I knew were tough little Australians with sun-tanned faces and bare knees and anything but the dispositions of young angels. This small child, with her soft face, her quaint clothes with long woollen stockings, and her pure white hair, seemed to me someone out of the wonderful world of adventure, as remote from humdrum everyday life as the lovely ship she sailed in, and the great man her father who sailed the ship. I decided to learn Norwegian, but could find no text-books – only books about Maori, and French, and Latin. I tried to start a movement at Essendon High School for the promotion of knowledge of the Scandinavian tongues, instead of dead Latin; but I found no supporters. Only I knew about the *Asmund* and that little girl.

Then the *Asmund* sailed, too, and she also went missing.

After Christian Christiansen came to our home my father decided that something ought to be done about my too great interest in ships and the sea, for the sea as a profession held no attractions for him. One day he brought a fellow-gripman home with him, a man from Wales who had sailed for years in clipper ships and West Coast barques, in the savage trade from the Bristol Channel round Cape Horn. I took an immediate liking to this big man, whose function was to talk me out of any wish to go to sea. Delighted to find so interested and knowledgeable a listener, he warmed to his subject and stayed hours, poor man, after his welcome was worn out, telling me of the great clippers in the China trade, and the rigours of Cape Horn west'ard roundings. It must have been years since he had been able to let himself go so fluently, for he was a married man with a family. He had a grand day, but my father was more worried than ever.

The old Welshman was a big man with enormous shoulders and a great chest like a Darling Downs bull, and all his discourse was of tops'ls and foaming seas, and of furling t'gall'nts, and running the easting down. I brought him out my secret book, in which were rigging plans of all the ships I'd seen, from the *Joseph Sims* – a tarred old-timer of a tops'l schooner in the Hobart trade – to the great four-masters *Howth*, *Rowena*, *Inverness-shire*, *Skansen I*. I noticed with regret that he did not share my regard for Scandinavian ships, which he called 'squareheads'. To him there was but one flag for ships, and that the Red Duster; but one nation of true seamen, and that the British. All others except Yanks were definitely inferiors, permitted to sail in old British ships on sufferance. Why, he said, there wasn't one of them who could sing a chanty, or build a clipper, except the British, and Blue Noses, and Yanks. I had no idea what a Blue Nose was and the prospect of learning about them was fascinating, but my father announced that the time had come for them to go to the tram sheds to begin their shift. The old Welshman departed, and I had visions of his huge bulk jammed in the driver's pew of a cable tram, flinging down grips round corners and picking them up again, while his heart heard the roar of Cape Horn gales, and in his mind's eye, great silent ships under a press of trade-wind sail followed each other through sunlit days, and he did not heed the grey buildings of the Melbourne streets towering over his small tramcar.

After that visit I was more than ever determined to go to sea in sail, to taste this grandly adventurous life for myself. My father said that it only seemed adventurous because I was building up my ideas of it from my own imaginings, fed on books, and the sight of ships in a safe port. The sea, he pointed out, was no safe port. But the cool loveliness of the silver-grey wind ships lying in the bay, and the song of the wind in their high riggings, stirred me deeply, and I vowed I would sail in such ships as soon as I could. My parents' pleadings that I should devote myself to school and win a scholarship there which would take me on to Melbourne University were largely wasted on me. The essential thing, said my father, was to become qualified in a profession. There was no way for the unqualified save Dead End Road, and the sea for me would be a dead-end calling. I knew that he was talking sense, but my ambition to go to sea in sailing-ships grew rather than lessened.

The years passed slowly – very slowly. Between the ages of ten and fifteen a year is a long, long time, and a term at school can be a drawn-out purgatory. In our home it was essential that the older children should contribute what they could to the family income; from the age of nine my elder brother and I had newspaper rounds, and when we were twelve we worked at the Spotswood glass-bottle factory. It was easy to get work there in the summer vacations from the high school, for the work was hot and trying, and no questions were asked. The pay was good and boys were much in demand there. It was forbidden, of course, for anyone under the age of fourteen to be employed in any factory. But we looked older than we were, and no one was particular. If a clerk asked for a birth certificate – which was rarely – we used each in turn to produce the elder brother's and he meantime was in the same factory under another name. The clerks never could get our name right. I must appear many times on the glassworks' books as Williams, or McVilly, or even Villari, from Kensington.

We worked, on the average, about two months of each year in the bottle works, most of it in the hottest part of the Melbourne summer when our high school was closed for vacation.

The work was hard, the hours long, and there was much night work. But the factory stood at the river's edge, and sailing-ships towed past. This was during the 1914–18 war, and though the *Lochs* and *Glens* and all the other sailing liners were things of the past, many deep-sea sailing-ships continued to trade to Melbourne. They came with general cargoes from New York or nitrates from Chile, and they loaded grain for Europe. Inside the factory it was hot and hellish, but the sight of a Cape Horner was compensation enough for me. Once the five-masted barque *France* towed past, and the sight was fascinating. The whole factory stopped work to look at her.

I did well enough at school, and won my scholarship. For this the credit was the school's and not mine, for I was not as interested as I should have been. My father allowed me then to present myself for the Australian naval college examinations, in which I was interested when I heard that the navy had a full-rigged ship, an ex-clipper from the passenger trade, sailing out of Sydney. This ship was named *Tingira*, but had been the *Sobraon*, a famous Cape Horner. Half-way through the examinations I learned with disgust that she was rigged down and sailed no longer. The naval college was nothing but a group of buildings at Jervis Bay, on the coast of New South Wales, where one would be expected to remain for a full four years. When I learned that I lost interest, and the selection committee, very wisely, decided that a naval life was not for me.

There was an election in the state of Victoria and my father, because of his years of service in the Labour cause, was selected to contest a hopeless seat. I suppose the idea was to try him out. If he did well there, then in the next elections he might be allowed to contest a seat there was real hope of winning. To his opponent's and his party's great astonishment, he almost won the seat. At last it seemed that he would find a greater scope for his immense energies than could ever be possible while he had to spend his working life driving cable trams.

But he had driven himself too hard. He had overworked consistently for years, without ever thinking of himself. Wherever there was a cause to champion for the underdog, he championed it by word and thought and deed; when there was a difficult meeting to address, I noticed that the party bosses came to our house with long faces, and he was selected to address it. It seemed to escape his notice – though it did not escape mine, even when very young – that he did a great deal of the donkey-work for a movement which, great as were its early aspirations, sometimes came regrettably short of carrying out its ideals. While he maintained his stout belief in the essential nobility of man, my father in his daily life made ample allowances for the dreadful mediocrity of most of his fellow human beings. He used to expound to us on our walks the duties of good citizens, and point out how here a railway had been ill designed through man's cupidity, or there a noxious trade had been allowed to permeate a poor-class residential area to the detriment of every home for miles around. He told us that these things ought not to be in a free, new land, and the way to prevent them was by the education of good citizens. Man in his profit-grabbing frailty would undo any good that was done by God, if he were allowed, and dissipate his whole heritage. He counselled us to lead purposeful lives, to fight for years if needs be towards some enlightenment of our minds that we might be the better able to give service to our community and to our fellow humans; to accept any privation rather than forgo education by which we could absorb something of the knowledge that abounded in the world. Above all, we must learn to think clearly, to reason soundly, to live the lives of worthy citizens.

'Never forget,' I can hear him saying now, 'that your time on earth is a gift from God which you ought to use, with His other gifts, to enrich all living, if you can.'

He was still speaking of such things when our first ride in a motor-car took him to the Melbourne hospital, a place for which he had no liking. My father was not a deeply religious man. I do not recall that he went much to churches. He used to give us his little harangues as we walked along, perhaps coming from the Victoria market, or a visit to the docks. Or he spoke to us while we clung to the side of his cable tram, after bringing him his supper in a small black bag. He would always end by saying that we must pay attention to what he said, not what he did.

'Do not take my conduct for your precepts, but my advice,' he would say with a grin.

When we reached the hospital, where he expected to be an out-patient for perhaps a few weeks, he was at once admitted. There was an operation for cancer, which was far advanced. It was hopeless. He was sewn up again. They gave him drugs. Within a week he had died. They brought him home in his coffin, which was left with the lid not yet screwed down, in our darkened front room. The Ballarat Irish uncles, the old colleague from the Welsh West-coasters and the clipper ships, the Labour politicians and the tramwaymen, and all his friends came to pay their last respects. I went in when they had gone. He looked peaceful lying there, and it seemed to my youthful eyes that he was better dressed in the undertaker's clothes than I had ever seen him in life. I touched the high forehead. It was cold. The lips were grey, and the blue eyes had smiled for the last time. What an end was this, to a full life of brave and unlimited endeavour! To be shut there in a long black box, helpless, hopeless, finished, gone. There was a plaque on the coffin-lid:

LEON JOSEPH VILLIERS,
BORN AT MELBOURNE DECEMBER 25, 1872,
THE SON OF FRANK AND CATHERINE VILLIERS.
DIED APRIL 10, 1918.

He was born. He lived forty-five years. He died. In the cupboard at his feet lay heaps of his manuscripts, his *Songs of Labour and of Love*, his poems of the Australian bush, now never to be revised. All his great hopes for his country and for us, his sons, were in that coffin too; somehow I knew that. He was an Australian of great vision and abiding faith in the destiny of the southern commonwealth; none of us would ever approach the standards set by him, or even begin to appreciate, for years, the values by which he had lived. He had risen above his environment, and he had taken us with him though we were all so young when he died.

Next day they threw earth down on the coffin, in a corner of the Coburg cemetery, and the dull thud of the clods was agony to hear. I thought of many things as I stood there. What was it he had said?

'Do not take my conduct for your precepts, but my advice.'

I knew that if the pattern of my conduct throughout my life came near to his, then I would have little heed to remember the advice.

CHAPTER TWO

LOOKING FOR A SHIP

FOR almost a year after my father's death I continued at school, for my mother said that I must give up the idea of going to sea, in respect to my father's wishes. I tried to put sailing-ships out of my mind, but they were still in the river. The class paid a visit to the Melbourne gas-works as part of a course in chemistry, and the four-masted barque *Caledonia* lay in the river near by. I found it difficult to concentrate on processes for the extraction of Melbourne's gas from Newcastle coal. We were taken to learn swimming in the South Melbourne baths, and a Swedish barque came sailing up Port Phillip Bay, and the stench of South Seas copra from the schooner *Lottie Bennett* filled the air. I became a poor swimmer. It was not long before I was pointing out to my mother that, with six of us to keep and educate, surely if one went it would make the maintenance of the others easier. This was an argument to which she gave no heed, though already life was difficult for her. My father had died just as he was about to reap some reward for his years of endeavour, and the family circumstances would have improved considerably if he had lived another year. His death left us almost destitute. The Labour movement came to my mother's aid, and established her in a small suburban shop.

My mother was a person of quiet pertinacity and infinite endurance, and she threw her whole energies into making a success of this shop. But she knew nothing of shopkeeping. The place was in a mean suburb. The oldest of her children was fifteen. We might have been useful enough on a newspaper round, or working through vacations in the glass-bottle works to earn something towards the cost of our clothes, but round a grocer's shop we were in the way. Just how my mother contrived to look after the six of us, and run that shop, I never have been able to understand. The effort wore down even her great constitution, and when the Spanish influenza epidemic struck Melbourne in early 1919, she was one of the first victims. By the time she recovered we had lost the shop.

Through that influenza epidemic I went to sea. Many of Melbourne's public buildings were hurriedly converted into hospitals to cope with the sick. My high school, being a fine modern building very suitable as a hospital, was among the first taken. This disrupted my schooling so severely that it came to a sudden end. I went off to work at the bottle works, as soon as I had recovered from my own share of influenza. Weeks dragged into months and there was no word of the school's reopening, or much abatement in the epidemic. The pupils were to be informed by mail when the school reopened. I never was informed. One day I got into the train at Spotswood station after the night shift at the bottle works, and seated in the compartment was a girl from my class at Essendon High. She was in school rig and she had her books. There was no mistake about it. Her hat-band bore the school's colours. She hadn't changed schools. I was black and sweaty from my night's work, for the factory provided no changing facilities. I sat in a corner seat and gazed out of the window, for I hoped against hope that the girl would not know me. The hope was vain.

Our high school was co-educational, but there was a stupid rule that the sexes must not converse together. In the difficult early years of adolescence the presence of girls became a torment. One looked at them, as the slow painful development of manhood increased the problems of daily life, not so much as fellow humans of a different sex, but as a different sort of human altogether. The girl in the carriage was a pretty blonde with a slight — very slight — trace of the child of the *Asmund* about her. I felt I was disgraced, in her eyes, and I took no steps to find out how long the school had been reopened. Nor did I ever go there again.

Instead, I looked about me for a ship to sail in, and changed to the night shift permanently in order to have the days to search in. There was no ship. What I could have done at the age of eleven or twelve, now, it seemed, I could not do. No longer did Cape Horn ships lie deep-laden in Port Phillip Bay awaiting crew to take them to sea, and offering a hundred pounds for the run to Europe. There were still a few Britishers about in which I might have become a premium apprentice, but we had no funds to buy a place in the half-deck of some miserable lime-juicer, to work four years there without pay. The fine big British sailing school-ships – the *Medway*, *Port Jackson*, *Illawarra*, and the like – were already a thing of the past. I should have to begin before the mast, but whenever I approached any Tasman Sea trader she was grossly over-manned, or about to lay up, or manned exclusively by clannish New Zealanders who had no place for a Melbourne greenhorn. New Zealand then had many lovely barques and I tried to ship in at least half a dozen of them, but was rejected by them all. The barque *Dartford* and the *Gladbrook* came in from Chile, and sweet-lined little timber barques came up the Yarra. The Australian barque *Shandon*, which was managed by the Government and sailed out of Melbourne, had a waiting list a fathom long. I tried every vessel in the Little Dock, even the lowliest ketch there, but they recruited all their small crews from Melbourne's doss-houses and had no place for a raw-boned boy. I began to fear that I should never get away. I loved the ships, though they rejected me, and I was still profoundly moved by the loveliness and by the sound of the wind in their powerful riggings.

The elderly master of the rakish schooner *Joseph Sims* at last set my feet in the right direction. He told me to get in touch with the Melbourne Ancient Mariners' Club, which ran a school for sea-minded boys at Albert Park, a suburb of the city. If the boys were any use, he said, they were shipped off to sea. The school was conducted by the marine surveyor of the port, an old sailing-ship man named Captain Charles Suffern.

I went down to Albert Park Lake the very next Saturday, and applied to the captain. I found him busily assembling the rigging of a small brigantine, which he had contrived out of an old lifeboat. My examination for enrolment in this school was very brief, for the captain was a man who wasted no words. All a boy needed were good health, his parents' consent, a Board of Trade certificate for good vision, and the desire to go to sea in sail. This last was most important. If you wanted to ship in steam, the school was not for you. You could find a steamer for yourself. But if you showed promise in the little brigantine and responded to instruction, then the captain and all the other ancient mariners would do their best to find you a real ship. You were expected to take the first place they found, regardless of ship or trade. The captain was very particular as to the ships he sent his boys in, and he always preferred the Tasman Sea barques. Most of the masters of these were members of the club, and did all they could to help. Several small barques and barquentines had installed half-decks for half a dozen boys, and when I joined, the scheme was thriving.

It was entirely unofficial, and had grown up through the energetic efforts of a seaman named Jones. Captain Edwin Jones was an officer in the Australian service of the White Star Line who had landed in Melbourne some years earlier, when his eyes failed him, and he could no longer follow the sea. He found the Australians doing little about sea training for their youth, apart from a sailing reformatory converted from an old *Loch* Line barque, and so he founded the Ancient Mariners' Club to foster the sea spirit and train boys for the sea. He launched a branch of the sea scouts with the same purpose, and to assist in the character-building of youth generally.

By the time I joined, Captain Jones had long returned to England; but the great spirit of that little man with the enormous eyebrows and the Cape Horn voice was still there, and the good work carried on. I was delighted to find the place, and sorry only that I had not known of it before. There were Ancient Mariners' boys then in half the barques in the Tasman Sea, in the Government's *Shandon*, and the German prize full-rigger *Cardinia* out of Sydney; in the little Tasmanian barquentines and a minute square-rigger running to the Gilberts and Marshalls for a Chinaman in New South Wales. None went in lime-juice ships, for the Ancient Mariners were opponents of the wretched apprentice system prevailing in them, to a man.

Those old sailing-ship captains were long-headed men, and it did not require much foresight or common sense to appreciate the very real need both for its own ships and seamen, in a continent with so long and vulnerable a shore-line and so weak a system of internal communications as Australia. The Ancient Mariners sought to build up good seafaring citizens, with broad minds, a thorough competence in their profession, and a stake in their country. Though at the time I could scarcely appreciate all the reasons for its being, I threw myself wholeheartedly into the school's activities and wished that it was residential. We attended twice a week and on Saturday afternoons. Captain Suffern, Captain Jones' successor, and an old sailing-ship boatswain were our instructors. Under their guidance we learned to pull an oar; to handle a boat under sail or oars; to worm, parcel, and serve both wire and rope; to do simple splices, the usual knots, and some fancy-work; to use the lead, read the log, box the compass; and signal by lamp, semaphore and with the flags of the international code. When we sailed the brigantine, the captain used the manoeuvres and words of command of a big sailing-ship, in order that when we went to sea the everyday orders about a square-rigger's decks would not seem strange to us.

Many seamen scoffed at the Ancient Mariners for their ideas, and said the modern steamship officer had no need of knowledge gained in sailing-ships. Such ships, they said, were doomed, and would soon be dead. Of what use was it to learn horsemanship when you would have an automobile to drive all the days of your life? In their turn, the old sea-dogs furiously rejected the very thought of motors. Such loathsome things were dependent upon petrol, and Australia had no fuel of that description. We went in sailing-ships or we went in nothing. The captain stuck to his guns. It was character he was after, he said. Any fool could have some knowledge. A year or so in a Tasman Sea barque would find what we were made of. As moulders of character and developers of the true sea spirit in keen boys, the sailing-ship stood unrivalled.

All this I absorbed and approved heartily, for all the sea books I'd read were of adventures under sail, and no wind sang in the bare riggings of steamers. I wanted to be captain of a sailing-ship, not just to sail in one for a year or so. If I wanted to be captain of a British sailing-ship, I had to hurry. That was just the thing I could not do. There were six or eight boys at the school before me, and berths were scarce. I had to wait my turn and be patient while I waited. It seemed to me, aged fifteen, that I had already been waiting a long, long time.

Months passed, and still I had no ship. A few boys went off in the *Louis Theriault*, an ex-Blue Nose schooner which the Ancient Mariner in command promised to convert to a barquentine, for she had three fine masts. Ordinarily, the Mariners regarded schooners as little better than powered vessels, because of their lack of square sail. But by 1919 they had to send some boys in schooners to get them under sail at all. Many American schooners used to visit Melbourne, but none of us went in those. The Ancient Mariners were suspicious of American sailing-vessels. The Yankee skys'l yard barque *Montauk*, a lovely wooden sailer, was looking for hands while I sought a ship. But when I approached her it was to see a man being carried down the gangway on a stretcher, after some altercation, and the ear-biting habits of her chief mate were publicized in the newspapers. Apparently the mate of the *Montauk* preferred biting off racalcitrant sailors' ears to knocking them down with a belaying pin. I saw plenty of spare belaying pins in the barque's rails. Her decks were beautifully white and her yards gleamed with fresh varnish, but the view on the waterfront was that she was a hell-ship. A boy had to use some care about shipping in Yankee sail, even then.

At last, about four months after I had joined the school, my chance came. The captain told my mother that if she would send me to Port Adelaide there was a place for me as a cadet in the half-deck of the barque *Rothesay Bay*, an old-timer in the trade between Austrailia and New Zealand which sometimes made voyages to San Francisco, or with coal among the islands.

CHAPTER THREE

THE *ROTHESAY BAY*

THE one-horse cab trundled slowly down Collett Street, bound in the general direction of the Spencer Street railway station, from which unpretentious collection of sheds the express for Adelaide departed daily. My sea-chest from the chandlers on Flinders Street was beside the driver. It was a fine old sea-chest with a painting of the full-rigged ship *Sörfareren*, done in ship's paint, on the inside of the lid, and the chest had sloping sides and beckets of fancy-worked sennit at either end, painted red, white, and blue. I was very proud of the sea-chest and the double-breasted plain blue jacket I was wearing.

My mother and the senior Ballarat Irish aunt – she who had presided over the establishment from which I first saw ships – were with me in the cab. Two envious small brothers, a scornful older brother (not for him any going off to be sea-sick!), and two small sisters had all gone off to school, earlier in the day. We lived too close to bare existence, then, for any show of sentiment. There were few farewells. My mother and all my aunts still regretted my decision to adopt the sea as a career, instead of something safe and profitable ashore. My aunt had something to say on the subject, even in the cab. But my mother said nothing. She had given me the best outfit she could, since I was determined to go; she did not want me to be a sailor but, since it was my wish, then I had her blessing. I missed the support of the adventurous uncles, but they were all away in the wilds of North-west Australia, looking for gold.

In the train I did not look much at Melbourne, except when the track passed near the glass-bottle factory at Spotswood. There was a big barque towing past, bound out to sea, and my heart lifted to think that at last I, too, was off to sail in a vessel like that. Finished with the bottle works! Finished with the land! My plans were all well laid (I thought). First I would serve four years in deep-sea sailing-ships, not a minute of it in a ship with an engine. Because of the cadet system, I did not know how long I might be in the *Rothesay Bay* – a year or so for a start, at any rate. Then any ship I could find that was bound Cape Horn, for that classic headland was beyond the range of the *Bay* barque in her last days. She was confined to the Pacific. I would use sailing-ships to wander as much as I could, as the old gripman friend of my father had done – I would go to California, to Chile and Peru, to the Scandinavian timber ports, to Buenos Aires and Rio de Janeiro, to Singapore and Cochin-China, and Delagoa Bay and Mobile, Alabama. I would sail in a barque, a full-rigged ship, and a four-masted barque – at least in one example of each rig – but no schooners, nor even a barquentine, if I could avoid it. I would learn all I could, and save every penny of my pay, first to reimburse my mother for the expense of my outfit, and then to finance the necessary spell ashore to attend some nautical academy to cram for a second mate's certificate. I was acquainted with the regulations for the granting of that certificate, and my books included several large tomes, most of them set out in appallingly dull questions and answers on what a second mate must know. After my second mate's 'ticket' was gained, I would find a berth as second mate in some deep-sea sailing-ship. A year or so of that, and then ashore again for the chief mate's ticket. Then another berth as officer in whatever sailing-ship I could find, and I would take my master's ticket just as soon as I was able. I had to do twelve months as a watch-keeping officer in a deep-sea ship, after gaining the mate's certificate, before being allowed to present myself for master. But I thought I ought to have all the certificates astern of me by the time I was twenty-three. After that, I would join some good sailing-ship line and work up to command.

Just what sailing-ship line there might be for me to join by then, or precisely how one set about working up to command at the age of twenty-three, or any other age, I didn't know. These things did not worry me much, as the Victorian country-side sped past and the sprawling suburbs of Melbourne were left behind. I thought that at any rate there ought to be sailing-ships in the Tasman Sea for another ten years, and if there were few other deep-water men about, there would be French-men, and West Coast Americans, and Norwegians, Finns, and Swedes. I did not then seriously contemplate going in foreign ships, except perhaps Norwegians, for I had the insular Aus-tralian's dread of most foreign things. There were nine big French Cape Horners in Melbourne and Geelong as I left, to say nothing of a dozen other big square-riggers, mainly Nor-wegian. A fellow-cadet from Captain Suffern's had written from the barque *Manurewa* at Newcastle that there were between thirty and forty big sailing-ships in the port, all in commission. I thought I should somehow find a sailing-ship to command when the time came. First I had to fit myself for command.

At Adelaide I met another lad from Captain Suffern's, Ginger MacNamara, also aged fifteen and also bound to join the half-deck of the *Rothesay Bay*. Ginger was a pale lad with red hair and bright blue eyes. His mother had packed his clothes in a couple of suit-cases, unmindful of the blunder she was making. Ginger apologized for the suit-cases and said he hoped we should be able to get our gear aboard by night, so that no one would see them. The barque was at an outport on St Vincent's Gulf loading some stuff called gypsum for a small place in the North Island of New Zealand. Neither of us had any idea what gypsum was, though I thought I remembered some of the stuff at the bottle factory. We made our way towards the outport – a place called Edithburgh – in a small steamer. The sea breeze blew fresh up the Gulf and brought up a nasty short sea, in which the steamer bounced along with a hideous motion. Both Ginger and I felt far from well, and another cadet, who was joining with us, felt greatly superior because he was not seasick. His name was Tom Germein. He was a South Australian, and his father was a master mariner on the coast. Tom had already made a coastwise passage or two with his father and had an air about him of the true seaman, though he had been only in steam. Ginger mentioned the matter of his suit-cases to the veteran, wondering whether he ought not to throw at least one of them away rather than commit the error of arriving at his first ship with his gear not stowed in the traditional chest, or bag, or – better still – no gear at all. But Tom said it would be all right. Lots of fellows were using suit-cases, even in the forecastle. Tom was a tall, dark lad with a likeable grin, and Ginger felt much relieved.

The *Rothesay Bay* had been years sailing out of Australia, when we joined her that day in 1919, but she did not appear in my book of ships. I had not seen her previously; probably she did not come much to Melbourne. She was owned, then, by a Sydney firm of timber merchants who had interests in sawmills in New Zealand, from which they stocked their lumber-yards in Sydney and elsewhere. They used the *Rothesay Bay*, and one or two other old sailing-ships, to bring their own timber from New Zealand, and sent her across to that Dominion with any cargo they could find. Sometimes high freights induced them to send her to California, or across to Chile. But she was less than 800 tons, and did not carry enough to pay on long voyages, even in 1919: her prospects of another run to the United States then were not good.

She looked the very embodiment of romance and sea adventure to the three of us as we surveyed her across the Edithburgh pier, though her hold was full of gypsum, her bow was unmistakably bluff, and her old iron sides and all her masts and yards were covered with paint of ugly war-time grey. She was a very ordinary sort of barque, as far as we could see – flush-decked, with a small raised poop a couple of feet off the maindeck, which did not break the line of her sheer. White railings round this poop and a white figurehead of a girl were the only relieving features in her drab grey. Even her for'ard house was grey. She had a spike bowsprit, being bowsprit and jib-boom in one spar, and she was rigged with two deep topsails, big single topgallants, and what looked like small royals on each of her two square-rigged masts. The mizzen-mast carried the standing gaff and boom of the typical lime-juicer, and the spanker was brailed in against the mast, and gaff tops'l stowed partly in the top, partly by the mast doublings.

She had two lifeboats carried on skids before the break of the poop, an open wheel, and only one capstan. This was on the forecastle head, where it was obviously placed to provide power for the windlass. Her sails were bent and, except for some of the heavier braces which were triced up, her gear looked clear for running.

I took all this in with a long, slow glance. There was nobody in sight on her decks, and as she surged the gangway to her rail squeaked slowly backwards and forwards on the quay.

As we struggled to the head of the short gangway lugging our heavy gear, we were met by a yellow-faced man, dressed in a singlet, a pair of very dirty nondescript trousers, a chef's cap, and a pair of carpet slippers. This strange individual came out of the galley and burst into loud laughter at the sight of us. He had a few straggly hairs on his very long chin, some yellow teeth stuck awry in his big mouth, and a laugh that was almost like that of a maniac.

In intervals between his silly mirth he shouted about us, and made offensive remarks.

'Gawd! More bloody boys! All right, you little barsteds, come aboard, but stay out of my bloody galley! Oh, look at Lord Ginger. Blimey! *Suit-cases!* Hey, HEY, Jack. Come'n look at this. Marchin' up the gangplank carryin' bloody suit-cases! Ho, ho, ho! Where's yer brass buttons, me lords? Sailors with suit-cases! Gawd!'

The appalling din he set up at least had the effect of bringing someone else on deck. A severe, thin-lipped man emerged from the companion aft, and walked to the poop rail. His savagely cold eyes showed no laughter, and looked as if they never had. He surveyed us with what might have been a look of deep contempt, or perhaps was just his ordinary expression. He had a lean, jutting jaw, and an expression on his whole being of cold and efficient ferocity. He was an oldish man to us. He must have been about forty.

His appearance sent the cook off the decks, still slobbering about the suit-cases and carrying on a long monologue about the uselessness of boys in general.

'You're the new boys?' The question was rapped at us.

'Yes, sir,' said Tom.

'Half-deck's aft. That's the way' – pointing to a teak companion immediately before the mizzen-mast, in the fore part of the poop. 'It's the old sail-locker. Captain will sign you on tonight, at eight. I'm the second mate.'

The way he said he was second mate sent a shiver through me, even on that hot afternoon. There was a bitterness in it I did not understand. Indeed, I was not prepared for either the welcome from the yellow-fanged cook or the apparent ferocity of the second mate. Somewhat taken aback, we made our way towards the companion he had indicated. Without a further word, he had turned and gone, leaving us to find our way as best we could. He gave poor Ginger's suit-cases a look that would have set fire to anything inflammable that might have been in them. Ginger quailed.

The companion leading to the half-deck was open, and we made our way down the steep steps into a gloomy, narrow compartment, lit by a couple of heavy ports. This compartment extended the width of the ship. A partition divided the sleeping quarters from a rude sort of mess-room, in which there were a bench and a long narrow table, and some utensils of tin and enamel. The sleeping quarters contained six bunks.

On the best of these, a slight figure lay asleep. There was no one else about. The sleeper looked nineteen or twenty years of age, a mature adult to the likes of us, much older than we had expected to find anyone in the half-deck. The noise of our gear clattering down the companion woke the stranger. He opened one cold blue eye and surveyed us without enthusiasm.

'New boys?' he said, at last. 'How many of you?'

'Three,' said Tom, who as the oldest was our spokesman.

'Gawd,' said the tired one. 'That means every bloody bunk. And I thought we were going to have some peace this voyage. Oh, well, find yourselves bunks, and stow your gear where you can. Mind you stow it tidily, though. How you're going to stow the bloody great shop you've brought aboard I don't know, when we haven't a spare bunk.'

He sat up in his bunk, which was fore-and-aft and immediately below the only port in the sleeping quarters, and gave us a closer look. The bunks were nothing but narrow wooden shelves, each six feet long and just wide enough for a boy. There were six lockers, secured with bits of wire, against the after bulkhead. A sea-chest was lashed in the space beside the fore-and-aft bunk below the senior boy's. The lockers, the chest, and the three tiers of bunks were all the half-deck contained. It was a bare place, but each of the bunks with a bed in it was arranged very neatly, with built-in shelves, photographs in frames, and the precious possessions of the occupant neatly stowed within his reach.

The only two fore-and-aft bunks were occupied, and there was nothing to choose between the others. We took one each, and Tom immediately set about making his comfortable, showing Ginger and me how to do the same thing. Within a remarkably short space of time he had his bunk looking ship-shape and ready for use. He stowed spare shirts and other clothing in a pillow-case, and this was the only pillow he had. Though he brought a large canvas sea-bag well filled with gear, somehow he managed to stow all of it away without seeming to encumber anything. Ginger and I tried our best to do the same, but failed miserably. This was obviously an art to be acquired with experience.

The young man on the fore-and-aft bunk surveyed our efforts without comment, other than to point out that he was boss of the half-deck, and everything had to be shipshape and apple-pie or we'd be sorry for it. Oilskins and sou'westers – he assumed we'd brought them – had to be hung in the minute space at the foot of the companion. We could have one locker each, and no more, and we were individually responsible for the safe stowage of everything in the locker, that nothing banged about when the ship got outside. Our eating utensils were stowed in racks on the bulkhead of the mess-room (and we ought to consider ourselves damn' lucky to be in a half-deck with a mess-room, said the boss, for it was the only one he knew in the whole bloody Pacific). We would get our 'whack' of food, and our bare whack – no more. As for wash-ing, we had better get ourselves some kerosene tins to cut down while they were to be had: these we could use both for bathing (when there was water) and for doing our washing (when it rained).

'The trouble with boys,' said our reluctant mentor, 'is they don't know how to live. Well, here you'll learn – and *bloody* fast. Just remember now, anything you want to know I'll show you – once. The second time I'll crack you.'

He further pointed out that the five cadets in the half-deck (he did not rate himself as cadet) took turns at bringing the food from the galley and cleaning out the quarters. The turns were a day each in port, and a week each at sea, in strict rota-tion, come day go day, seasick, homesick, or just plain lazy. The work must go on regardless of all other considerations, and the quarters be clean – all shipshape and apple-pie, and no damned Irish pennants! Ginger and I didn't know what an Irish pennant was, for there'd been none about the Ancient Mariners' establishment. Tom Germein confided that Irish pennants were untidy loose ends of anything left flapping anywhere.

'Sailors don't like 'em,' said Tom.

It was beginning to be obvious that there were many things sailors did not like, which had never bothered me in the past. I began to wonder just how accurate a picture of the sea life the books I'd read might have given me. I racked my brains, and could recall no yellow-fanged sea cooks, cadaverous and savage-eyed second mates, half-deck bosses aged twenty with the ideas of cleanliness of a hospital matron, and an air of re-lentless efficiency which was almost frightening. But perhaps it was only an air. True, I saw no Irish pennants about the old barque, and her decks and rigging were certainly 'shipshape and apple-pie' enough for anyone. Everything was neat and clean and properly secured.

The arrival of the evening meal and the two other cadets, simultaneously, gave a more cheerful prospect to things, for the two cadets were both thoroughly likeable young fellows of little more than our own age. They had each been only one previous voyage in the barque, and were therefore infinitely closer to us than the twenty-year-old 'boss'. One of these boys was from Captain Suffern's, the other was a cheerful young New Zealander named Dave Freeman. They made us welcome, and we were grateful to them.

Dave Freeman soon disposed of any fears we might have had about the half-deck boss. 'One of the best chaps in the world is old Wally,' said Dave. '*And* a first-rate seaman. But he just can't get his "ticket" and he's got soured a bit. So he pretends to be tough. Crack you? Crack any of us? Not on your life! He'll show you things until he's blue in the face. But at least ten times every day he'll shout the old formula. "I'll show you once; the second time I'll crack you!" That was his welcome when he went to sea and he thinks it ought to be ours.'

'The half-deck would be a pig-sty without him,' put in another cadet. 'Just you wait till we get to Sydney and he goes off, and see.'

'But what about the second mate?' I asked.

'He's all right, too,' said Dave, who refused to see anything whatever wrong with the *Rothesay Bay*. 'Just do your work and keep on doing it, and he won't worry you. His trouble is he hasn't any ticket and he can never take a job that calls for a qualified man. And his wife's in this port. If you think he's tough, you take a look at her!'

In the evening Ginger, Tom, and I met the captain in the panelled saloon, and were signed on the ship's articles. His wife read them, in a low, gentle voice. The captain's throat was heavily bandaged and there was obviously something seriously wrong with him. He could scarcely speak. What was in the articles which we cheerfully signed I didn't know, but we had not come from Melbourne and waited for a ship so long, *not* to sign them. I would have signed anything.

As night fell and for'ard hands began to return down the small jetty, singing and shouting, I stood by the rail at the break of the poop and listened to the quiet sighing of the wind

in the rigging. Aboard ship at last! True, she was a smallish
barque, not much more than 700 tons. She was a bit bluff in
the bow, too, and her harsh war-paint showed her to scant
advantage. But she was a real square-rigged ship, with a sweet
cutwater and a carved figurehead at the bow. She had cat-
heads for her big bower anchors, and though she was certainly
a little wall-sided, her rigging was stout and trim, and her
decks and all her being breathed to me of adventure. It was a
great day, though the half-deck boss and the second mate obviously didn't think much of it, and now the drunken sailors
for'ard were kicking up a dreadful row.

We sailed in a day or two, right from the pier. The afternoon breeze was off the land in that corner of the Gulf, and
the way to sea was simple. The barque's offshore anchor was
down well clear of the pier, so that she could be warped out
to that while the sail was loosed, and when the anchor was
ready to be broken out, working canvas would soon have her
under way. We tramped round the capstan heaving the cable in
while the mooring lines were let go, and experienced boys
loosed sail aloft. Our for'ard hands were drunk again, very
drunk, though not incapable. Several of them had run together
from the hard square-head ship *Margarita*, and these were
drunkest of all. They galloped up the rigging with such gusto
that all the shrouds and ratlines shook. They ran along the
yards, scorning the foot-ropes, and they danced and sang,
laughing to think themselves free of their great Cape Horner
and in this handy, small Australian barque. I feared to see
them fall, but soon realized that they would not. To them,
come straight from a ship with a mainmast 170 feet above
the deck and a maindeck 300 feet long, our barque was a play-
thing, almost a toy.

The cook was drunk too. So was the second mate. So was
the mate, an ancient sea-dog whom I now saw for the first
time. He was a tiny, wizened man with a thin grey moustache,
one watery blue eye, and a queer stance up on the poop like
a sort of movable stanchion, a two-legged maritime appurten-
ance which bobbed up and shouted, when the ship was getting

under way. He had very short legs, a bull voice, and a terrible vocabulary. He seemed extremely annoyed at the idea of the men being more drunk than he was, and he kept shouting to them not to fool about aloft, or he'd have them down sweeping their own pieces into the scuppers. The captain stood by the rail aft, a quiet, bandaged figure. He could not shout, and the mate was doing the shouting for him. Shout! The enormous bellows from his great lungs seemed to startle even the seagulls. The sailors ran from line to line, from halliard to tack and sheet and brace, letting go this and hauling on that as the old barque, hove short to her port bower, waited for the life-giving sail to be set to give her way. At a bellow from the mate the cook rushed out of his galley to tend the fore-sheet, tripped over a bollard and fell head foremost into the scuppers, where he promptly went to sleep. The second mate shouted at boys aloft to overhaul buntlines, clear gaskets, see what the hell was in the way of the t'gall'nt sheets. The strong young sailors, drunk to a man, manned the halliards lustily and mastheaded the two tops'l and t'gall'nt yards as if they had been broomsticks. They went at everything with such a will that they never finished a chanty, and the chanties they sang were such as I had never read in any books. Canvas boomed and thundered until restraining tack and sheet took charge and made it work: hundreds of fathoms of line of all shapes and sizes cluttered the decks where they had been flung down from their pins: chain sheets rattled in their leads: and now the merry song of the capstan pawls took up the riotous chorus of our sea-going as the anchor was tripped and we were under way. Now she had the three headsails up – inner and outer jibs and the fore topmast stays'l – and the mate bellowed orders for the mainsail to be set. The spanker was sheeted home, and the royals mastheaded, a Norwegian and a cross-eyed Swede from the *Margarita* loosing them and waltzing on the yards until the mate roared up at them, 'Get down out of that, you bloody fools!'

Then they shouted something in Norwegian, and balanced on their bellies one on each truck at the very tops of the masts holding out their arms and legs like trapeze artists doing an act. What a going to sea! I had learned nothing to prepare me for this at Captain Suffern's school, or from any books.

But the wind was good, and the sound of the sea breaking before the bluff old bows was sweet and glorious, though before long the sea crashed there with a loud banging and clouting and sprays began to cloud over the fo'c'sle head. Course was set to go through Backstairs Passage inside Kangaroo Island, and all hands worked on the fo'c'sle head to get the anchors secured while the water was comparatively quiet. They were secured for the time being by cockbilling the flukes over the t'gall'nt rail, and lashing them with chain and wire. The heavy anchors were handled by means of a 'fish' tackle, a ponderous contraption of fourfold gear and enormous blocks which hung suspended from a wire pennant secured in the fore topmast-head. I thought it expert and dangerous work, manhandling this great thing, which now and again, when it was free for an instant, took a murderous swipe across the deck. But the thin-lipped second mate and the Scandinavian seamen knew their work, drunk or sober. These weren't the first anchors they had catted and fished in a seaway; I thought I saw a gleam almost of satisfaction in the second mate's eyes as he conducted operations. The tumult and the shouting had subsided by that time; Dave Freeman was at the wheel, and the little barque was bounding along.

When the anchors were secured, all the sails set and trimmed to best advantage, the buntlines overhauled and stopped with a turn of sail-twine to the jackstays that they might not chafe the sails, and the decks cleared up with all the gear clear for running and everything secured, and when the cook had been revived with a bucket of sea-water and hustled back into the galley (where he immediately carried on with his work as if nothing had happened), all hands assembled at the break of the poop for the division of the watches. There were fourteen of us, all told. We boys stood at the back while the mate and second mate did their selecting – a man each called by name, or beckoned. The mate took first choice. The cadets were left until last. The mate took Tom Germein. Ginger MacNamara and I went to the second mate together, to compensate him slightly, I suppose, for the mate's having taken the lion's share of the able seamen. The second mate gave no sign of thinking himself compensated for anything.

By that time it was well into the first dog-watch. We were still in the sheltered water inside Kangaroo Island, and except for her list to the wind and her way through the water there was little motion in the barque. This is the life! I thought. But I reckoned without the morrow. Then it was cold and grey, and raining, and the wind from the west had brought up a great sea from across the Australian Bight. This was the great Southern Ocean where the wild west wind blows, and the wild west was blowing. The sea fumed and leapt at us, and now and again lopped its crests inboard over either rail. There was now no shelter from the land, and for the first time I felt the savage, endless enmity of the real sea. The barque, with her royals and all her lesser sails now fast, was dipping and rolling, and her motion was such as I had never dreamed of. Many of my books had spoken of the motion of a ship in a seaway, but somehow the real import of the endless heave, lurch, and roll had never once occurred to me. I had not thought of seasickness. Usually when I imagined myself at sea, the sun was always shining, and I was in a brass-bound uniform strutting the deck somewhere with a polished telescope (not polished by me) with which to admire the beauty of attractive islands on the horizon. The mundane details of seasickness, heads-cleaning, deck-swabbing, and the like had not really bothered me, though I had heard about them often enough. Here now there were no islands, attractive or any other kind; nobody wore brass buttons; there was no telescope. The wind screamed and the sea rose, and the ship lurched and stumbled across the creamy, bitter waters. A callous, oil-skinned figure on the poop was shouting, 'You there! Boy! Lay aloft and overhaul those tops'l buntlines! *Not* with bloody rope-yarn, now! Sail-twine! Oh, for Chrisake! Don't you little barsteds know anything?'

All this because I fished out a rope-yarn from my pocket first, in a quick hunt for twine. Aloft I was violently seasick, and an albatross, cold and austere as the infernal second mate, looked disgusted.

Ginger and I being considered useless, I suppose, for more skilled employment, were put to scraping pitch from the planks of the poop, where the seams had been very badly caulked – obviously by a drunkard – during the ship's stay at Edithburgh. Down on our hands and knees, with blunt scrapers, we toiled in the rain. My oilskins leaked. Up there on the poop it seemed to us both that all the wild motion of the ship was viciously concentrated. As she lifted her stern out of the sea and threw us to the grey skies, my stomach left me. I felt faint and light-headed and careless. From the depths of my innards a nauseating slime arose, and nearly choked me. Ginger looked like wet death, and his red freckles mocked his green, drawn countenance. Sprays drove across the poop, and all was misery. The second mate allowed us to stop work to go to the rail only, and that very briefly. To look aloft at the swaying masts and yards was to be giddy; to feel the constant rising of the ship up, up, up into the pressing dome of the grey sky while my whole digestive processes howled in agony, was torture almost beyond enduring; to realize that this would go on for days, weeks, months, *years*, was to be depressed profoundly.

'Take off the spilled pitch, not the goddam' wood! We can't spare wood,' snarled the second mate. 'I want the poop finished *this* voyage. Get on with it!'

There seemed to be acres of poop-deck, and all the pitch was malevolent glue, and all the poop planks splinters.

But a watch was only four hours long at the worst. After that, we dared not face the midday meal. The half-deck boss and the other cadets laughed with real glee. 'Plenty for us,' they said. 'Don't you b——s get better while the fresh grub lasts!'

The captain was ill, too, though he was not seasick. What he had in his throat was a cancerous growth, poor man, and he should not have gone to sea at all. The mate now had real charge of the ship. Old Jackie Shimmins, mate of the *Rothesay Bay*, had lost more sailing-ships round the Southern Ocean, probably, than any other ancient mariner. He was a man then long past seventy. For years and years he had had commands, of brigs and barquentines and small barques, and schooners. He had lost the lot. He'd piled more than one up in the Bass Straits, that island and rock-strewn stretch of storms that torments travellers between the Australian mainland and Tasmania. The way through Bass Straits was the best way for us to go on our passage from St Vincent's Gulf towards New Zealand. The wind was fair. But when he knew he had the responsibility of the ship, Jackie brought the old barque up to the wind, and shaped a course across the great sea towards the south of Tasmania. It didn't bother him that now the west coast of that island was a lee shore. It was several hundred miles away. He had sea room, and that was what he wanted. In Bass Straits are too many unlit islands, and the bones of quite enough barques and brigs.

The next week or two are best forgotten. I was seasick for four or five days, but they seemed like five months. I missed no watch and I missed no work, and I did my turns of lookout and all work aloft. Nothing else was to be thought of in that ship or any other sailing-ship.

'Here nobody gives in,' laid down the half-deck boss. 'No, my sons, not to anything.'

So Ginger and I stumbled about and suffered, and were nuisances in general; until suddenly one morning I awakened at one bell – quarter to four – to find that I could raise my head without wanting to be rid of it. I had lost all desire for the ship to sink beneath me, and life seemed again a grand gift to be enjoyed to the full. My head and my stomach were normal again, and I felt abominably hungry. All the half-deck offered in the way of food at that hour in the morning was a bite of hard biscuit, full of weevils. I didn't worry over the weevils. Some kind-hearted soul had drawn my 'whack' of condensed milk three days before and had not yet consumed the whole of it. Before two bells I had polished it off, with all the biscuits in the kid as well. That morning the smell of the coffee in the galley at half past five seemed glorious, and as the grey dawn slowly drifted over the cheerless sea and lit the sodden, straining rags of the barque's canvas I knew the life was wonderful.

At four bells we sweated up the gear of everything that was set and saw that the sails were drawing to perfection. Even the second mate, superintending this, seemed almost human, and at a word from him I bounded into the mainmast to see that all was well there. Ginger, also recovered, ran up the fore, and we made a race of it. Our job was to see that all gaskets were properly made up and on the fore part of the sails where they could cause no trouble, that buntlines and leachlines were overhauled and not chafing anywhere, that all the mousings were in order, lest a shackle or a hooked block work itself adrift at an awkward moment – in short, that all the wonderful machinery of the rigging was as it should be, ready for instant use and in good order. Our concern was with the running rigging only. Able seamen looked after the standing rigging. The second mate's sharp eyes could detect a worn-out mousing at the bunt of the main royal yard, from his place of authority on the poop. There was no skimping anything; he saw to that.

The rain had eased a little, and from the main t'gall'nt yard the streaming deck of the old barque seemed slim and almost clipper-like, as she lurched and rolled along on her way towards the south of Tasmania. The oilskinned figure at the wheel far below was the embodiment of romance, and even the burned salt pork and sickly sweet beans of that inadequate breakfast failed to dispel the aura of enchantment that clung to the ship from that time onwards. My body was adjusted to the life now internally and externally; my stomach was at peace and my feet balanced me despite the most violent motion. Spiritually, I felt nearer the Creator of things on the high yards and astride the bowsprit-end than I ever had felt ashore. This was the life! Drive on, good barque, I am where I want to be! This is contentment.

CHAPTER FOUR

OVER THE TASMAN SEA

CONTENTMENT it was and contentment it continued to be. But it was not without blemishes. Life in the *Rothesay Bay*, bound round the south of Tasmania towards New Zealand, was hard, and there were one or two shocks in store for me. It was summer when we sailed from Edithburgh, but there was nothing summery about the Southern Ocean or the Tasman Sea. Both of these were notorious storm-breeding areas, summer and winter, and the South Cape of Tasmania is a miniature Cape Horn. The wind blew from the south-east for days, and we were almost jammed on the coast of Tasmania. It sleeted and rained, and the high wind blew a mournful dirge in the rigging. We beat about under shortened canvas, and the maindeck was constantly awash. It was a good thing that there was no break in the poop bulkhead giving access to our half-deck, for it would have been impossible to keep the sea out and it would have flooded us. The one port, over the boss's bunk, leaked a lot, though it was puttied up and the steel dead-light was in place over it.

Now that I was recovered from seasickness the inadequacy of the food was trying. I discovered that the tin of milk I scoffed was intended to be my 'whack' for three weeks. We were on strict allowance measured out by pound and pint and not a morsel more. Ashore, a poor breakfast might not matter much when one had had at least a good night's sleep. But at sea there was never a good night's sleep. The ghastly business of never having the chance to get more than three and three-quarter hours' sleep was very difficult to become accustomed to. The barque was on the two-watch system, four hours on duty followed by four hours off, with the four hours from four to eight PM broken into two two-hour dog-watches. All the watches and reliefs were contrived so that meals were eaten in watch below. We worked a full ten hours one day and four-teen hours the next, day and day about interminably, but we did not enjoy uninterrupted watches below. It always took a few minutes to change the watches, and if there was any heavy work to be done (like getting in a tops'l, or the mainsail, or to put the ship about) it was usually left to the change of the watch in order that both watches would be awake and available. This was hard on the watch which was supposed to go below. Not only were all meals eaten in watch below (this did not take very long), but all 'peggying' was done then, too, and with the redoubtable half-deck boss always about, clearing up had to be highly efficient. The cadet whose turn it was to clear up was called the 'peggy'. Being highly efficient at that kind of thing was a trial, but it was excellent training.

Everything from bringing the food from the galley to trim-ming the half-deck's only lamp was done by the peggy; noth-ing was easy. To bring the food from the galley nearly always meant to pit one's skill again the old devil sea, as the barque lurched along and leapt and rolled, and tried her best to fetch both peggy and dishes into the cold scuppers. Lamp-trimming was done with inadequate gear, and the standard of lamp-oil was the lowest procurable. Things were done the hard way, and those who were accustomed to that standard took a fierce interest in its maintenance. A second-voyage cadet was as con-servative an old shellback, in his own opinion, as the most ex-perienced able seaman, and at sea the half-deck boss developed into something of a martinet, as did everyone else with any authority aboard.

The wind howled all the way down the Southern Ocean and across the Tasman Sea, and the effort to induce it to give us sufficient progress in the right direction was immense. Old Jackie Shimmins might have lost a lot of ships, but he was doing his best not to add the *Rothesay Bay* to the list. He kept a press of canvas on her until we cleared Tasmania, and then he drove her towards the north-east at her best deep-loaded speed, which was about nine knots. All this meant a great deal of extra work. If Jackie held on to his sails, it took all hands to fight them when they had to be taken in. The *Rothesay Bay* had deep upper tops'ls, with single reef-bands. Reefing these tops'ls was heavy work. Day or night, it required all hands. We had plenty of practice at fisting sail. In all watches below it was 'Keep handy for a call'. A boy snatched what sleep he could, always in his clothes. I didn't like being awakened after three fitful hours of tossing sleep, in the middle of some black and blustery night with the old barque trying to stand on her head and at the same time roll both rails under, while the wind shrieked and the spume was everywhere. It was always worst when you woke. Once you were out on deck and joining in the fight yourself it was never so bad. But that wakening moment was sometimes terrifying. What, get used to this? I thought. Deliberately choose such a life? A lurch of the barque sent my head smack against the bulkhead. You *have* chosen it, the wind screamed at me. Stick it: stick it! Fight it! It's never so bad then.

'Come on, Snow!' shouted Tom. 'You won't have time to get those soul-and-body lashings on. It's all hands reef the main tops'l at eight bells. Here, give 's a hand to get these oilskins on.'

Out I'd roll, and for a few moments join the wild scrimmage on the inadequate space of the half-deck, wrestling with oilskin jackets and pants, and lashings of rope-yarn and marlin round the wrists and trouser-legs to help keep out the sea. Tom had a wonderful suit of oilskins in reeking yellow stuff. The trousers had a great apron, and the jacket, instead of buttoning down his chest, fitted over his head in one large enveloping bag-like fold. They might have kept the rain and some of the sea-water out, but they did their best to keep Tom out, too. It took five minutes for even an agile boy to put them on.

Eight bells! Struck mighty fast, and the clock flogged by the impatient mate.

'All hands close-reef the main tops'l!'

We struggled up on deck, where the fierce wind cut into us after the fug of the half-deck. A hurried muster; no shout of relieve the wheel and lookout as usual (they could remain where they were until the tops'l was subdued), and all hands hastened in their heavy oilskins and sea-boots to the main rigging, port watch to port and starboard to starboard, and in a moment the melodious shouts of the chanty-singers rose against the tumult of the west wind. The yard was lowered to its lifts, the reef tackles manned, and the reef cringles in each leech hauled snug to the yardarms. All this was done from the deck, for all the lines and gear by which the sails were controlled led there. That was why there was such a maze of them.

'Aloft and reef her!'

Away up the weather rigging we all ran, the port watch anxious to have the job done that they might go below, and we starboarders keen to show them who were the smartest sailors in the ship. Not them! Second mate at the bunt in charge of the job, the best able seamen to the earings at the yardarms, and the rest of us strung out along the yard fisting the sail, skinning that part of it which was to be reefed and getting the reef-points well secured – in ten minutes or so, with any luck, the job was done. Then down on deck again to stretch the reduced area of the sail, steady the braces, and – if no other sail urgently required attention – the port watch could go below.

'Relieve the wheel and lookout! Handy for a call, the watch – no one in the half-deck now, you boys!'

But sometimes it took half the night to fight one sail.

The half-deck boss called work aloft and jobs like splicing 'sailorizing'. So did everyone, and they all liked it. There was a fierce exultation in the rush aloft, a wild delight in the fight with the mad canvas, a joy in shouting down the gale while one's feet streamed out on the foot-rope and, far below, seas crashed aboard over the high bulwarks and the foam streaked past. There was a sense of achievement in the team-work of the sailors, pride in a hard job well done, as one climbed down from aloft.

But our work was not all sailorizing. Far from it. Ginger and I had deck-brooms, soogee swabs, or scrapers in our hands far more often than we ever touched a marline-spike. The ship had only one marline-spike, and that was kept locked in the donkey-room. Only the experienced able seamen did any splicing, sail-making, or important jobs in the rigging. We boys scrubbed out heads, scrubbed the second mate's cabin and the pantry, carried coal and water for the silly cook (who always grabbed a meat chopper as we approached the galley, ready to defend whatever he was cooking lest we steal some of it), trimmed lamps, helped to scrub down decks in the morning watch, and swept them again in the second dog, soogeed the paintwork inside the bulwarks, cleaned out the boats, sand-and-canvassed off the ancient varnish from the teak fire buckets which were ranged in immaculate order by the break of the poop, scraped capstan bars, and wire-brushed the capstan. We hated soogee, which was paint-washing.

'Why do sailors keep everything so beautifully clean at sea and then get drunk in port?' I asked Dave Freeman.

'They're only drunk on Saturdays,' said Dave.

'And sailing-day,' said Ginger.

'And any other day they can get some money,' said Tom. 'I expect they keep the ship so clean because they want to be able to sleep anywhere aboard when they roll back drunk. In the scuppers, f'r instance.'

'Well, it seems silly to me to go off and get drunk when you've got a lovely clean ship to stay in,' I said.

'You get sick of that, Snow,' said Tom, from his vast experience. 'Then when you go ashore the lousy people *make* you get lit up, so's you can suffer 'em. You see, in a ship like this – any sailing-ship – you get to be part of a real gang. But ashore most people don't even know they're born. Every bloody thing's so soft for 'em, and they try to make it softer. So sailors get drunk, you see . . .'

I didn't see, quite.

'Well, you see, that's why Wally says he'll show you once and the second time he'll crack you, if you don't know,' Dave piped up. 'Life doesn't show you once. It cracks you the first time. This's life – real life. We get some cracks, and the shore people don't even know we take the cracks for 'em . . .'

'You'll take some cracks from me if you don't cut the yapping and get on with that soogee-moogee!' shouted the second mate. 'Don't you useless bloody soldiers know that soogee's strong? It'll burn the good paint if you leave it on. Wash it off, now! Get on with it!'

For a few moments we bent in silence to the job in hand. Useless bloody soldiers, indeed! This was a foul insult. As for the infernal soogee burning off the paint, what about our raw wet hands? Didn't they burn, too? But that was the sailing-ship attitude – the ship first and the humans a long, long way astern. It had to be the ship first, for if the ship were not looked after thoroughly, soon there'd be no humans with her. For the ship of sails all things had to be done thoroughly and with competence, whatever the sacrifice.

I began to understand why the Ancient Mariners were not interested in boys who wished to go in steam. It wasn't because sailing-vessels were 'romantic'.

Though all of us felt the constant interruptions to our rest, we must have had enough. Our boss permitted no sleeping in the forenoon watch below, unless the weather was atrocious or the night had been unusually hard. It wasn't much use trying to sleep then, anyway. It was always nine o'clock before we were finished with breakfast and the necessary peggying. The midday meal was at seven bells, which were struck at 11.20 AM instead of 11.30, to give the watch forty minutes to fetch their food, eat it, and prepare for the four hours on deck. If you turned in at 9 AM the longest uninterrupted sleep you could hope for was two hours and twenty minutes. Then you'd waken with a dreadful furry taste in your mouth, from undigested breakfast, and have to fall at once upon dinner however unpalatable it might be. It wasn't worth it. So Boss Wally ordained that the forenoon free watch should be given up to study. We took the sea profession very seriously. No course of study was provided by the ship, though the boss was always willing to help. He took a delight in teaching, since he was anxious to get his own certificate for which he had already failed on two occasions. To teach was the best way to learn.

On the last try he had failed over the Rule of the Road, and he was for ever muttering pages of these technicalities to himself in his sleep, and cursing himself for getting something wrong. It seemed to me, at the age of fifteen, that getting a Board of Trade certificate of competence must be an alarming business. The boss said the examiners in Sydney and Melbourne alike were the biggest bunch of bastards unhung, and recommended Hobart in Tasmania as the best place to get our tickets. The examiners there, he said, were not a bad bunch of cows. To our Sydney-side boss, everything and everyone was either a 'bastard' or a 'cow'.

What the state of wedlock had to do with the tempers of Board of Trade examiners I didn't know, but I studied laboriously in such works as Reid's *Seamanship*, Nicholls' *Concise Guide* (which was far from concise and guided me, at any rate, to very little), and Brown's *Signalling*. The boss had many more books, many of them on navigation.

'Don't bother about navigation,' was his advice to us. 'Not the first year, anyway. Any fool can navigate if he can add up, read tables and use a sextant. Seamanship! That's the thing. Seamanship and the Rule of the Road. Only don't learn that all off by heart at once. If you do, some cow's sure to change it. And don't think you know all the answers when you've mastered those books — if you ever do.'

If the theoretical side of our profession was neglected by everyone save ourselves, the practical side was advanced daily. There was no nonsense in the *Rothesay Bay* about looking after boys and lessening their risks. We stood wheel turns, lookouts, and all the rest, with the men, and did more than our share of the work aloft. The flying-jib, gaff tops'l, and the two royals were left entirely to us. No able seaman ever touched any of these sails. We loosed all the sails, as it was necessary. Sometimes when the braces were heavy and it was necessary to square in — always a laborious task when the wind was fresh, though a welcome one for it betokened fair wind — one of the boys was sent to the wheel and left there until the job was done. The wheel was exposed to the wind and rain and sometimes it kicked viciously, as a following sea flung itself at the rudder. It often took all my strength to hold the ship to her course.

The worst trial about steering was the poor light in the binnacle. Whenever one of the binnacle lamps blew out it was a cadet's job to relight it immediately. There was no house on the poop, in the lee of which there might have been some shelter to strike a match – if we had a match. There was a small canvas dodger lashed in the weather mizzen rigging, but that was for the protection of the officer of this watch and we dared not go there. So we would try to light the lamps in a lee made by our own oilskins. They were kerosene lamps, but there was no kerosene for them. Instead, an inferior substitute smoked and fumed, and imparted a dull and fitful life to the best of wicks perhaps for four hours, under the best possible conditions. The *Rothesay Bay*'s were not the best of wicks, and the Tasman Sea rarely provided good conditions.

This problem of keeping the binnacle lamps alight was another of which I had not heard before, and its solution defied not only me but everyone else aboard. Time after time we'd struggle aft, Ginger and I, one of us going first holding up an oilskin to make a lee, while the other followed, clutching both lamps to his breast beneath his short oilskin jacket. Time after time we would struggle against the wind as far as the binnacle, only to have the infernal lamps blow out just as we tried to transfer them to the brass cylinders in which they were supposed to function. This was in the days before the common use of battery torches. I do not recall anyone using an electric torch in the *Rothesay Bay*. By night she was blacked out; either you had superb vision or you had not. If you had not, it was too bad. It was all very well to say steer by the stars, but on most Tasman Sea nights no star was visible. I must say I was never able to detect much anxiety in old Jackie Shimmins or the second mate when the compass was in darkness. They were accustomed to minor ills of that sort, and both of them seemed to have an instinct for feeling that the barque was reasonably near her course. The feel of the wind on their faces, the behaviour of the ship, the sense of the swing of her – they were ultra-sensitive to these things, for they had spent their sea-lives by them. It took a major accident to shake the second mate out of his savage calm. Old Jackie would not have batted an eyelid had the barque been dismasted. The second mate's cold eyes glared at the sea with a ferocity of intense and knowledgeable hatred, nourished by years of hard servitude in ships. Just why he had no Board of Trade certificate I never found out, for the man was a splendid seaman, and had been thirty years in sailing-ships. I never saw him with a sextant. Perhaps he couldn't read, which was a common enough state among the older mariners.

In the cold mornings, at many a one-bell shake, I dreaded that I might some day be like him.

Time passed, and the winds blew, and we blew along with them. On the twenty-eighth day after sailing from Edithburgh we came round the cape named by Tasman for Maria van Diemen (who had never been near it), which is at the northern tip of the North Island of New Zealand. By Cape Brett a great wind blew, coming up ice-laden from the Antarctic. It was right in our faces. Jackie shortened down, and we thrashed about off Cape Brett for days. What an effort we had to make to bring a thousand tons of gypsum to New Zealand!

'Strewth! How I'd like to have those bloody bastard Board of Trade examiners out here!' yelled Boss Wally when for the fourth time in two days it was all hands reef tops'ls. 'Six months o' this! That's what they're always giving me. I'm going to be a farmer.'

The spray and the rain dripped off his face and his oilskins were ripped beyond repair. All the finger-nails of his right hand had been torn out by the roots, when a fold of wind-mad canvas ripped away from him; his finger-tips were a mash of blood and raw flesh. The topmast rigging had worked loose and was trying its hardest to twist his wiry body as he fought his way aloft, now far out over the sea as she rolled back to wind'ard, now over the decks when she rolled a'lee. On the yard, feet balanced on taut foot-ropes which violently imparted the motion of all the other sea-boots upon them, the mastheads describing anguished circles in the sodden sky and the barque leaping and lurching about as if she were tired of the whole voyage and wanted to fling us all into the sea, and the masts after us – oh, for a farmer's life and the firm earth to stand on!

Yet how grandly the old ship fought for us, too, and how fine a band of brothers we were on those high yards. I looked down at old Jackie Shimmins' lean and small, mean figure, huddled by the weather-cloth on the wet poop. He wore no oilskins. The rain beat upon him and the peak of his ancient cap dripped heavy water. Jackie would not wear oilskins, saying he would be wet through anyway and the oilskins would keep the wet more surely in, not out. So long as he was well wet with sea-water as well as rain, he did not mind. Sea-water would never harm anyone it did not drown, he said, and it had been a long time drowning him ... Now and again he turned his grizzled head to wind'ard, watching the squalls, alert for any that meant a shift of wind. His feet were planted apart, firm upon the reeling poop. One hand clung to a batten of the mizzen rigging. He face was red and raw. The second mate was saying something to him. I saw Jackie gesticulate, pointing to wind'ard.

Somehow I felt a great pride to be sailing there with Jackie Shimmins, and I redoubled my efforts to fist the ironbound sail. The great sound of the wind in the rigging was a threat no longer but a symphony of strength and power, and I knew that in a world beset by wars and mounting daily difficulties, the sailing-ship was still a triumph of man's seafaring genius. To be one of a band of men who conducted such ships upon their voyages was to me also triumph – it was fulfilment of life such as I had dreamed on. Here in the battered barque all men mattered: by the sure efforts of our own hands we survived. By the excellence of our efforts, directed by the unquenchable spirit of old Jackie in the poop, we drove that old barque of gypsum to her destination. The skill and the sure loyalty to their calling of all the seamen and the shipbuilders, the riggers and the sail-makers who had gone before us, the essence of whose work and devotion were in that ship, bluff poor old barkie as she was, helped us at every turn. We were not alone. The brave spirit of seafaring man, handed down through the ages, was abundantly with us. We sailed on under God; and the storms departed.

On the thirty-sixth day we came to the bay of Whangarei, and on an arm of those lovely waters there was the cement works to which we were to deliver our gypsum. Apart from the blot of factory the surroundings were beautiful and New Zealand, in those parts, a lovely land. The sun shone; the smell of the bush was fragrant and attractive. In the harbour tasty fish abounded.

'Here is the place for your farm!' said Dave to the half-deck boss.

'Farm? What cow wants a farm?' said that young man. 'I'm a sailor.'

I thought I was beginning to know just what he meant.

CHAPTER FIVE

'THE SET OF THE SAILS!'

LIFE at Whangarei was good, though we worked all the cargo out, and those sacks of gypsum were heavy. Working hours were from six in the morning to six at night, every day except Sunday. Sometimes, as a concession, we finished at four on Saturday afternoons. We worked the cargo, and we looked after the ship. With fish in abundance and plenty of fresh vegetables, the food was good. We slept like logs all night every night, and this was heavenly. We ate ravenously, worked hard, and grew lean and sinewy. We did not go ashore much, except to take walks in the bush, for Onerahi, where the cement factory was, had little to offer. There were no distractions. The crew could not get drunk and, for the moment, this did not bother them.

When most of the gypsum was out, the royal yards were sent down. Great was the competition to come to old Jackie's eye to be selected for this job. Cadets did the work, with an able seaman to superintend. Then we began to load timber, stacking each plank carefully in the hold. I was astonished to notice with what care this was done. I could appreciate why the rigging was looked after so thoroughly, and the sails, and the steering gear, and so on (except the binnacle lamps), but at first I failed to appreciate why so much pains should be devoted to the stowage of planks.

'Look, you silly little cow,' the boss said when I approached him on the subject. 'Won't you ever understand that in a sailing-ship everything – *everything* – has got to be done properly? If we don't jam every possible plank into the hold, then the bloody lot will shift when we get in a seaway outside. And who suffers then? Ships can fall over, capsize, founder, open up. Who looks after 'em, except men? Sailors. Us. And by cripes, we bloody-well look after the one we're in, too.

Everything has got to be apple-pie, shipshape, and Bristol fashion, even though you can't see the reason why.'

The sawmill was slow delivering the timber and we had time to set the rigging up. The *Rothesay Bay* had lanyard rigging, and some of her shrouds and backstays had worked a little slack in the Tasman Sea blows. Setting this up again was a highly skilled operation, and Jackie, the second mate, and our Scandinavian able seamen were experts at it. We boys learned a lot helping them.

'The job of the rigging is to support the masts, not to add to the strain on them,' the boss explained. 'It isn't a lot of rope and wire looking pretty. Everything – every part – has its job to do, and it must be just so. If any cow puts an undue stress on any stay, why then the wood will go, and we'll have a sprung topmast some day when we can't afford to have one. Then we'll have the whole bloody rigging about our ears. And who'll suffer then?'

'Sailors. Us,' I said. I was beginning to know the answers.

'You're darn right we will. And now you just make your life's work aboard here, and every other ship, seeing that sailor's *don't* suffer, or I'll cuff your ears until there's no brain left in between, if there ever was any.'

With that the boss got on with his work, which was trying to get the broken-down donkey engine to function. Somehow he always managed to do that, though the boiler and the winch with it looked dangerous heaps of rust.

When the rigging was set up, which was not before both Jackie and the second mate had been pulled many, many times round the ship, while they examined the stance of her masts with the eyes of experts, the foot-ropes were set down for overhaul, the wooden battens in the shrouds and the ratlines in the topmast and t'gall'nt rigging overhauled, the wire beckets on the yards (through which we would thrust an arm in wild weather, the better to work with both hands and yet not be flung from aloft) were all thoroughly examined, and re-seized to the jackstays. Meantime sails were carried ashore and spread out on a green, where they could be gone over meticulously. The standard in all these jobs was perfection. A great deal of the charm of the life was based upon everyone's cheerful acceptance of this. All things had to be done well lest any of importance be left ill done, and kill somebody or destroy the whole ship. The 'machinery' of our ship was in sight before us constantly, and its care was our first charge. In the old barque we got down to the very anatomy of our profession, and we found great satisfaction in the achievement of difficult jobs, well done. There was a real feeling of responsibility, too, about the sailorizing jobs. Everyone aboard, I believe even the cook, took a pride in his work. Our able seamen took as great a delight in the jobs as the keenest boy tried to do, though they were strange men, without ambition, with no clothes or anything else beyond their immediate needs, and no letters ever came aboard for them.

In our free time we fished and swam, and sailed one of the lifeboats. On Sundays we took walks ashore. Sometimes with the smell of the bush in my nostrils and its beauty all before me, spread below some hill which Dave and Tom and I had mounted, I wondered a little about the sailing-ship life. Surely similar satisfactions were to be had ashore. Here also there must be delight in the achievement of real things, growing and raising, and taming perhaps, some corner of this bush for a generation or two. The birds sang and the earth was soft and warm and the bush was almost welcoming in a way the restless sea could never be. Yet I knew the attractions of the land were not for me. The wind rustled quietly in the high trees and in the fields of corn and reminded me of the wind in the rigging, powerful, majestic sound which was now more stirring and compelling to me than ever.

We moved down, after many weeks, to Auckland, to complete our timber cargo for Australia, for the little sawmill at Whangarei could not produce our fill. We sailed down with a quiet fair wind, and tied up at a wharf in the heart of the city. Round us two-masted scows and clean little coastal steamers, with black-topped white funnels and green and gold hulls, lay at their berths, with here and there a deep-sea steamer loading or discharging overseas cargoes. One of these was a Sunderland tramp which was discharging coal from the United States, across the berth from us. Mounds of her coal covered the wharf between us, and coal dust blew everywhere. There was a coal-miners' strike in New South Wales, and no coal was being shipped from Australia.

'The mate wants to see you,' the boss told me when we were secured alongside.

I approached old Jackie with some mild alarm. He did not often send for boys.

Jackie took me along to the after-end of the for'ard house, silently. The doors at the end of the house were open to allow the donkey-engine to work.

'What do you see in there, boy?' asked Jackie.

I took a good look.

'An old winch, sir. Empty bunkers. A rusty boiler. Empty sacks.'

'Never mind about the rusty boiler and the old winch. Now take a look up on the wharf. What have we there?'

'Coal, sir. Plenty of it.'

'Aye, plenty of it. Here empty bunkers, there plenty of coal. Now, boy, understand that I don't want you to do anything dishonest. That would never do. But this is a poor ship. We can't pay for coal. It's scarce ashore, and expensive. There's more coal on that wharf than the people in Auckland could possibly want, and there's thousands more tons of it in that dirty steamer. I want you to be night-watchman here in port; and in the night, after it's well dark, you fill those bunkers with that coal. It's not dishonest, now! There's the coal. We need it.'

I was taken aback, not at the thought of taking the coal, but by the prospects of nocturnal coal-lumping. It was very dirty coal.

'Yes, sir,' I said. 'Fill the bunkers.' One was required to repeat the gist of orders to show they were understood.

'Turn to at six,' said Jackie. 'Six PM to six AM. That's the hours. Don't start on the coal until midnight. Keep the galley fire going, and have it cleaned and ready for the cook at half past five, when you call him. And see he gets up. He'll put a bite of supper out for you. You'll also see there's a hurricane lamp burning by the gangway, so the men can see to come aboard. They mustn't fall in the harbour. We can't spare 'em here. And tend the lines. You know what that means? Call me if there's anything ever bothers you.'

'If a policeman sees me with the coal, sir, what do I do?'

'You see the policeman first. Don't worry. You haven't far to lift the stuff. It isn't stealing. It's just an old custom of the sea, but maybe only seamen would understand that, so you'd better not let any of the shore bastards see you. All right?'

'All right, sir,' I said. But I was a bit dubious about it.

However, all went well with the nightly coal-lumping. About half an hour after midnight, when the wharf was in darkness and no one but myself was about, I set about transferring as much of that coal as possible from the nearest dump into our galley and donkey-room bunkers. They were big bunkers. I must have moved about a ton a night. Each day what was not used was transferred to the barque's coal store, in a part of the fore-peak. The bunkers were always empty for me. Jackie was very pleased and so was I, thinking I was helping the old barque to compete with steamers in a hard world. I did so well that Jackie got me to replenish the fresh-water tanks in the small hours, too. There was a tap conveniently placed on the wharf. I didn't know that fresh water, like coal, ought to be paid for.

Being night-watchman was a busy job, and it was hard to get a decent sleep in the half-deck by day. I was glad when our cargo was completed and it was time to go to sea. We moved to anchorage immediately the last plank was stowed. By that time our decks were filled with stacks of timber, which was jammed into and onto the ship in all directions, until the cook had to climb down into his galley and all the belaying pins for the running gear were shifted six feet up to special rails which were lashed in the shrouds. Wells were left round the main and fore fife-rails for access to the gear there, and the pumps, and all the spare chains and heavy wire in the ship were lashed round the cargo. It was lashed down with the utmost thoroughness so that not a plank could move – we hoped – even if the barque fell on her side, and precautions were taken to see that the loose ends of running rigging – braces, halliards, buntlines, downhauls, and the like – could be triced up and secured, lest they trail away through the washports behind the timber and be the very deuce to get back aboard again.

'If one plank can move, so can the bloody lot,' said Jackie, 'and they will take us with them.'

As soon as we were out in the stream, the captain, still with his throat heavily bandaged and his brave wife looking after him, appeared from somewhere, and went immediately below again. The barque took a bad list, for the timber we had loaded at Auckland was much heavier than that from Whangarei. With this stowage, naturally, she was cranky. She took a list to port. This appeared to be accepted and to alarm nobody, but I did not like it.

'Timber ships often list,' I was told. 'Can't blame this poor old bitch. There's more on her head than in her belly. We might list, but we won't sink. Not with this cargo.'

We sailed as soon as we could, going out with a land breeze on the port beam which held the ship upright and prevented the authorities ashore from noticing our list. Perhaps they would have paid no attention to it had they seen it. But there was a very general distrust of all shore authorities, and a unanimous desire to do them down. It didn't seem to occur to anyone aboard that sailing with such a cargo might be dangerous. At any rate, we knew it was well stowed. It wouldn't shift. If she didn't blow over she wouldn't capsize. We were bound only for Sydney, little more than 1,200 miles away. We ought to make it in a fortnight.

We were, in fact, nearly two months. The passage across the Tasman Sea became a drifting crawl. The tops'l schooner

Huia, a vessel not a third the size of the *Rothesay Bay*, had made the passage once in four days and a few hours; but the *Huia* was a lovely old bird at sailing. Even had the *Bay* been a clipper, we could set little sail unless the wind blew from the port beam, or right aft. As it was, she often rolled in the most alarming manner and seemed to me to be about to fall right over. Her list grew worse rather than better. Nothing could correct it, and we did not try. Complete restowage of the cargo was the only answer, and that was not possible.

So we drifted about the Tasman Sea, that stormy basin which lies open to all the Antarctic gales at its one end and the Coral Sea cyclones at the other. We could not put the ship about by any means other than painfully wearing her – running off before the wind and then slowly coming up on the other tack. We could make no pretence at beating. Jackie was a cautious mariner and every night we shortened down to tops'ls – the fore and main upper and lower tops'ls, the fores'l, and the sturdier fore-and-afters.

'I'm an old man. I need some sleep. Call me if there's any sign of a shift of wind,' said Jackie. But he didn't sleep.

We never saw the captain during this stage of the voyage. He was reported to be dying. Jackie's command was absolute in everything but name and pay. Our half-deck boss was acting second mate, and shared the watchkeeping with the real second. After a while we began to be short of food. Day after day something would run out, until we had to draw in our belts pretty tight, and there were rude comments in the chanties at the many pulley-haulie jobs. The soloist in the chanties had traditional liberty to improvise and was free to criticize anything. In this way the sailors let off some steam. No one ever paid any attention to their broad and frequently blasphemous hints, though even old Jackie often grinned as some well-oathed complaint was shouted lustily across the sea.

The favourite time for a rousing chanty was when the tops'l halliards were manned, which was generally at the change of the watches. There was a Welshman for'ard – one of our few

Britishers there who sang extremely well and was a first-rate improviser.

'Oh, our Old Man he don't set no sail!' he'd begin, all hands trailing on the stout line ready to come in with two mighty shouts of 'Leave her, Johnny, leave her!' and two hearty, synchronized hauls which would shift the yard about a quarter of a foot.

'An' I could'a stayed in a lovely jail!' Again the soloist sang melodiously.

> 'Oh, leave her, Johnny! Leave her!'
> *'With all night in an' plenty o' ale.'*
> 'Leave her, Johnny, l-e-a-v-e her!'
> *' 'Stead o' drifting about the Tasman Sea,*
> *'Oh! A jackshite's life it ain't for me!'*
> 'Leave her, Johnny, leave her!'
> *' 'Cos there ain't no grub and there ain't no pay!'*
> 'Leave her, Johnny, leave her!'
> *'But they tell me we'll come in some day.'*
> 'Leave her, Johnny, leave her!'
> *'Before then we'll be eating hay!'*
> 'Leave her, Johnny, l-e-a-v-e her!'
> *'Now it's time for me to shout belay!'*

'Belay the halliards there! Do you want to jam the parral in the bloody cross-trees?' Jackie would shout, and a couple of strong men would run to the fore-part of the halliards, by the block, while at a shout of 'Come up there!' all the others let go, and the line was quickly belayed round its pin. Then they'd all grin, and on to the next job, while one of the boys coiled the halliard down clear for running, but not so clear that it could roll over the side.

'There's one dam' bad thing about a timber cargo,' said Tom one day. 'You can't make much soup out of it.' There was not much sustenance in New Zealand pine.

A sudden, dirty squall in the middle of the twenty-sixth night nearly blew us right over. What a night! Wind howling and shrieking as if it had a personal animosity against us, the infernal timber cluttering up the decks fore-and-aft adding greatly to the difficulties of working, the barque listed over until her lee sheer-poles were below the water and the timber to wind'ard looked like giant stacks in a nightmare, all the movable gear streaming off to leeward in a boil of foam, both binnacle lights blown out and the binnacle itself adrift from its fastenings, and the rudder so far out of the water as to be useless.

It was a good thing Jackie was a cautious mariner. Had we been carrying a press of sail we should certainly have gone over. The fore tops'l blew to ribbons and so did the inner jib. I should have been frightened, going aloft to get the remnants of the tops'l in and to save the bolt-rope, if there had been time, and had I not absorbed something of the confidence of the older men. Why they should be confident I don't know, for it seemed to me that all hell was loose and the barque would roll over in her own foam at any moment. The spray and spume boiling along her side set up a faint green light the effect of which was most uncanny, like a ghost-ship raging in a turbulent sea-cemetery. How cold and murderous was the devilish sea! There had been a lumpy, bad-tempered swell before the wind came, and now the old barque jumped and floundered in a leaping storm of waters as if she did not know what to do next to keep her head above the sea. Now her bluff bows leapt a great sea until the weather bow must have been exposed to the keel; missing the cold embrace of the sea, she hastily flung her cut-water in again as a wall of water rose before her and swept bodily over the fo'c'sle head. All the time she seemed to be lurching farther and farther over. The wind was on the wrong side and she would not pay off. The tangle of gear flowing out to leeward made it almost impossible to work the braces. The shrieking of the wind and the crashing of the seas made it impossible to hear any orders. We first-voyagers stumbled about in the wake of the men who knew what they were doing. Once I was down in the well of timber by the main fife-rail, and the noise of the timber working, with alarming creaks, crackings, and groans, was almost terrifying.

But the lashings held. Nothing shifted. Nothing gave. And the old barque was tight. She made no water. The rigging was well stayed. Nothing carried away, though the stresses at the mastheads as she jumped and quivered through the night must have been enormous. Most of the time she was over thirty degrees.

When at last the grey light of first morning came and the squall had settled into a sullen gale we were still afloat. More than that, we were still floundering on, more or less, in the rough general direction of Australia, for her leeway was that way. The weather side was out of the water like the cliff face of a half-tide island. Aloft the ribbons of the blown-out tops'l screamed and thrashed where they had blown adrift from the too few gaskets. Aft, all hands were huddled round the bole of the mizzen-mast, with lifelines round them to keep them aboard. Jackie had the barque hove-to, and he clung in the weather mizzen rigging by the dodger, his one eye red and his ancient face almost as grey as his stubbly moustache. He seemed his usual self. The for'ard house was washed out. The half-deck was a wreck. There would be no breakfast. But we were hove-to in safety; and we had ample sea-room. All the sea-room in the world, if we wanted it.

We were at sea for the best part of another month. Then one day we sighted a steamer. She came close. There was an exchange of flag hoists. I noticed with mild wonder that I no longer knew the flags of the international code, which I had been able to recognize so glibly back at Captain Suffern's. This was the first time I had seen the flags since joining the ship. No matter; I had, I hoped, learned other things. We were about a hundred or a hundred and fifty miles from the coast of New South Wales then, somewhere to the north of Sydney. I don't think Jackie believed very much in, or ever practised precise navigation. Nobody in the ship, probably, knew exactly where she was. Our boss could navigate quite well, but the only chronometer was in the saloon and no one might go in there save Jackie. In a cabin off the saloon our cancerous captain was slowly dying.

We must have asked the steamer to report us. A day or two later, in fine weather with a flat calm, a smudge of smoke on the southern horizon grew into a Sydney tug, and the tug approached us rapidly and gave us her line.

'The owners want their bloody wood,' said Dave. 'What we go through to bring it to them! What an amount of work and worry, just to bring a stack of timber a thousand miles!'

The tug's people gave us some fresh food. Next morning we were anchored in Rose Bay, Sydney. The smell of copra from an Islands barquentine near by to windward was sickly sweet, and the lovely coves of Port Jackson were a delight to see.

'Damme!' said the boss, who had been a magnificent acting second mate. 'I've forgotten that useless bloody Rule of the Road again.'

Within a day or two our unfortunate captain went ashore and died. The owners fired old Jackie, not in the least aware of the prodigious efforts he had made on their behalf. At the age of seventy-one he was on the beach again. Well, he had his mate's wages, I suppose, and such odd perquisites as he could get his hands on (such, for instance, as at least half the purchase price of that galley coal I'd laboriously removed from the Auckland wharf). Jackie was an old, old hand, not accustomed to much generosity from ship-owners of from anyone.

When he was given notice the crew was reduced to a few cadets, for all the men had been paid off the day after arrival. In a flurry of good cheer and bad whisky they had gone ashore, singing and shouting. Only Dave Freeman, Tom, and I were still aboard, with Jackie. Ginger MacNamara had gone to Melbourne on leave with the other Melbourne cadet, and our boss's home was in Sydney. He was taking a few days off before facing the Board of Trade examiners again.

Jackie sent for us boys. We found him seated on his settee, in the hutch off the poop mess-room which served as his cabin. The cabin contained a bunk with a mahogany board, some drawers for clothes beneath the bunk, a bit of 'thwartships settee, a swinging lamp, a small desk to write at, and a tiny closet for clothes. It was all incredibly neat. On the desk the ship's log lay open at the page of entries for her last day at sea.

'Barque *Rothesay Bay*. Auckland towards Sydney. 53 days,' it read.

'Auckland *towards* Sydney? Why not *to* Sydney, sir?' I asked.

'A sailing-ship isn't bound *to* any place until she gets there,' said Jackie in a loud voice. Usually he was far from loquacious. This seemed to be his talking day. Perhaps the whisky had something to do with it.

'Steamers think they are bound to places,' he went on. 'Sailing-ships know they are only bound towards. Towards! That's the thing. Always towards – and do your damnedest to get there. But you aren't sure of anything until you arrive. When you come to make log entries, remember that. Things have to be shipshape and seamanlike in the log. Do you boys like sailing-ships?' he broke off suddenly.

'Yes, sir. We do!' A chorus of approval, thoroughly genuine.

'Well, now, listen here. I've called you young fellows together to offer a little advice. I know we haven't done much to help your training here. But the ship's done that. The ship and the sea, and you yourselves. I've seen you studying in watch below. That's the way to get on. I never tried it myself. But don't try to learn too much out of books. You stick to sailing-ships and learn all you can while you are able. Because they'll soon be gone.'

'What, all gone, sir?' asked Tom as the old mate stopped.

'Yes, all gone. The shore bastards haven't sense enough to keep them,' Jackie went on. 'Everything's power now. You mark my words. Within twenty years, thirty years, forty years, there'll be such a craze for power, and every damned thing will be so mechanized, that there won't be sources enough for all the power the shore sods'll want. Then they'll be sorry they gave up sail, and lost the skill of using natural things which didn't let 'em down. They'll let the whole damned world down yet ... I'm an old man, but I'm a lucky one. I've been able to serve my life in natural things, to serve in sailing-ships ever since I can remember. You won't be able to. You're the unlucky ones. So for God's sake stay in them while you can. Finish your time in them. Seek out the last one on earth, if it's necessary. Only stick to sail! I'll help you all I can,' the old man went on. 'I wish it was more. But I've still a little influence where men are still men.'

He stopped a while. We looked at each other, wondering.

'This ship is finished,' Jackie began again. 'She might make a passage or two more. But there's a dam' fool coming here in command and he'll sail her under, if she isn't hulked. Did you see the *Daniel* as we came in? She's hulked. I'm hulked. We'll all be hulks. The dam' fool coming here doesn't like cadets. My advice to you is to find a better sailing-ship than this while it can still be done. This one's all right, but there are better. I'll help you find one. You must finish your time in sail. It's a man's life. It'll make you fit to stand up to the shore bastards. Never trust them! Never trust the shore bastards; they'll do you if they can. That's what they're at all day and dream about all night, doing each other down, while sailormen bring them the cargoes they couldn't live without, and are thrown out on the beach every day. Remember that, my boys! Learn your business thoroughly. Learn to look after your own sails, and make them take you where you want to go. The set of the sails! That's the thing. Aye, aye, it's the thing I've given my life to. You could do worse.'

I hoped to do a great deal better than old Jackie Shimmins as I thought over what he had said. Perhaps a fifteen-year-old hasn't sense enough to appreciate real character. I thought the old man was raving because he had been fired. Towards the end the fumes of whisky had been almost overpowering.

He was right about the new captain. I was working in the galley getting a bit of a meal for the few of us who were working by (as standing by a paid-off ship is called) a day or two later when I became aware of a peculiar stranger, prancing about the decks and behaving queerly. He kicked the bulwarks, shouting that they ought to be white, not grey, which was a colour fit only for bloody ships-of-war. He flounced up on the fo'c'sle head, jumped on the bowsprit, and peered down at the figurehead. That figure of a Scots lass was the only decently painted thing in the ship, the only part of her that wasn't grey. It was painted in what were meant to be lifelike colours, with eyes, lips, nostrils, and so on all shown, even to the rouge on her cheeks. She was a bonny lass and we were all proud of her. The stranger dropped to the steel bobstay, took a horrified look at the figurehead's face, and scrambled back aboard, hopping about in a fury.

'Bloody girl's cross-eyed!' he shouted to all the seagulls and passing ferry-boats in Johnson's Bay. 'Poor old bitch! No wonder she took two months trying to find the way from Auckland!' And so on, and so forth, with oaths and blasphemy. He was saying, I gathered, that figureheads ought to be gilded or plain white. Perhaps he was right about that. But he had no business to be abusing our ship, nor any part of her. Besides, *I* had painted that figurehead and it had been a real labour of love, a dog-watch job, in my own time. Even old Jackie had approved.

During all this I had no idea who the obnoxious stranger could be. He was in plain clothes (like all sailing-ship people, except apprentices), and he had not announced himself. So I spoke up, and asked him who he was, to come aboard our barque and swear at everything. At this he checked his eloquence, stopped hopping about for a moment, and gave me a cold stare.

'Look here, my boy,' he said, after a pause. 'I don't know who the hell *you* are. But I'm the new captain of this ship, and you're fired.'

That evening, when Jackie came back from the shore, drunk again, I told him what had happened and asked about another ship. The captains of the Islands barquentine *Ysabel* and the Tasman Sea sluggard *Senorita* were old boys of his, he said. I could go in either. They might last four years. Or if I could stand the bagpipes, there was the barque *James Craig*. She had good owners; aye, perhaps she was best. The mate of her was looking for some likely ordinary seamen, and her master was a grand Scot named Murdo' Murchison.

CHAPTER SIX

A MOVE FOR'ARD

THE *James Craig* was a lovely little vessel, as much a clipper as the *Rothesay Bay* was a warehouse. I looked back on that old warehouse with affection as I pulled across to my new ship. Her war-time grey was streaked with rust. Ugly flat punts full of New Zealand timber cluttered her sides. Her royal yards were down, but there was still a graceful rake to the high masts, and a lovely line to her sheer which spoke of sea-kindliness. I had not been with her very long – only one voyage – but I felt that as long as I lived I would owe her something. Something of me would be with her so long as she survived; something of her would be with me, too, as long as I survived.

The *James Craig* looked a thoroughbred, the poor old *Bay* a workhorse. The lines of the *Craig's* hull were extremely lovely. She sat gracefully and light even upon the waters of Johnson's Bay, with the hulk of the *Daniel* beside her and her sharp bows high out of the water where the coal had been discharged for'ard to get at a leak there. Her rigging was new, and lofty. The line of her sheer was unbroken, for she had neither a raised fo'c'sle head nor poop. Her iron hull was painted black with a gilt line of beading. A scroll-work ornament decorated her sweet bow.

'D'ye like the look of her, lad?' a bewhiskered old Scot working on a stage by her side addressed me, as our boat came alongside. 'Ye should ha' seen her in the old days. She'd a wunnerful figurehead then. Aye, 'twas Steel of Greenock built her, away back in 'seventy-four. He built some lovely 'uns. But she's just a rigged-up hulk now. Ye should ha' known her in the 'seventies when she was a Glasga' West-coaster. Did ye ever hear tell on her figurehead, now? Did ye not?'

I said I was sorry I had not.

' 'Twas a full-length figure of a Highland chieftain,' said the

whiskered one, 'and wunnerful well carved. 'Twas the McLeod
o' McLeod, in his full regalia, an' the tartan an' all was there,
proper an' shipshape. The old man thought so on it that 'twas
kept covered up at sea, wi' a special sort of canvas cloak f'r its
protection, an' to keep the McLeod man war'r'm. An' in ports
'twas only uncovered of a Sunday moor'rnin', sharp at eight
bells. The old man'd lift his hat an' say a greetin' as a 'prentice
boy took off the coverin'. "Guid moornin', McLeod," he'd say,
takin' his old hat off. I mind a time when I was in her in Newcastle in 'ninety-six when a de'il of a young 'prentice boy tied a
whusky bottle to the spor'r'r-ran an' put a beard o' tarry
oakum on t' face, an' a clay pipe on him an' all. 'Twas a joke,
he thought. But we all thought the old man'd gone mad, when
he saw it. He was ravin' there an' cussin' in the Gaelic for a
week. D'ye have the Gaelic, now, ye'sel'?'

I couldn't answer that because I had only a vague idea of
his meaning.

'Do you speak Gaelic? he means,' whispered Tom Germein
at the oars. 'You know, Gaelic, like they speak in the High-
lands of Scotland and at the smoking concerts in the Cale-
donian Club.'

I had to reply then that I regretted I did not. The port of
registry on the *Craig*'s counter was Hobart, not Glasgow.
Gaelic, now? What had that strange tongue to do with the
pretty barque, lying in Sydney harbour? I had great difficulty
in understanding the old man even when he thought he was
speaking English.

The bewhiskered mariner noticed my bewilderment.

'She's still a Scottie,' he said, 'though there's stars in yon
Red Duster she's flyin' now an' she's been lyin' a coal hulk in
Rabaul these dozen year'r'rs. Aye, laddie, once a Scot always a
Scot, ships an' men. An' the Gaelic's guid aboar'rd here.'

I realized why the figurehead was the Chief of the Clan
McLeod when I read the name on the bell by the antique up-
and-down windlass immediately abaft her low fo'c'sle head.
'*Clan McLeod*,' it read, '1874.' The old name was still there
though she had been the *James Craig* since 1903. At that time

– the middle of 1920 – the line of lovely little barques which (with a sprinkling of barquentines) flew the J. and J. Craig house-flag out of the port of Auckland, had been dispersed, and the *James Craig* had been rescued from service as a coal hulk in New Guinea, rerigged because of the shortage of shipping and the temporary harvest of good freights. When I joined her she belonged to a firm of Tasmanian jam merchants and shipping agents, who had financed her refit. The refit must have been skimped somewhere, for she had almost foundered on her first passage – from Newcastle with coal towards Hobart in Tasmania – and had run back in distress to Sydney, from off the Gabo, with her forepeak full and many of her shrouds so slack as to be useless. They had been cut too long, or perhaps her lower masts might have settled a little. She was in the process of a second refit to put these defects right when I joined her, and the old wooden Norse barque *Daniel*, which had been an inter-Colonial trader since 1907, now cut down to a hulk, was alongside to store her coal while the hull was made seaworthy.

I swarmed aboard, throwing my new sea-bag (which I'd sewn myself) and bedding before me. I'd sold the big chest, which was really an encumbrance in a small ship. The *Craig* was a good hundred tons smaller than the *Rothesay Bay*, and she had no half-deck. I made my way along the deck to stow my gear in the forecastle, approaching that historic domicile with interest. In the *Bay* the cadets had never gone into the for'ard house. This was not actually forbidden, but it was not done. The 'squareheads' and 'dagoes' in there were left to themselves in their free time, as far as we were concerned, though we were all good friends on deck.

The *James Craig* had no half-deck and only the smallest poop. Her fo'c'sle was a house on deck immediately abaft the foremast. It was obvious that it was a new house, built to replace an older, smaller one which had been removed when the barque was a coal hulk. The new house took up most of the space between the main hatch and the fore fife-rail. It served to accommodate crew, galley, and cook, and to carry the two double-ended lifeboats. The after-part of the house was a small galley, with a coal stove. Adjoining the galley, on the port side, was an airy mess-room for the crew. This was an innovation. There was a sliding hatch through which the cook could deliver meals, piping hot from the stove. The mess-room was enamelled in white and was spotlessly clean. The remainder of the house, forward of the galley and mess-room, was the fo'c'sle proper. It was divided into two sections by means of a bulkhead down the middle. The starboard side, with six bunks, was for the starboard watch, and the port side, also with six bunks, for the port watch. All the bunks were fore-and-aft. There was a good stowage for oilskins. There were several large ports on each side, and it seemed that the designer had really had the well-being of sailors at heart. I never saw a better fo'c'sle in a sailing-ship anywhere. A locker was provided for each man to stow his gear, and the mess-room was also a recreation-room. I was pleasantly surprised.

'You'll be starboard watch. Take any free bunk. They're all the same. No water comes in here,' said a cheerful young Englishman who was repairing some sennit on his ditty-bag. 'Grub's good, too. No "whack" here, though we signed for it. She's on "sufficient without waste". Do me, too, after the hungry *Cumberland*. You're from the *Rothesay Bay*?'

I said I was.

'You'll find a good crowd here. My name's Keen – Sharkey Keen, they call me,' said my new friend. 'The old man's one of the best. The mate's a lanky Tasmanian. He's a grand fellow to work for. Gets things done without yelling. She's got a bos'n. Doesn't carry a second mate. Bos'n is a very old Scot, name of Sandy McNab. Sandy is a good one, too. There isn't much he don't know about sailing-ships. He's over eighty and he's been in 'em since he was ten. We're in Sandy's watch. That's him you can hear now, making that awful row on the pipes. You've got to put up with that. Never let on you don't like it! It stops sometimes. Not often, though.'

Sharkey Keen was quite right about the *Craig*'s crew. They were a very decent set of men, most of them much older than

the Scandinavians who manned the *Rothesay Bay*. The fo'c'sle
was inhabited by twelve men, eight of them able seamen – real
able seamen – and four ordinary seamen. Half the men were
over forty, two of them over sixty. They were old sailing-ship
men who had never been in steam. They were the real faithful. The bewhiskered mariner who had hailed me in the boat
was Dan Murchison, a distant clansman of Murdo' Murchison,
the master. There were several others named Murchison, all
distantly related and all from the same part of Ross-shire.
These spoke Gaelic among themselves, and were much given
to playing upon a reed they called a 'chanty', which seemed to
be the mouthpiece of a set of pipes without any pipes to it.

'They sold their pipes,' confided Sharkey. 'That's all they've
got left – thank the Lord.'

I soon discovered that life in the fo'c'sle was well regulated
and, except during bouts of drunkenness among the Scots
(which were rare, because it cost a great deal to get them
drunk, and they had very little), good manners prevailed. The
place was kept to the same standards of cleanliness which our
half-deck boss had insisted upon in the *Rothesay Bay*, except
that the men were neater than the boys, and the place was less
cluttered with gear. The older they were, the neater were the
sailors, and the less gear they had. Whatever else they might
not have had, each treasured a small canvas bag, liberally
decorated with sennit and fancy work, in which he kept the
tools of his trade – his fid and marline-spike, a palm and a few
needles, a piece of beeswax and a sail-hook on a lanyard for
holding the seams when working on the sail-maker's bench.
By that time I had one of these bags myself, though there was
little in it.

The boss of the starboard fo'c'sle was a Belgian named Bert
who had run from one of the big Bordes four-masted barques
at Hobart. Bert ruled the roost thoroughly, but with benevo-
lence. It was queer to hear him remonstrating with the Scots
for using what he called 'Garlic'. English, he said, was the
proper language of the ship and they should use it. But the
Scots were intransigent. Bert's own version of English was

rather astonishing. An argument between him, big Dan Murchison and an old Russian Finn named Gus was a delight to hear, provided one was not expected to follow it.

At the meal table, if there were any ignorant departures from the men's own code of good manners, Bert's rebuke was instant and severe. Our code could be summarized very simply. Eat quietly; waste nothing; allow elbow-room to all. These were the basic rules. There was no tolerance of any departure from them. It was, for example, definitely not the thing to cut half a piece from the loaf of bread.

'If you only vant an 'alf-slice you don't vant any,' Bert laid down. 'If you vant an 'ole slice cut it flush-decked an' eat the lot. No fo'c'sle 'eads on de bread!'

As with the bread, so with everything else. Tidiness reigned. On deck, and in the quarters, everything was shipshape, and the Lord help any who (while sober) did anything out of place.

It took a month to get the little barque squared up for sea. Mr Carver, the Tasmanian mate, and Sandy McNab, the bos'n, superintended the rigging work day after day, and I learned more about rigging in that month than I ever learned in the rest of my life. Mr Carver was one of those sailor-Tasmanians who used to abound in the Tasman Sea and round the Islands. Tasmania, then, had a few remnants left of the island's once great sailing fleet, which in former days had rivalled the clippers in the wool trade round the Horn, and there was still some tradition there of following the sea under sail. Mr Carver knew his business, though he spoke no Gaelic and could not blow the pipes.

In port there we did not see much of our captain, who was a dark and very pleasant Scot from the barque *Lobo*, and the Scottish *Lochs* before that. He hailed originally from Ross-shire, but had been in colonial barques since 1903. He spent much of his time ashore on the ship's business, as a shipmaster must. The men said he had been magnificent when she'd been struck by the southerly buster off the Gabo and they thought she'd sink. She would have sunk, they declared, under almost any other man. They swore by Captain Murchison to a man.

My own stay in Sydney was spoiled by an incident ashore very shortly after I signed in the *Craig*. I went to the city (which I seldom did) in order to send my pay home to my mother in Melbourne. Sharkey Keen came with me to show me the way, but soon after we landed a pretty girl smiled at him, and that was the last I saw of Sharkey. I had not sent money by mail before, never having had any, nor had I been in a post office. I proposed to send the cash, which was in six new crisp notes, by money order. I drew a bad blank in the first post office I tried.

'Get a form,' snapped the clerk when I asked how I could send my wealth.

I looked about. There were a lot of forms. Most of them seemed to be intended for writing telegrams.

'What sort of form, please?' I asked.

The clerk gave me a scornful glance and went on with his work. After a few minutes I left that post office and searched for another, somewhat bewildered. As I looked about the busy Sydney streets a cheerful stranger, very affable and pleasant spoken, chummed up with me. He looked like a seaman, though somehow not quite the type I should expect to find signing in the *Craig* or the *Bay*. He was a little oily in his manner. I was glad of his friendship. He soon discovered what I was trying to do, and, saying that he had a lot of experience in such matters, offered to help.

'I know just where there's a good quiet post office,' he said. I'll be glad to help. Those forms take careful filling in, you know. Least thing wrong and those pig-headed cows behind the desk won't send your money for you. A nasty lot, son, a nasty lot. So you're in the old *James Craig*? I knew her well when she was one of J. and J.'s. She's a lovely one, if you like. And sail! She used to offer her mooring lines to half the steamers on the Tasman Sea, to help tow 'em along as she left 'em behind. Aye, son, you're the lucky one now, to be in a little honey of a windbag like that! Are there jobs in her, you say?'

We got along famously, though we seemed to be walking a long way, and I thought I had already noticed two post offices we had passed.

'It's a special one I'm looking for, son,' said my cheerful guide. 'Aye, a very special one.'

When at last we found the special post office of his choice I readily accepted his suggestion that he could deal with the cows of clerks better than I could, and the best thing to do was to hand him the money to buy my order for me.

'Just wait in the sun here,' he said. 'It's no use depressing yourself inside. I'll be out with the receipt in two shakes of a dead lamb's backside. That I will.'

I handed over my six crisp notes, and in he went. He never came out again. I waited and waited, at first sorry that he should be put to such trouble on my behalf, for I thought he was having an argument with some dreadful clerk. But after a while I began to be a little anxious. It must be an awfully long argument. Perhaps there was something wrong.

I looked inside. There was no sign of my kind-hearted friend at all.

Then I saw that the post office had an exit to another street. I'd been fleeced by a shore bastard! I felt as if I had been let down by the whole human race. The mean, thieving rascal had pretended to be a sailor. I found my way, hungry and depressed, back to the ship; it was years before I landed in Sydney again.

At last our hull was tight again, our rigging set up, the coal all back aboard and trimmed under hatches, and off we sailed. Going through the Heads we passed the tops'l schooner *Dart*, outward bound towards the Islands. There on her small poop was old Jackie Shimmins, waving his ancient cap. The *Dart* had been a Government Survey ship once and was a lovely model, finer in her lines even than the *Craig*. She was said to be a bit wet in a real seaway. With a bellyful of coal, so was the *James Craig*. It blew again off Gabo, and she wallowed and rolled heavily with the seas coming green over either rail. But this was only one night. She sailed like a little witch and handled beautifully, though the older men complained about the cotton canvas in her tops'ls and courses.

'It should be good Arbroath flax,' said old Dan. 'This snowy cotton stuff's f'r cir'cus tents. It's har'der than the hobs of hell an' the de'il himsel' wouldna' get a good stow on the cur'rsed stuff. Och, noo! Me lads! R'R'Roll an' bust! Heave, an' she must!' Dan was at the heavy bunt at the time, with a southerly buster shrieking in his ears while we tried to get the upper tops'l in. His enormous voice blew away with the wind, and the night came down while we were still fighting the cotton canvas. Cotton canvas was very, very stiff, and it ripped out finger-nails with the greatest of ease.

For a boy, the *James Craig* was a delight, despite the cotton canvas. In the first place, it seemed to me to be a good thing to have no half-deck. There was no sub-division of the crew into mariners and pseudo-gentlemen. There was the crowd for'ard, and there was the afterguard aft. Each knew exactly where it stood, with no extraneous elements. A boy was a real part of the ship's company. I'd been that in the *Rothesay Bay* too, to some extent, but there the boys were rather a gang apart in anything other than the ship's work. In the second place, the *Craig* was a lively, lovely, and highly responsive thoroughbred of a ship, and her captain got the best out of her. She tacked like a yacht and ran like a greyhound. She was a delight to steer, and her binnacle lamps did not blow out. Her steering compass was inside the after-end of the saloon skylight, which meant that it was lighted by the well-sheltered saloon lamp. True, by the four-to-eight watch sometimes the light had burned very low and it was difficult to see the compass. But even in the worst weather the light did not go out. The *Craig*'s standard compass was slung in gimbals inside a ring on a high wooden pole at the break of the poop, which was an arrangement in the earlier iron vessels. Exactly how a compass perched up there could be used for taking bearings and the like I did not know. Sometimes I saw Captain Mur-

chison or Mr Carver peering up at it, but Sandy McNab had
no truck with it at all.

When we picked up the Tasmanian coast and came sailing
up lovely Storm Bay into the River Derwent and old Hobart,
I was in love with the *Craig* and hoped I could finish my time
with her. But there were rumours that she would be laid up, or
cut down to a hulk again. Already she had cost her owners a
great deal of money. We had been told that we were to load
cased jam in Hobart for Liverpool, round the Horn, but when
we were at Hobart there was no mention of this cargo. We lay
at Hobart a long time and I took a great liking to the clean
southern city, at the foot of Mount Wellington. It was an attractive and cheerful spot, full of small ketches and schooners.
Hobart was a real seafaring place and Tasmania could easily
have developed into the cradle of Australia's seafaring manhood. A grand air of the adventurous past still clung to the
clean waterfront, though the schooners were in the firewood
and apple business now and no longer went blackbirding to
Melanesia, and the port's last whaling barque was long since
broken up. The infamous hostelry of Chopper Cross, known
throughout the seven seas, still stood, and there was still at
least one slipway for building the beautiful little sailers for
which the port had been long famous.

We loaded no jam for Liverpool, or anywhere else. For a
while it was feared that we might be laid up, but a cargo of
timber was arranged from outports towards South Australia.
There were still several small sailers engaged in this trade. We
towed to a sawmill in the Huon River, and the scenery that
lovely day was so beautiful that it seemed incongruous to have
a sawmill there at all. I thought that when the time might
come, many years afterwards, for me to leave the sea, I would
retire to somewhere down the Huon or on Bruny Island. The
whole of southern Tasmania then was a wonderland, a rolling
forest land of beautiful wooded hills, fern-lined gulleys, and
high mountains.

Quite close to our sawmill was a new ship, a lofty barquentine which had just been completed there, built from Huon

pine which the mill had dressed. The name on her counter was *Amelia J.* As the sun set over her she looked almost fairy-like, a dream ship; the news that she was destined for the coal trade from Newcastle was a rude shock. She had just been commissioned and was about to sail on her maiden voyage. She was so attractive a model that our old Finn could not resist her. He packed his bags and joined forthwith.

'In many ships 'ave I bin, for sixty yars,' he said, 'but neffer one like *dat*. I go.'

She was his last. The *Amelia J.* went missing, deep-laden with coal, not long after she was launched. Perhaps she did not care for her cargo of coal. At any rate, when she went our old Finn was still with her. So were some boys from Captain Suffern's.

While we were loading in the Huon River the captain's wife and family joined, and Sandy McNab left. He did not hold with women in ships. We shipped a young Tasmanian able seaman, named Johnny Gleeson, in place of the Finn. Johnny was about twenty, fair as a Scandinavian. He had already been with Captain Murchison's brother Finlay in the barque *Wathara* on a Cape Horn voyage, and had been sunk in the *Pinmore* by the Graf Felix von Luckner in the war. He came to us from the brigantine *Rachel Cohen*, a queer little black wall-sided thing which was in the Macquarie Island penguin oil business. She was commanded by an ancient named Joe Hatch, who looked like St Paul and made his living boiling down penguins in the sub-Antarctic for their oil. Poor penguins! The white-whiskered Hatch had a runway contrived for them on the beach at Macquarie Island, up which they ran to fall into the boiling vats, alive. Johnny made only one voyage with him. The penguins were too much like sailors, he said.

Tasmanian timber was very different from New Zealand's. It was heavy stuff, and the barque was loaded to her plimsoll mark without deck cargo. We sailed on a quiet morning round the south of Tasmania and up to wind'ard across the Southern Ocean, towards Spencer Gulf and Port Pirie. It was like beating to the west'ard past the Horn. Gale after gale swept down on us. It was midwinter, and savagely cold. The wind'ard road from South Tasmanian timber ports towards the Leeuwin, wild as it was, was well known to Captain Murchison and his mates. Many a small Colonial barque had eked out a hard living in that trade over the past two-score years, and they had been in most of them. The new bos'n was a Tasmanian known as Dimple Smart, a hard-bitten mariner out of the barque *Wild Wave*. The Roaring Forties were Dimple's home.

We were about a month beating across the Southern Ocean. Sometimes it blew so hard and the sea was so great that we were all but hove-to. On one such night, a fresh-water tank which had been secured on the fore part of the house broke adrift, and washed about the decks threatening to break the watch's legs.

'Overboard with the bastard!' shouted Dimple.

We got after the tank, to push it outboard with a roll to leeward before it maimed somebody. But we could not get near it, or hold it when we were near it. It seemed possessed of the spirits of the South Seas demons, now rushing at us on the foaming sea which broke over the rail, knocking us down; now making a wild sweep towards the lee main rigging; now rolling about the decks as they were momentarily dry, with a fearsome clatter as if it wanted to summon up the host of dead from the floor of that great ocean. Once we got the thing to the rail, and Sharkey Keen and Johnny Gleeson pushed it outboard with capstan-bars. Then the ship rolled under it again, and scooped it out of the sea. Once more it careered wildly about the decks, knocking old Bill Barrett down and taking a swipe at Dan Murchison which would have killed him had he taken the full force of it. Dan swore in Gaelic. Old Bill raved like a madman. A giant sea filled the decks again while the wind screamed and the ship lurched violently, lying far over to leeward. Aft swept the tank, fetching up against the poop bulkhead with a crash that awakened all hands. Now the barque rolled to wind'ard again with a wild swing. Across the foaming decks the tank swept, murderous and determined.

'Out of its way!' screamed Dimple. We jumped for the rigging, waiting for a lull to descend to the decks again and man-handle the tank once more into the sea. A second time we had it overboard: *a second time it rolled inboard again*, for the ship was drifting bodily to leeward and scooped it out of the sea.

'All right, you insufferable bastard!' roared Dimple. 'If you won't go overboard, you'll bloody well stay inboard! After him!'

The tank worked into the lee corner of the maindeck by the break of the poop. Cautiously we made our way towards the thing, as a brief lull and a dry deck kept it stationary a moment. We were almost round it, each with a lashing to try to secure it somehow to a ringbolt or bitts, or to several pins in the rail, when the ship fell down in the sea and scooped up a green one, which plucked the tank off the deck and at last took it away. The last we saw of it, it was rolling over and over in an absolute hell of foam.

'That's what you get,' gasped old Bill Barrett; 'that's what you get f'r shippin' out in a thing that has a bloody mess-room! 'Tain't right! 'Tain't right, it ain't! Bloody mess-room in a sailing-ship – bound to be trouble!'

Bill was a sour and disconsolate man with a great distrust of the Southern Ocean and an immense hatred for the sea. He was the only sailor I remember like that. His hatred was in-cessant and intense. It was a personal thing that lived with him, and he could not get away from it. He had been at sea for more than sixty years. There was no other calling he knew, no other way for him to gain a livelihood. He spent every minute of his night watches on deck, walking by the break of the poop, unlike we others, who generally sought what shelter we might find when there was no work to be done. He looked upon the sails as personal enemies and the sea as an arch-fiend. His language, if one stood beside him on the foot-rope getting in a fighting tops'l, was almost maniacal. In his watch below, Bill always kept an ear cocked for calamity. At the slightest sound of change of wind or sea, out he jumped and was on deck in an instant. His hatred allowed him little sleep. He ate his meals in a tin plate on his knees, outside the galley, no matter what the weather. He would never go in the mess-room.

Bill Barrett neither yarned nor listened to yarns. I wish he had passed on some of his stories. Later I learned that he had plenty of them. He had been A.B. in the sweet Tasmanian *Harriet McGregor*, in the Hobart–London trade, in the *Lufra* and *Wagoola*, and the *Brier Holme*. He'd been a whaler in the *Flying Childers*, and many more. He had been a sailor in the queer old barque *Royal Tar*, on the extraordinary voyage when she took the Utopians to Patagonia (perhaps this had helped to sour him, for the visionaries of the New Australia Coopera-tive Settlement Association must have been difficult for an old salt to tolerate over a long voyage). Bill was in the *Royal Tar* earlier, when she sailed from New Guinea to San Francisco with all the crew down with blackwater fever, drifting about the Pacific for months. He'd been with Jackie Shimmins in the *Edward* and the *Natal Queen*, and had shared in the loss of both.

Sometimes Bill would awake with a violent start and spring from his bunk like a madman.

'He's at me for it!' he would scream. 'He's at me! At me innards!'

I thought he had delirium tremens. Later, when he had left, I learned that once, when much younger, he had been thrown away on the island of Kerguelen from the wreck of some Hobart sealing and whaling barque, and was one of the sur-vivors who made a small boat in which they sailed through the Roaring Forties the 3,000 miles back to Tasmania. There was some cannibalism. They ate a boy. It was the boy, perhaps, who was at the old man.

Bill left in Port Pirie the day we arrived, still cursing the sea and trying to forget the Kerguelen voyage. He wanted to get some sleep, he said. Instead, he got violently drunk. The last I saw of him he was asking the mate of the Scots ship *Kirkud-brightshire*, astern of us, for a job. Poor Bill! He was a small man with short, fat legs, and enormous twisted hands. He had a grisly grey moustache, always drooping, and he kept an old

felt hat jammed on his grey head. He could neither live with
ships nor without them. He was a magnificent hand aloft; but
we were glad when he had gone.

Our Tasmanian timber was part-cargo for Port Pirie, remainder
for Port Adelaide, where we loaded superphosphates in bags
for New Zealand. At the wharf in Port Adelaide the *James
Craig* was one of a trio of square-rigged ships. The others were
Wild Wave, a stub-toed Tasmanian ancient with a round
English stern, and the big four-masted barque *Mariechen*. Her
port of registry was Mariehamn, a place of which I had not
previously heard, and from her gaff a strange flag flew. It was a
pale blue cross on a clean white ground.

'That's the new flag of Finland,' said Johnny. 'She's a square-
head.'

I looked at the big ship curiously. She was a massive ship,
manned by young fellows with white hair and pale yellow eyebrows. The name on her bell for'ard was *Glenericht*. She was
very clean, and scrupulously well kept. She looked a fine ship,
but I did not ask for a job aboard. The tow-headed young men
spoke a peculiar language.

The little *Craig* tramped pleasantly about the Tasman Sea
for several voyages, and I continued to be very happy aboard.
I liked the life. Our crew became younger and younger, as
the older men left. Both in New Zealand and Australia we
shipped young men from the colonial barques, the *Dartford*,
the *Gladbrook*, the *Rona*, and the *Raupo*, all of which had
been reduced to hulks again or were about to be. Our fo'c'sle
was full of a pleasant crowd, and all good sailormen. One of
them, a Port Chalmers man from the barque *Gladbrook*, had
an album of photographs from that old-timer's Pacific voyages.
Such an album was a rarity then. No one had a camera aboard.
The older sailors had no photographs, but they had prodigious
memories, and I listened to their yarns with the greatest of
interest. As an ordinary seaman it behoved me to be silent
when my elders were speaking. That was no hardship. I knew
no yarns, and theirs were fascinating. I wish now that I had

recorded them. I kept something of a log, for I knew that I was sailing at the end of an era; but the log was not detailed enough. At the time I did not sufficiently appreciate how rich – and how rapidly disappearing – a vein of source material I was allowed to know. Nor did it ever occur to me that some day I should be something of a sailing-ship historian. I was still studying laboriously to become, some years hence, a square-rigged second mate, and had much in mind my ambition to become a sailing-ship captain, like Murdo' Murchison or the captain of the *Glenericht*. But not of the *Wild Wave*, nor the *Rachel Cohen*, nor the tops'l schooner *Joseph Sims*. When I knew them, these were lowly and ungainly little wagons.

It seemed to me that our Captain Murchison in the *James Craig* led a highly satisfactory and very useful life. She was a small barque, only 640 tons. But she was a handy one, and she did her share of the world's work efficiently. Her master navigated and sailed the ship, and had a beautiful panelled saloon to live in with his family. The saloon was painted white and gold, and there was much plush and mahogany. Off it were the captain's sleeping quarters, a small bathroom, and a tiny spare cabin, where his little daughter lived. She was perhaps five years old. Mrs Murchison was cabin 'boy' and looked after the quarters and her children. She had enough to do. She was a pleasant young woman who kept out of sight, and her influence aboard was good. The small children had the run of the ship in good weather. They often played in the galley or scampered into the fo'c'sle. They were great favourites with the sailors, who made them little ships to play with. The happy laughter of tiny children in the old ship fo'c'sle, reeking of Stockholm tar and marline, was perhaps a strange sound, but it did not seem an incongruous one. Some of the Scots there were their clansmen.

Perhaps the *Craig*, sailing in the South-west Pacific in the early 1920s, was an unusual old barque. At any rate, she was a very happy one and I don't recall that any of the more experienced men remarked on this as unusual – not, at any rate, in the colonial barques.

'Are all ships like this?' I asked Johnny Gleeson one day.

He laughed. 'All ships like this? I should say not! Go in a miserable lime-juicer, or a goddam' Yank!'

It seemed to me that the fo'c'sle of a happy sailing-ship at sea was one of the more pleasant abodes of labouring man, where the sailors of all nations had learned through the centuries to work and live amicably together. Here there was true democracy, true international cooperation. At least all were equal in their lack of possessions, their pride in their great calling and their skill, and their spirit of service in the ship. It has often seemed to me since, when as a newspaper-man in Fleet Street it was my misfortune to attend international conferences and the like, that those old sailors knew more about the realities of cooperation than the self-seeking politicians ashore ever dreamt existed. A sailor was a man for his own sake; one of a team. He lived a full life and he looked four-square upon the world, a world from which he sought no false distractions except in the frightful mediocrity of ports. And the high standard of real good manners – not a lacquer of standardized behaviour, painfully acquired and even more painfully transparent, but based upon genuine consideration and respect for the problems of one's kind and a real ability to share the life of his own small community – was astonishing to me, whose previous ideas of sea life had been gained from books and a brief experience in the half-deck of the *Rothesay Bay*.

Perhaps I was lucky in Jackie Shimmins' choice of ship. But I was to serve in many fo'c'sles, and the life in them all, *at sea*, was well ordered and mannerly.

Then one day we sailed into Port Phillip Bay with a cargo of planks from New Zealand, and we towed up the Yarra past the glass-bottle factory at Spotswood, and secured alongside a berth in the swinging basin between the squarehead ship *G. D. Kennedy* and the *Bohus*, a barque. No sooner were we tied up than word came for'ard that the *Craig* was to go to Hobart as a hulk, and she would sail no more.

CHAPTER SEVEN

LIME-JUICE VOYAGE

THIS was a mess. How was I going to complete my four years' time, which I must serve before being allowed to go for second mate? There was a council of war in the *Craig*'s fo'c'sle, for I was not the only one there still short of sea time.

'It looks as if we'll have to go in a Limey,' said Johnny, disconsolately. 'We'll feel it after this one.'

'That we will,' put in Sharkey Keen. 'Well, whatever one we go in, it's no *Cumberland* for me! Or the *Terpsichore*, or the *Wiscombe Park*, or any other dirty, great, single t'gall'nt bitch! But isn't there one of these inter-colonials left, after we're gone?'

'There's the *White Pine*, somewhere,' suggested Duncan McKenzie, a New Zealander who'd joined us one passage in Auckland. 'But where? I dunno. She'd do us. She's a lovely little thing. Captain Proctor has her. He's all right.'

'Well, she isn't in Melbourne,' I said. 'And according to Tom Germein there's nothing left out of Sydney either.'

Tom had written me that he had shipped in the *Amelia J.*, but had the good fortune to leave just before she went missing. He was then in the barquentine *Alexa*, trading to the Gilbert Islands. He said he'd thought of joining, the British *Monkbarns* at Newcastle, but was told she was going home to be laid up. He meant to stay in the *Alexa* as long as he could, though he would like to serve some time in a big Cape Horner. For the time being, it was not possible. The bottom was falling out of world freight markets, and steamers were driving the last of the small barques from the Tasman Sea. The *Rothesay Bay* was already a coal hulk at Wellington. The *Shandon* was a hulk in Melbourne before our eyes. There were a few barquentines and schooners still in the trade, but none of these was then in Melbourne.

There were, however, several deep-sea sailing-ships in Melbourne at the time. In the swinging basin where the *James Craig* lay, the Swedish *Svithiod*, *G. D. Kennedy*, and *Bohus* were all discharging Baltic pine. Two four-masted schooners down from Puget Sound were putting out for Oregon. They were the *Resolute* and the *Carrier Dove*, which did not look very dovelike. They were both American. We did not consider shipping in a schooner, or a Swede, though all three squareheads were lovely vessels. Two of them were school-ships, full of boys. They were all old British ships. The name on the *Svithiod*'s bell was *Routenburn*, and she had a particularly beautiful hull. On the *Kennedy*'s bell we read the name *Dunboyne*. She had a white hull, spotless decks, and yellow masts and yards, all beautifully kept. But she must have had a hundred boys. There would never be any jobs with her.

Johnny and I were appointed a committee to go to Williamstown, at the mouth of the Yarra, to see what was there. In the distance we could see the masts and yards of two big square-riggers in that direction. We found they were the four-masted barques *Hougomont* and *Bellands*.

'Let's look 'em over close,' said Johnny. 'It'll be one of these.'

We walked slowly along the railway pier, where both were loading grain in sacks. They were fine, large vessels. After the *James Craig*'s 640 tons they looked tremendous. They were each about 3,000 tons and they looked like liners to me. I liked them both, and would gladly have shipped in either. Both were reported to be in need of hands, as many of their crews had deserted – an old lime-juice habit in Australia.

'I'm for the *Hougomont*,' I announced, after a very cursory inspection. I liked the long sweep of her open decks, her nice sheer, her steel wheelhouse, and the general appearance of her. The other ship was much larger and had a built-in midships section, like a three-island steamer. To my mind, this spoilt the sweep of her decks. Both ships were strongly rigged. Both had double t'gall'nts and royals on all three square-rigged masts. But the *Bellands* looked clumsy to me beside the *Hougomont*, though neither was a clipper.

Johnny took a much longer look at both ships before venturing his own opinion. His narrowed eyes took in details alow and aloft.

'The *Hougomont*, did you say?' he said at last. 'No. I think I prefer the other. And look here, Snow, here's why. First, take a good look at your *Hougomont*. I guess it's the wheelhouse and the nice long maindeck that took your fancy. But the maindeck will fill with water as soon as she gets outside. These are Cape Horners, and they'll have a full gut before they leave this wharf. They'll be wet ships, both of 'em. But the *Hougomont*'ll be the worst, you mark my words.'

'But why, Johnny? What's the difference?'

'I'll tell you why. Look at her low bulwarks. Look at the low freeboard she'll have, when she's down to her marks. Think of the sweep the sea'll have, galloping around that great deck. Her houses will be unlivable and all hands'll be half-drowned. Then look at her braces. All the old hand stuff just like the *Jimmy Craig*, leading to the rails. Heavy as hell! Lee fore brace in her running for the Horn will drown somebody, and weather crojack brace'll rupture 'em. And I'll bet she steers like a bitch.'

I listened with astonished interest. What Johnny said about the open deck was right. The small decks of the *Craig* were dangerous enough when they were full of water in a heavy sea. Why he condemned the poor *Hougomont*'s steering qualities I did not know, and he did not explain. He went on to expound the merits of the *Bellands*, where there was a pleasing sound of caulking hammers, and the gentle breeze blew a quiet symphony in the high rigging. The *Bellands* was the largest sailing vessel (except the five-masted *France*) I had seen, and that in itself had put me against her.

'Size isn't everything,' said Johnny. 'Indeed, it needn't be anything at all. Just look at these points. First, she's got a Liverpool house. Now that house means a lot of good dry bunks for the Jackshites many a time when the *Hougomont*'s

crowd'll be bailing their fo'c'sle. I don't say it can't be washed
out, too, but it's obviously a lot less likely than in any ordinary
sort of ship, like the *Hougomont*. She's like a three-island
steamer on deck, except she'll never be pounding into the
weather the way a steamer does. That's point number one.'

'But, Johnny,' I said. 'That may be so. But every time you
work the braces or have to go along the deck for anything you'd
have to gallop over the midships structure. There's no way
around it. You'd be up and down companions all the time.'

Johnny snorted.

'What do you want, lifts up the masts? Get this, you lazy so-
and-so! That structure means less sea aboard. Seas knock you
down, sweep you overboard, break your bones. Running up
and down ladders might be inconvenient, but it won't hurt
you. And see here too,' Johnny went on, warming to his subject, 'do you notice anything peculiar about those braces?
Have a good look now – not the t'gall'nts and royals. The
heavy ones. The course and tops'l braces. There's something
about them that ought to appeal to your lazy nature.'

'Why, they're all wire. And they lead strangely. Some of 'em
seem to be double-ended – one end of wire leads to blocks at
the tops, and t'other leads – why, let me see. I can't make it
out at all.'

'What she has is brace-winches,' said Johnny, with an air of
knowledge. 'You haven't been with them. They don't have 'em
in little wagons. But, you believe me, they're good in big ships.
They take the drudgery out of bracing. And I'll bet she's got a
capstan for every course tack and sheet. Here, let's go aboard
and see.'

We marched up the steep gangway, past the notice which
said NO ADMITTANCE EXCEPT ON BUSINESS. Johnny and I were
on very serious business indeed, investigating the merits of a
Cape Horn ship. On deck she was like a liner. The massive
masts and yards rose to the heavens, and the maze of her rigging seemed to allow no clear space for slinging cargo in. The
great sweep of her seemed as long as the straight at Flemington, but much more exciting. Her huge fo'c'sle head lifted a

long steel bowsprit high over the end of the wharf, and her lower yards looked at least a hundred feet long. (They were, in fact, 92 feet.) She had a sort of cat-walk bridge extending fore-and-aft the whole length of her, so that it was not necessary to descend to the main deck to get about. As Johnny forecast, she had seven capstans, and abaft each fife-rail except the fore was an ingenious hand-winch of wire drums, the functions of which, my shipmate explained, were to pay out and heave in the wire braces, as a few men turned the handles. Well-kept wires from these drums led into the rigging, where they passed through blocks to reach the yards on the mast next ahead. Johnny was enthusiastic about the brace-winches, pointing out the brakes on them and explaining how they simplified the work.

'They're dandy for going about,' he said. 'Instead of half the watch having to take in the braces, one man can stand by the winch here at the brake, and she'll do the job herself. Only you have to be careful to slack away a little on the whips first, to allow a bit of play. That's the whips, by the rail there. You set 'em taut afterwards, and that's all the pulley-haulie there is. And look up here at all the gear for the sails. Every buntline in her is good steel wire, and plenty of 'em too. Look, five to each tops'l, five and two leachlines for the courses, four for the t'gall'nts, five for the royals. She'll do me, I tell you. And I'll bet she has crew enough to eat her.'

'Maybe they won't have too much else to eat,' I suggested. 'Didn't you and Sharkey say Limeys were the hungriest ships afloat?'

But nothing would quench Johnny's enthusiasm.

'Don't be always thinking of your guts,' he said. 'Of course she'll be hungry, by Australian standards. She'll be on bare "whack". You'll get your pound and pint, and nothing else. English chaps don't get as much to eat as we do, ashore or afloat. Well, men have stood that for a good many hundred years. I reckon we can take a year or two of it, too.'

We looked all over the ship, except in the poop. The officers lived there, although everybody else was accommodated in the midships section. There was an alleyway running through this giving easy access fore and aft (in port), and we peered into her big fo'c'sles and the galley. The name on her bell was *Forteviot*. There was another name painted in heavy black lettering on the lifeboats. It had been painted over but could still be read. *Werner Vinnen* it said.

'So she's been a German,' Johnny commented with satisfaction. 'They knew good ships. She'll be all right.'

Johnny had a great deal of admiration for the seafaring Germans, based on his experiences with Graf von Luckner after the *Pinmore* was sunk by the *Seeadler*. Von Luckner might have sunk his ship, but he was a hero to Johnny.

As we were about to go ashore a short man standing by the break of the poop hailed us.

'You young fellows looking for a ship?' he said. 'I've been watching you.'

He looked like old Jackie Shimmins, perhaps five years younger.

'Yes, sir,' said Johnny. 'We're looking for a ship to serve some more time for our second mate's tickets. Are there any berths here?'

'Yes, my boy, if you've been in sail. We need several able seamen. Have you your papers with you?'

Johnny and I fished out our discharges. 'We're from the barque *James Craig*, up the river sir,' he said. 'She's going to be hulked. Do you have any idea how long this one may stay in commission?'

'Ah, that no man knows. I'm the mate; nobody aboard here knows how long she'll fly the Red Duster. We'll be taking this grain to Falmouth for orders. Pay off in Europe, you know. That's our articles. Sixty North to Sixty South, sign for three years, wages of the port. Pay off in Europe.'

A minute or two later we had arranged to sign on, Johnny as A.B. at fourteen pounds ten a month, myself as ordinary seaman at eight pounds ten. These were good wages.

'Bring all the other young fellows you can get,' said the old mate. 'We can do with 'em.'

We brought Duncan McKenzie, and a Swede, and a couple of young chaps from the ship *Cardinia* (which had thrown herself on a reef in the Fijis) who had been pestering the *Craig* for berths. I still had a sneaking regard for the fine sweep of the *Hougomont* and regarded the *Bellands* as somewhat mechanical. But the decision was made. It never occurred to me to stay ashore, though this was my first visit to Melbourne since I had gone to sea. I went one evening to a school concert at the Moonee Ponds town hall, to find myself among a horde of callow youth, with whom I had nothing any longer in common, though I had been at school with them two years earlier. They were already the landsmen. A pimply youth near me who had a teacher's scholarship was shouting derogatory views on women. I felt his test was to come.

The *Bellands* moved out to anchorage in Hobson's Bay on Christmas Eve, and we began to prepare her for the long passage towards Falmouth for orders. We lay in the bay for eleven days. As my suburban home was in sight from the yards and I had not been home for Christmas for some time, I asked for leave. This was curtly refused. Until then I had not seen the captain, who spent most of his time ashore. He was a cold man with protruding eyes. He looked more like a suburban grocer than a Cape Horn sailor. The official reason for refusing leave was given as fear of desertion. Those of us who came from Melbourne were all very young, and we were not drunkards. Having just signed on, and being committed to a sea career, we were scarcely likely to desert.

But there it was. We were in a lime-juicer now, and before the mast at that. I quickly gathered that, as far as the afterguard was concerned, we were less than the scupper-dirt. After the free acceptance of man and boy at their own worth, fore and aft, which prevailed in the Tasman Sea barques, this brusque intolerance struck me as strange. It was not the only shock the big *Bellands* brought me. I looked about me at the big four-master, lying idly with 5,000 tons of wheat which a hungry Europe urgently required, and wondered what I had let myself in for.

I wondered a great deal more a day or two later, when there was a row in the port fo'c'sle and a Cockney able seaman led a deputation aft about the food (which was atrocious). The immediate cause of the trouble was a kettle, in which the watch was supposed to draw its tea. The kettle leaked beyond repair. As spokesman for his shipmates, the Cockney requested a new kettle and better food, as it was the holiday season. The mate said there were no new kettles, and they were already getting all the food they had signed for. The Cockney demanded to see the captain, saying that they might as well have things put right before they went to sea. There were a few words.

The captain's answer was to make a hoist of flags, requesting a police boat. Off came the Williamstown police, full of fire, expecting to deal with at least a mutiny. But there was only poor Cockney. He was taken away under arrest. In a few days we heard that he had been sentenced to a month's hard labour.

We young Australians and New Zealanders thought pretty furiously about this. To us, this was a new way to treat mariners. We felt the cold hand of class distinction descend upon us, and resented it sharply. Our food was the minimum scale laid down by the Merchant Shipping Act for the sustenance of deep-sea mariners. It was of the poorest quality, parsimoniously distributed. Every possible distinction was made between the poop and the fo'c'sle. Our stores were labelled 'crew' this and that, crew coffee (the sweepings of some warehouse with slight connexion with the coffee trade), crew marmalade (a mushy brown oil in stone jars, made in Dundee), crew everything else that a wily ship-chandler could produce in a state of sufficient inferiority to bear the label. Even the fresh potatoes, after the first few days, were strictly reserved for the afterguard. We had some dried and preserved muck which was war surplus, and must have been raised beneath the sea. This sort of thing was new to me. The Tasman Sea barques had not been mean, though we knew what shortage was in the *Rothesay Bay*. The English, it seemed to me, were a strange lot. That well-found great ship, paying high wages to an abundant crew, had a good freight and could save very little by meanness with the food.

'It's hunger and ease aboard lime-juice ships,' said a Seattle Yank whose last ship had been one of the Hind, Rolph skys'l-yard barquentines out of San Francisco. 'Yeah, hunger and ease. Plenty of hunger and not much ease. Too big crews, not enough to do, and not a goddam' sailor in the poop at all.'

'But yez wouldn't go back in the Rolph ship,' said a Peruvian from the *Guaytecas*.

'Waal, there was 'nuff to eat there, and to spare.'

'Aye, and belaying pin soup for an appetizer. Ze Limeys ain't ze worst.' The Peruvian was not impressed.

'They was sailors in the afterguard, too,' the Yank went on. 'We never hung around an anchorage with a bellyful of cargo. It was sail her, load her, and sail her again with them.'

'Aye, on flying-fish v'yages,' a Swede commented. 'Dis ship ain't on no flying-fish run. It takes time to get a big ship ready for Cape Horn.'

She certainly was put in a state of readiness for heavy weather. All the best sails were bent and these were practically a new suit, all the gear overhauled, everything about the decks secured, and the hatches caulked and battened down, and then breakwaters were built up over them to prevent the breaking seas from stoving them in. When all this was done we were towed down to Melbourne Heads. There the four-master waited another week; why, I don't know. The weather was good. We had a full crew. The ship was as completely stored and provisioned as she was ever likely to be. When after several false attempts we did make a start at the end of the first week in January, we were towed through the Heads and several miles outside, though the *G. D. Kennedy* came sailing past us, under a press of sail. The weather was fine and there was a fair wind. Towage was an expensive item in Australian ports. A good proportion of the sum the *Bellands* spent on tugs in Melbourne could have been saved.

I was surprised to notice how little difference the extreme size of the vessel made to the actual amount of work on sailing-day compared with the handy barques. Indeed, there was considerably more work in them. In the first place, the *Ballands* had a large donkey which was used to weigh anchor and get the heavier yards aloft. She had eighteen able seamen, all skilled sailing-ship men except one. She had two bos'ns, both good organizers and leaders. She had half a dozen apprentices besides, to do the donkey-work. The brace-winches and her ample deck capstans lightened the braces, tacks, and sheets. I noticed with amazement that the youngest apprentice was not allowed to go to the higher yards, though he had been in the ship a year and was an alert and agile boy. Truly the ways of the lime-juicer seemed strange.

The wind blew from the north-east, light and fair. We headed south-west down the Victorian coast towards Cape Otway, though the *G. D. Kennedy* sailed the other way. What now? I asked. Were we going the Jackie Shimmins way round Tasmania to avoid Bass Straits? But surely that did not make sense. Leaving Melbourne Heads, we were already well into the straits; it was asking for trouble to shape a course then to make a lee shore of the stormy west of Tasmania.

'He's going round Good Hope, if the wind holds.' It was Yank who brought the news for'ard after his first dog-watch wheel.

'Good Hope? Corblime,' said Johnny. 'Oh, well, more days more dollars, I suppose. But I've never heard of a ship out of Melbourne going that way. From South Australia, yes; and from the West it's shortest. But what's all the hatches caulked and breakwatered for, and us setting out on a flying-fish passage, after all? He'll never make it.'

'You're dam' right he won't, Tassie,' said a young Australian from the barque *Inverneil*. 'Our last run we were bound t'wards Bunbury from Melbourne here. That's only 3,000 miles. But we were so slammed about in the westerly gales in the Bight that the old man put up the helm and we ran for it round the Horn and Good Hope, the whole bleeding way round the globe.

Sixty-five days we were. And the *Inverneil* could sail rings
around this hog-gutted warehouse.'

I had not heard of the Good Hope route for sailing vessels
bound from Melbourne towards the English Channel. I thought
we should have to go round the Horn because there was no
other way. Johnny explained that if a square-rigged ship,
leaving with an easterly wind which she could hold a while,
could only get across the Australian Bight and past Cape
Leeuwin, then she could stand up to the nor'ard there in the
Indian Ocean and pick up the tail of the trades to carry her
westwards towards the Cape of Good Hope. There was a
favouring current to help round Good Hope, and after that
southerly winds could be relied on, more or less, to sail up to
the Atlantic trades. When they'd sailed that far they were
nearly home. It was a risky way to go, though, from Melbourne.
It would be difficult to get across the Bight; even after that
the passage, if it were feasible at all, would be a slow one.

No Cape Horn! I was disappointed bitterly. I had looked
forward to this first chance of making that classic rounding. I
was, however, alone in my chagrin. The older seamen were well
pleased at the news, or indifferent to it. Most of them reckoned
a west-to-east run round the Horn no rounding, anyway.

That was before they knew there was no tobacco in the slop-
chest. When they discovered that, there was an uproar. No
tobacco! It was the only real comfort the men knew. Sailors
in deep-sea ships relied upon buying their tobacco from the
slop-chest kept by the captain of the ship, where it was available at the captain's interpretation of duty-free prices. Price
was a secondary consideration, since no money was actually
handed over. The captain kept an account and charged purchases against wages. Tobacco, clothing, blankets, oilskins,
knives, soap – all the everyday necessities of the sea life
(usually the scourings of some dreadful chandlery in a slum
port) were supposed to be available. It was in a captain's interest to conduct a good slop-chest, not only for the sake of
morale and welfare generally, but the profits were his. These
could be considerable.

We crossed the Indian Ocean in the Trades. A weather-side view
of the *Parma*

The *Beatrice* was lovely, and she could sail. She had an especially clean-lined Scotch hull, and graceful bows

There was plenty of work aloft. Here three boys work on the high yards of the *Grace Harwar* to get an upper topgallant-sail fast

With her long poop she ran dry. The high freeboard kept all but the heaviest seas from breaking aboard – a view of the *Herzogin Cecilie* from the fore-top looking aft

The news that there was no tobacco in the *Bellands'* slop-chest was not believed at first. It was too fantastic. Not even the oldest hand had ever heard of such a thing. No tobacco, and the ship was not a week out from port, bound on a passage that might take four months, or seven! The men off watch crowded aft to verify the news. It was true. There *was* no tobacco. The miserable captain had forgotten to take in a sea stock.

Morale took a steep decline. It had quite recovered from the shock of the Cockney's imprisonment in Melbourne. The weather was good. The easterly wind held, and we were having the most famous luck with the sailing. The big wagon lurched along in the Australian Bight like a steamer, her sails bathed in sunshine day after day and scarcely water enough on deck to help with the washing down. The news that there was nothing to smoke struck the men hard. They cursed and growled, and became furiously bad-tempered. A few were for going aft in a body and demanding that the ship put into Albany, or Bunbury, or Fremantle. But, for the time being at any rate, the shouting was confined to the fo'c'sle. No one went aft. The chantymen in both watches added verses to their chanties drawing pointed attention to the need for a smoke. But that was as far as it went. The good discipline of the sailing-ship men kept things going, though as day followed day and the weather continued monotonously good, some of the men grew so morose that they began actively to dislike the few non-smokers who did not share the general misery.

One and all set about the search for a substitute with resource and determination. But there is no substitute for good tobacco. Some made mixtures of which the main ingredient was their own hair. Some teased out rope-yarns and mixed a few shavings and bits of sail twine. Several tried tea-leaves, but the tea in the *Bellands* was atrocious stuff, both as tea and as tobacco. Some stuck to brown paper and cane, but the supply of both was very limited. As we passed the Leeuwin and came up to the good weather of the Indian Ocean, turning westwards on about 27 degrees south, and the moss and barnacles began to gather on the ship's sides (she had not been dry-docked in Melbourne), some optimists scraped the moss up and dried it in the sunshine. They tried even this as tobacco. But it set up a poison gas which nearly suffocated them, and made the fo'c'sle where they were experimenting unliveable.

With the tail of the south-east trade as a light fair wind, we sailed on westwards. We were in a lonely part of the ocean and sighted no other ships. Day after day the trade wind blew and, upright and lovely, the big four-master slipped quietly along. Her speed was rarely better than seven knots, but it never dropped below five. Flying-fish skimmed before the great cutwater, and the conditions were excellent. Week after week the main deck was dry and there was never need to touch a sail. The huge crew was divided into watchkeepers and daymen, though there was not much attempt to get a fair day's work out of either. The ship was in good order; the sails and rigging were well kept up; soon there was a shortage of jobs. The working routine was easy – too easy, with the too-large crew and all that good weather – and the life should have been pleasant enough. But instead it was wretched. I had no idea tobacco could mean so much to men, and resolved to have nothing to do with it for the rest of my life. All the petty annoyances and slight frictions which normally they would have taken in their stride were magnified into excessive hardships.

In any other lime-juice ship the poor food and the ordinary discomforts of the sea life would have formed the basis of dog-watch songs, to be sung round the main hatch to the accompaniment of 'music' played on dilapidated combs. Except for chanties, there was little singing in the *Bellands* that voyage. The older apprentices who had been in the ship nearly four years (and were treated as extra ordinary seamen) were masters of the art of thieving cabin stores, The sailors raided the fresh potatoes, and ate them raw. To the for'ard hands, the steward was a bitter enemy: the cooks were enemies: the officers were enemies. The galley was locked by night and given up to the cockroaches; the cooks – there were two of them – had no friends. The petty officers were not enemies, but they were not friends, except the two Norwegian bos'ns. These were referred to as Dutchmen or Squareheads, neither epithet being intended as complimentary. But they were a good pair, and generally respected. There was a harsh insistence by both the sail-maker and the carpenter on the formal limits of their work. Neither did very much. The ship's sails had been sewn expensively ashore, and the sail-maker spent much of his time sewing an enormous sea-anchor, and making storm stays'ls which were never used. The carpenter took soundings, oiled the steering gear and the gear aloft once weekly, kept an eye on the windlass, sometimes turned out something for the improvement of the saloon, and made a sea-chest and various gewgaws for himself. Both he and the sail-maker tended their few privileges with greater energy than their skill; that seemed to be the way of things in that ship then.

Half-way across the Indian Ocean the carpenter was set to joining baulks of lumber for an enormous sea-anchor to be used, I gathered, off the Cape of Good Hope. Fifty-four days out from Melbourne Heads we sighted the bulge of South Africa. Three days later we were round the Cape. There was no occasion to use the sea-anchor. When we saw the land there was again a lot of shouting about a deputation aft to make the captain put into Table Bay to buy tobacco. This time a small committee went aft. Its members were a Yankee, a Russian, and a Finn. They got no further than the mate. He had some tobacco of his own and sent them brusquely for'ard. Sailing-ships made no deviations from their voyages not forced on them by act of God; our shortages were very much the act of man, and no captain would admit himself in error by standing into any port to buy comforts for his crew.

We sailed on. Nothing could stop the ship. There was a little head wind, but even then the favouring set carried her onwards. When the wind came from ahead, it was typical of the ship that she was put about by wearing – a clumsy, time-wasting manoeuvre for a ship which can be tacked. She was never tacked. Our bos'n said the captain was afraid of the brace-winches, fearing they would take charge. The sailors, already fuming at the lack of a smoke, openly sneered at what they thought an exhibition of poor seamanship. A good ship handled sloppily is an aggravation to men who take a pride in their calling and are ready and profoundly happy to take a pride in their ship also.

The head wind was soon gone. A southerly came, which grew and grew until it became unmistakably the south-east trade. In little more than a fortnight we were approaching the island of St Helena, which was then still a place of refreshment for long-voyage sailing vessels. The same deputation which had approached the mate off Good Hope now saw the captain and respectfully requested that he touch at St Helena to buy tobacco. Since he was anxious to make the ship's number to the signalling station there, the captain said he would stand close in, and if it was possible to stop a bumboat and get tobacco from it, then he would back the mainyards for a few moments.

Tobacco from a bumboat! What a hope! Any bumboatmen met off St Helena would be on the lookout for duty-free tobacco from us.

The island looked good as we sailed up close, after ten weeks steadily at sea. The weather was pleasant and the sea flat. Sure enough, we saw some bumboats. The first was missed, for the ship had too much way and sailed past before a line could be thrown. The mainyard was backed for the next, which was not missed. As soon as the boat was alongside there was a furious yelling. It was a lively cutter, manned by four large negroes.

'Wantem plurry baccy, Jackie!' shouted an Australian A.B. who must have thought we were off Samarai or Tulagi. 'You fellas savvy baccy! Big fella plurry ship no' got 'em!' And much more in the same strain.

The rail was lined by shouting seamen, all yelling in peculiar English which some used because they thought it appropriate, and others because they had no better.

In the midst of all this, the coxswain of the boat, a burly

great negro with a straw hat carrying the name band of HMS *Lowestoft*, suddenly made himself heard, in a powerful, resonant voice.

'Am I to understand, gentlemen, that you wish to buy some tobacco?' he began, using English with an accent far better than any with which he had been addressed. 'That is about the only thing we do not have,' he went on. 'Indeed, we had hoped to get a little pipe tobacco from you.'

With that he leapt aboard. There was a long palaver. The negro coxswain offered to sail into Jamestown and buy what we wanted, if we would pay for it. As a guarantee of good faith, he wished to leave one of his men aboard. This the captain would not hear of. The coxswain said he would be back with our tobacco by nightfall. It was then about noon.

Some ten or twelve pounds was quickly collected, most of it from the fo'c'sle, and off went the boat on its long pull to windward. All this time we had been drifting steadily to leeward. We continued to drift throughout the afternoon. No attempt was made to stand off and on. By nightfall we were miles from the island, and we saw nothing of the boat again. A deep and abiding gloom settled on the fo'c'sle, and the smokers flung curses at St Helena which would have surprised Napoleon. When a week later we picked up the island of Ascension none of the smokers as much as looked in its direction.

It would have been a simple matter, with the conditions of settled weather and assured fair wind then prevailing, to have sailed close in by the port of Jamestown. There was not much risk about it. But it was perhaps too much to expect from a man who did not like to put his ship about, and spent a flying-fish passage making a sea-anchor for a magnificent great ship which could have ridden out a hurricane.

On the eighty-sixth day out from Melbourne Heads we reached the Equator. Until then the passage had been good enough. But we languished in the doldrums for the following three weeks. Our captain tried to cross the Line too far to the eastwards, not wishing to lose too much longitude, and he allowed the ship to drift into a windless zone where we wallowed for twenty days. A great part of the art of sailing a wind-driven ship consists not so much in using the winds that God provides, but in knowing where He provides them. The main wind-systems of the world are fairly well known. An essential in working any ship through the doldrums is so to plan her course that she gets across where the zone of calms is at its narrowest, regardless of distance lost. There is plenty of information available – the weather charts issued by the United States Hydrographic Office, the bulletins of the Deutsche See-warts, the recommended sailing routes laid down in the British Admiralty's *Ocean Passages of the World*.

Perhaps we had no copies of these publications aboard.

There was one good thing about our long spell in the dol-drums. We drifted into the company of the Norwegian full-rigged ship *Maletta*, forty-four days out with a cargo of maize from Algoa Bay towards Falmouth for orders, and she gave us all the tobacco she could spare. This was enough to last all hands for the next three weeks, and the name of the *Maletta* was blessed among us.

Eventually we picked up the north-east trades. They set in fresh, and the big ship showed that, given a chance, she could sail all right. She soon left the *Maletta* hull-down astern. We were nearly four months at sea, and all hope of a good passage was lost. Any passage of more than four months from Australia to the English Channel is bad.

On May 4th, when our noon position was latitude 28 degrees 26 minutes north, longitude 41 west, we sighted a burning sailing-ship which our appalling afterguard sailed by and abandoned to its fate. This so infuriated the men for'ard that there very nearly *was* a mutiny to compel the captain to allow the ship to fall off a little and at least investigate the ship afire. But the arms were aft. If a poor Cockney went to jail for a month for complaining about the food, where would we be in a mutiny? The merchant shipping acts stand four-square be-hind fools, as well as able master-mariners.

A rocket was seen by one of the lookouts in the middle watch. His report was ignored on the grounds that he had seen either a shooting star, or nothing. But at daybreak the burning ship could clearly be seen. She was about four miles away, then, on our lee quarter. The weather was perfect. She had a few rags of canvas set, and smoke was belching from her main hatch, sometimes black, sometimes white, as a cloud of steam arose when her people pumped water on the flames. Our second mate was an apprentice whose time had expired while the ship was in Melbourne, where he had hastily acquired a certificate. He had the watch. He climbed to the jigger-top with the ship's telescope. From there he could see that the stranger was a big barque, seriously afire. He called the mate. The mate had very bad eyesight, and a poor opinion of the second mate. He could see nothing. This he would not admit, for he stood in peril of being forced out of his livelihood if his poor vision was advertised.

'Nothing but an auxiliary steamer,' he said with a grunt. 'Ocean's full of 'em.'

'Surely, sir, auxiliary steamers generally use funnels as smoke-escapes, not their hatches,' said the second mate, who knew quite well the mate was almost blind.

'That's enough out of you! When you've been at sea as long as I have, you'll know an auxiliary when you see one.' With that the mate stumped down below. I did not see the captain on deck until seven bells. Apparently he also refused to accept the second mate's account, though he must have been aware of his chief mate's very poor eyesight. We sailed on, though we would not have lost more than an hour or two, falling away from the wind and dropping down to offer help.

Months afterwards, when we had come up to Europe, I learned that this vessel was the Dane *Lysglimt*. A notice in Lloyd's List Weekly Summary, dated June 17th, 1921, reads as follows:

From Delagoa Bay. March 6: *Lysglimt* (s.v.) to Kristiania. Abandoned on fire 27.55 North 41.1 West 4th May.

Seeing us sail by, the poor fellows had abandoned their burning barque, and taken to the North Atlantic in boats. They were later picked up, I am glad to say, by the French steamer *Souivah*, and landed at Marseilles.

I was heartily sick of the *Bellands* long before we reached the Bay of Biscay. Food was very short by this stage of the voyage, and morale was extremely poor. What annoyed me was that the stupid privations practised aboard, and the whole unsatisfactory spirit of the ship, were so unnecessary. The voyage was, at any rate, a good object lesson in what *not* to do, if I ever became a sailing-ship captain myself, as I surely proposed to do. In the Bay, where we could reasonably expect good westerlies to blow us in, the wind blew fresh from the east and we beat about for days. Every time the ship was put about she was worn round, true to the *Bellands*' tradition, though a small grey barque close by, under all sails but the gaff tops'l and her royals, was tacking easily enough. Ill-sailed *Bellands*! The great ship had no chance that voyage.

As at last we warped her through the lock gates at St Nazaire, the chantyman shouted verse after verse of long-prepared imprecations upon her, for her tobaccoless voyage, her ham-fisted sailing, her food shortage, her long swelter in the doldrums. I sang the choruses as loudly as the rest, but it was not the ship which should have been criticized. The ship was all right.

We were 151 days at sea, well over 160 from anchorage to anchorage. Across the dock lay the *Hougomont*, her people grinning at us. She also had used the Good Hope way, but she had been 138 days, for she had not sailed until January 17th. The barque we saw beating outside was the *Bohus*, which had barely begun the discharge of her outward cargo when we sailed from Melbourne and yet beat us by a day into the Loire. The *G. D. Kennedy* had long since discharged her grain and was already outward bound again with Baltic timber towards Melbourne. The Finnish *Marlborough Hill* had been only 91 days.

'That'll do, men,' said the mate, coming for'ard when the ship was secured. The sails were still aloft and the decks were a mess. But these words were our release from bondage, our notification that not only was the voyage ended, but our employment. The young men from the Dominions were so thoroughly disgusted with the way the *Bellands* was handled that even the certainty of being thrown out on the beach did not worry us. On the morrow we would sign off and receive our pay. We were finished, thank God, with the *Bellands*. A couple of pimps primed bad whisky into all who would take it, in the fo'c'sles, and a milling crowd of harlots smiled at us from the wharf. The dock was lined with Cape Horn sailing-ships laid up in tiers, and out in the river were a dozen more. Apart from the *Hougomont* and ourselves, none seemed in commission. But, at any rate, a good number of big sailing-ships was still in existence.

I would, I thought as I packed my bag to go to England, soon find another ship to sail in.

Looking back on her voyage now, it seems to me that the unfortunate *Bellands* suffered from a malady which put many a lime-juicer and American ship out of business, in the first two decades of this century – poor officers. It was difficult to induce good men to go in deep-sea sailing-ships when it was to their professional advantage to join one of the big steamship lines. There were plenty of exceptions, and some fine shipmasters and officers remained in sail until the last. But there were more than enough of the other kind; a bad master could ruin the best of sailing-ships, and once he was at sea, his owners had no control over him. The 1914–18 war, with its brief revival of sail and its endless demands for more and more officers to man all kinds of ships, gave commands to some who were unfitted for them; it was, perhaps, inevitable that some of these would be found in sail. The *Bellands* had been a German prize, officered and manned hurriedly. I wish I had been in the *Mount Stewart*, at her best, or in one of the smart *Glens* or *Shires*.

CHAPTER EIGHT

ON THE BEACH

IT was not my idea to go to England. When we were paid off the whole crowd were sent from St Nazaire to our 'home ports', a term which was loosely construed to give Australians and New Zealanders domicile in England, and half the Scandinavians as well. Only the mate and one apprentice remained by the ship. Perhaps the apprentice was allowed to go aloft, now that the ship was safe in dock. We were, I gathered, shipped out of France at the Government's expense, for it was then the middle of 1921 and it was forbidden foreigners – even such cosmopolitans as sailing-ship seamen – to seek work in post-war France. We were shipped off like labelled stores, going across France by train via Nantes, Orléans, and Paris. It was a mistake to send a sailing-ship crew via Paris. Big men from the British Consulate met us at each stop to speed us on our way and make sure we went. But at Paris our score-odd lusty seamen descended from the overnight train from Nantes with a whoop and a wild exuberant surge which broke through the Consul's men's defences. With a rush, they were gone. Three of us from the *James Craig* stayed together, and though we had our fling in Paris too, in due course we went on. Paris was a delightful town, but there were no Cape Horn ships in the vicinity.

In Le Havre were two small barques, *Alastor* and *Shakespeare*, both registered at Kristiansand. We boarded them, for they were fine little ships, like the *Craig*. But they were laid up with no prospect of employment. There were no jobs for them, or likely to be. The ship-keeper aboard said he doubted very much whether we should find a square-rigged ship in commission anywhere.

'The world's gone crazy,' he said. 'There's no work for sailing-ships.'

We went on to Southampton and thence to London. Going

up in the train, I was amazed at the beauty of the lovely English fields. The green land looked like a well-kept park to my Australian eyes. It was all so neat that I wondered whether half its inhabitants spent their evenings sweeping it with loving care, to see no slightest thing was out of place. How could this beautiful land produce the wretched sea cooks of the *Bellands*! How could any meanness spring from this? But in due course we began to enter the sprawling surroundings of the enormity of London, and I could well understand why English people went to sea.

We were far from being a gloomy quartet, though none of us knew what the next move would be. Three of us were ship-mates from the *James Craig*. The fourth was a cheerful youth who had been ordinary seaman in the *Bellands*, though he came from an excellent family which could well have afforded to apprentice him. He was against the apprenticeship system, holding it morally wrong; with this we were in full agreement. This youth surprised us by remarking that his town house was not occupied, at the moment, and we could bed down there if we wished. Town house? What was that? Did people in England live in two houses? Johnny asked.

Our shipmate said his father was headmaster of a co-educational school at Hampstead and, as such, he had a small house in that neighbourhood. But the family lived in the countryside whenever they could. So they had a rambling old house there too. Anyway, the town house was in a suburb of London called Golders Green. It was a long way from the docks, but if we took his advice we should make our temporary home there. Things were very bad in England. We might be looking for a ship a long time.

'There are very few British sailing-ship lines left,' said our shipmate. 'Only four, I think. You've just seen what one of them is like, but for Pete's sake, don't go and form your impressions of England from a miserable passage in an ill-managed four-masted barque. It's our misfortune that we have to sail in great ships at the end of their days. In their heyday it was different!'

'Yes,' agreed Johnny, sitting in a corner looking out at the fields, 'it's too bad that we just grew up in time to find 'em at their last gasp. I'd give something to sign in the *Cutty Sark*! Though the old-timers gave her a good cussing every time her name came up in any fo'c'sle I've been in.'

'What are we going to do now, in London?' I asked. 'Did you say there were four lines left, Porky?'

'Oh, we'll find a ship some time. You can always do anything you stick at long enough, and believe in. Yes, there are four lines – Stewart's, Hardy's in Glasgow, Tommy Law's *Shires*, and Bell's. There's also a Canadian outfit that calls all its ships *Garth* something or other. Stewart's is a London company,' Porky continued. 'Their office is in Billiter Street. We can look in there. They've lots of ships. The *Monkbarns*, *William Mitchell*, *Kilmallie*, and *Falkirk*, at least. As far as I know, though, none of them's in England. Hardy's still have at least three I know of, and there are three or four Scots *Shires*. As for Bell's, maybe you won't be interested. But they still have four sailers. And you must remember an owner can't always help what his captains do, once he appoints them and they get away to sea. You mustn't be biased. All Bell's ships aren't sailed by dug-outs. They're good ships, too – the *Bellas*, *Bellhouse*, *Bellpool*. You'll agree that as a ship, there was nothing wrong with our old *Bellands* either.'

'There were one hundred and twenty Cape Horn ships in, or bound towards, Australian ports when we left,' said Johnny. 'I read that in a shipping paper. They can't *all* just drop out of commission at once, just when I want only three months' more sea-time.'

'There's always steamers,' said Sharkey Keen, from the other corner. Sharkey had been drinking in the delights of the English countryside and had contributed little to the conversation.

'Steamers! Take back that horrible word!' shouted Johnny.

'Gosh, you Aussies are a biased bunch,' said Sharkey, lapsing back into silence.

*

We lost no time putting up at a seamen's home in the East
End, and went out to look for a ship the first afternoon we
were in London. But looking for a ship in a London full of
ships was no easy task. In the first place, getting at the docks
at all was a difficult and mildly depressing business. Here was
no clean waterfront to stroll around, as in Auckland or Wellington, or Sydney, or Hobart. In London, which was then the
busiest and largest port in the world, ships were shut away,
tied up in grimy basins behind vast areas of slums on both
sides of the river. The whole locality where ships and seamen
went about their business was one great array of dirty streets,
dingy back alleys, smelly shops, depressed citizens, and poor
communications. Great ships, even liners whose names were
household words, came creeping stealthily up the bleak river
where the sun rarely shone, past factories and oil-dumps and
groups of laid-up vessels, and were pushed and pummelled by
tugs which reeked smoke all over them, into locks and into
docks, to lie forlorn and dejected a while remote from the freedom of the sea.

London was full of ships, but it was also full of stranded seamen. The janitors at the seamen's home looked at us sharply,
wondering, I don't doubt, how long we could pay our bills.
After a few days we three from the *Craig* moved to the Scandinavian Sailor's Home overlooking the West India Docks, to
be nearer such few sailing-ships as we had discovered. The
fruit of many bus rides and much foot-slogging round the
docks was one full-rigged ship, one four-masted barque, and
one barque. They were all laid up. The barque was the little
Oaklands, the four-master the big *Peking* of the German Flying
'P' Line, which then flew the Italian flag temporarily, and the
full-rigged ship was the *Windsor Park*. When we first saw her
we could not make her out at all. Her national flag was tied in
a knot and could not be distinguished. The port or registration
on her counter was an extraordinary place called UUSIAKAU-
PUNKKI, which Johnny suggested might be in Wales or Ice-
land. In fact, she was a Finn. The bankrupt status indicated by
the knotted flag made her useless to us. There was a writ

gummed to her iron foremast, and there were no jobs in her. The *Peking* was well manned by a full crew of Italians, and the *Oaklands*, which was Norwegian, had failed to find a charter.

Well, we had a little money. We did not squander our pay. We were young and full of optimism. If the worst came to the worst we could accept our shipmate's offer of beds in his place at Golders Green, and continue to look for a ship from there. True, Golders Green was a longish way from the docks, but by that time we were well aware that in London no nice family sought a home with a view of the docks. Much of Mr Golders' green was a dormitory for the more successful graduates from the East End of London, and the North End Road was nine miles from any ships. However, we were caught in the collapse of the post-war boom. The world was in the first of the steadily deteriorating messes which were to follow one another for at least the next twenty-five years. We were soon without money to pay for lodgings, and little enough to buy food. We could choose the Embankment, or Golders Green. We thought we would put the Embankment off as long as we could. Johnny said it was no place for sailors. So we went to Golders Green. A good deal of interest was taken in us by the local policemen, who doubtless made sure that we were lawfully on the schoolmaster's premises. Our neighbours gave us no welcome; but we had beds and good shelter. No one else was in the house, and we were very grateful to our shipmate.

Another disadvantage about Golders Green was that fares by underground railway or bus to the dock area were high to such poverty-stricken young fellows as we were then. So we walked. The summer of 1921 was hot and glorious in England, and each morning as we strode across the Hampstead Heath the great metropolis looked wonderful and romantic, spread out before us. The great dome of St Paul's, the high tower of Big Ben, the whole panorama of the great city looked its entrancing best. But we never reached the wonderful London which we saw from Hampstead Heath. Our way was through mean streets, round Mornington Crescent way, and towards the south-east. It was a long, long walk, and those pavements were hard.

Every day we visited the *Oaklands* and *Windsor Park*, and had a look at the *Peking*. Johnny Gleeson found a small back-room office somewhere near Fenchurch Street where a very old master mariner, long retired from the sea, had set himself up in the business of providing 'runners' to move awkward ships. We registered our names with him as square-rigger men, for he hoped to get the running of the *Oaklands* across to Norway. If so, he would hire us. Running was a lump-sum business, and there were no articles. We should be paid an agreed sum for each job. When I learned that I lost interest, for the loss of time worried me even more than being without funds. There was neither profit nor security in working for the provider of runners, but we put our names down with him for the *Oaklands* (it would provide a week or two's food), an old dredge which was to go to Saigon, a small tug for the Mediterranean, and a ferry for Sydney harbour. The old master mariner, for a sufficient consideration, undertook to deliver any sort of vessel, craft, or lighter anywhere there was water, so long as it was afloat and could be made reasonably seaworthy. But the ferry was still on the stocks, the tug had been condemned, and the wrong monsoon was blowing for the delivery job to Indo-China.

When we had money we ate in cheap places where the food was cooked in the windows. In restaurants such as these the main dish was sausages and mash. You could both see and smell the quality of the food as you entered. But any food was good to us.

How long we might have gone on looking for a ship in London I don't know. The state of Europe grew daily more desperate, though the recent war was supposed to be over at the time. There were coal strikes, Sinn Fein troubles, troubles of all sorts. With national economies out of joint everywhere, there was little work for ships, and seafaring men were stranded everywhere. We allowed no grass to grow under our feet, and were quite prepared to walk to the Bristol Channel or to Scotland, if we heard of a sailing-ship in need of hands in either direction. But we never did. We called at agents' offices, as well as visiting the ships. The kindly Finnish mate of the *Windsor Park* gave us the address of that ship's brokers, Clarkson's, then of Fenchurch Street, who looked after many ships. We called there, and though we were probably a nuisance, we were well received. One of the managers made copies of Lloyd's List available to us, and offered us all the information about ships which they had at their disposal. But even he could not tell us where there was a sailing-ship left in commission in British waters.

We called at the office of John Stewart and Co, in Billiter Street, and again were well received. Their *Falkirk*, a kindly old Scotsman told us, was bound for France, but they did not know of any further charter for her. Others of their ships were on the west coast of South America, trying to get nitrates or guano to carry to Europe. Even when they did eventually reach Europe, prospects for further voyages were very slim.

Then one day a chance meeting with a Norwegian acquaintance in the Commercial Road put us on the track of a big sailing-ship in the river, of which we had no previous knowledge. She was reported to be in commission, and she was lying at the buoys off North Woolwich. Her name was *Omega*, and she was flying a flag which was unknown to the Norwegian. He thought she was Panamanian, or perhaps Estonian. She was a four-masted barque in ballast.

We hurried towards North Woolwich, looking sharply out for the masts and yards of a strange four-masted barque. Sure enough, there she was – a big, wall-sided lump of a thing with huge single t'gall'nts and deep royals above them. She was grey-painted, looked reasonably well kept, and was flying a flag in three vertical stripes of red-white-red which was unknown to us. However, square-rigged ships were always international. We were not worried about such details as flags.

We managed to get out to her in a tug that was towing a garbage barge.

'*Omega*, Callao,' we read on her counter. At least we knew

where Callao was. She was Peruvian, then. I hadn't known that Peru owned any big sailers which sailed as far as London.

At the gangway-head we saw, coming out of the quarters in the poop, a brawny large Cockney barmaid. She was a cheerful lass we had seen at a pub called Charlie Brown's, where sailors foregathered. Charlie's was a cheerful place, and she was a girl who took life very much as she found it, and left no man better, or much worse.

'Blime,' she said, staring at Johnny. 'What brings you here?'

'Blime to you!' said Johnny. 'Where's the mate?'

'I'm the mate here,' she said, striking a pose to look what she imagined to be the part.

'Come off it, old girl! The dinkum mate, we want. We want a job.'

'You and your dinkum mates! Why don't you learn to speak English?' At that, she stood under the boat-skids and surveyed the pair of us. 'Hans!' she shouted in a great voice which startled a negro working on a brace-block by the jigger-top. 'Hans!'

A bleary individual, looking very much as if he were just beginning to recover from a long, happy binge – or had given up hope of ever recovering – came to the washboard at the entrance to the poop alleyway. He had been a handsome figure of a man once, probably not long ago.

We said we were looking for jobs. We'd heard there might be some in his ship.

'Sailors?' he said, as if he were too tired to waste any words.

We showed him our papers from the *James Craig*, and the others. We always carried our discharges.

A very cursory glance at these documents, and at us, seemed to be enough for Mr Hans. He asked us to follow him into his cabin, our friend the barmaid coming too. Well she might; she lived there. His cabin was a spacious place with a port in the ship's side and another looking out on the maindeck. Its furniture consisted of a large wooden bunk which had been rigged out to double, but could be rigged down at sea. This great bunk surmounted a set of drawers, contrived so they would not roll open at sea. There were a desk, a comfortable settee, a chair or two, a large wardrobe, and a place to hang oilskins. On the bulkhead were photographs of a five-masted full-rigged ship and a five-masted barque, both under full sail. Between these was a small silken German flag.

We took a good look at the two five-masters, in many ways the greatest square-rigged ships that ever sailed.

'I was in them both – once,' said the mate. There was a depth of feeling and a sort of hopeless bitterness in his voice as he said that.

He explained to us that the *Omega* was a former German ship, a West Coaster, now seized in prize and allocated to Peru, in whose ports she had been laid up throughout the recent war. She was under charter to load coal at Barry Dock for Callao, and she needed crew. But there were difficulties. There was a coal strike in South Wales which might be settled any day, and might not. Though the ship needed crew, her articles could not be opened until it was known that she could load. We could have places aboard on the same conditions as the men already in the ship – to work by for our food, signing for the wages of the port as soon as her articles were opened. We should not, he said, find conditions irksome. There was a lot of sailorizing to be done aboard her, and we'd like that. The food was tolerable. He was sorry there would be no wages, but there it was.

We accepted his offer on the spot. We liked the look of the *Omega* and her mate, and the wholesome smell of a real ship was welcome in our nostrils after the long spell ashore. And, as Johnny said, the *Omega* was a dam' sight nearer other ships than Golders Green.

We moved aboard next day. There was about half a crew working-by. Those who were coal black lived in the starboard fo'c'sle; the browns, copper-coloureds, and whites were in the port fo'c'sle. Most of the whites were Finns or Norwegians. The *Omega* was a happy ship, at any rate off the Woolwich buoys. Her officers and all the afterguard were Germans who had remained with her throughout the war. It was a tribute to their characters that they had not gone quite to pieces, and seemed to be holding the ship and her queer company together very well. We turned to strictly to time and worked a full day. There was no advantage taken of the fact that we were not on articles, and the subject of wages was never mentioned. There were several barmaids aft, as well as the young lady from Charlie Brown's. These went marketing for the ship each morning and brought back fresh vegetables for the meals. This was an excellent idea, and one I wondered was not used in other ships. Instead of taking anything a profit-seeking chandler chose to overcharge the ship for, good fresh food was bought as required in the markets ashore. We had plenty of salads and meats prepared with chilis and peppers.

Our shipmates, white and black and in-between, all spoke a sort of English, which was, at any rate for the time being, the official language of that Peruvian four-masted barque. There was a Norwegian A.B. who had served for three years in the clipper *Cimba*, and an old Finn who claimed service in the *Thermopylae*. While I could listen to their yarns I sought no distraction ashore. The old Finn had almost an obsession against the *Cutty Sark*, which he declared could not follow the lovely *Thermopylae* in light winds or strong, even if the *Thermopylae* were half dismasted. Be that as it may, the subject was entrancing. The old man said there was only one sailing-ship worth sailing in left in the whole infernal world. There were lots of sailing warehouses, and worse, but one ship, thank God, still remained. At least he thought she was still about somewhere. She was then Norwegian.

'What was this ship?' I asked.

'De four-mast full-rigger *Lancing*,' was his reply. 'She vos built for a steamer and sailed like hell as soon as dey rigged her, so's she could forget she ever had an engine. Six days eighteen hours New York to Liverpool. Seventy knots in a watch. A flyer, I tell you! Find her, young fellow. Find de *Lancing* an' dere you have a *ship*! Dere'll be no more.'

I had not previously heard of the *Lancing*. But the other sailors agreed that the old Finn was fairly right, though several spoke well of other ships they had been in, which were still afloat. They mentioned the *Coriolanus*, the full-rigged *Mount Stewart*, the *Dundee*, the *Marlborough Hill*, the Chilean barque *Nelson*, the American wooden ship *Benjamin Packard*, and the *Star of Russia*. The Finn scoffed at all these. He stood by his declaration that the *Lancing* was peer of them all. But where she was to be found he had no idea.

The *Omega* herself was certainly no clipper, and had never been intended as one. She had once been a Scot, as the name *Drumcliff* on her bell indicated. In Britain's great discard of sail she had gone to those judges of a good ship, the Germans. We liked her well enough, but for a ship bound round the Horn to the west'ard there were a few disadvantages about her. Those huge single t'gall'nts, for instance – they would be a handful. That big open wheel, as exposed as it could be; the unusual arrangement of working deck above the midships house, giving the appearance from outboard that she was a three-island ship, like the *Bellands*, which in fact she was not. There was only a skeleton deck carried out to the bulwarks from the house, and it seemed to us this place could be a deathtrap when the great seas ran, for the water would smash against the deckhead, the ship's side, and the side of the house, and maim anyone who got in the way.

No seas broke aboard the *Omega* at the Woolwich buoys. I never did see a sea break over her, for the strike on the coal-fields of South Wales steadily worsened and her prospects of sailing were correspondingly slim. This was irksome. True, we had plenty of interesting work to do aboard, for after her long lay-up her rigging required a great deal of attention. The summer months of 1921 continued warm and pleasant until there was a serious drought in London. There was plenty of time for study; but since her articles were not yet open, working-by the *Omega* did not count as qualifying service towards a Board of Trade certificate. Only indentured apprentices could reckon such time. The nebulous status of ordinary seaman working-by was not to be unduly prolonged.

But what could be done about it? The *Windsor Park* was

still bankrupt. There had been no call to run the *Oaklands*
anywhere: if one came it would merely be to some small port
in South Norway where one would be stranded all over again
or shipped back to England as a distressed British seaman –
a DBS, as it was called. We had no desire to become distressed
British seamen, or to remain unpaid Peruvian seamen for too
long either.

Then one day the old Finn had some news for me.

'I've heard of de *Lancing*,' he muttered hoarsely as we were
working together, putting up an overhauled foot-rope on the
fore lower tops'l yard. 'She's in France. Go over and join
her.'

'France?' I said. 'How do I get to France? I've been shipped
out of there already.'

'Dere's ways,' said the ancient sailor.

A couple of weeks later I slipped ashore quietly by night from
a little weekly steamer at the port of Nantes, a seventeen-year-
old ordinary seaman stealing into France in quest of a four-
masted full-rigged ship which had been converted from a
steamer. I had very little money and very little gear. On such
an expedition there was no need for gear. I had a blanket and
a change of underclothing. With me was a most unusual young
man, who was leader of our little expedition. Johnny Gleeson
and Sharkey Keen had both elected to stay in the *Omega*,
where there was at least a certainty of food. My new companion was known to me only as Lusitania. That was not his
name. He was a Finn, about twenty-six, dark, lean, lithe. His
story was that he was a lesser greaser in the liner *Lusitania*
when she was torpedoed, and he survived by being blown clean
through one of the funnels. After this he was always known by
the name of that ship. It seemed strange to me that a sailing-
ship sailor – and that the strange young man certainly was –
should ever have shipped in a steamer at all. If he did go in
steam it was unlikely that he would accept employment in the
engine-room, or be competent to do the work of a greaser
there. But Lusitania was a very strange young man. Perhaps

he had his own reasons for being in a Cunard trans-Atlantic liner, when his rightful employment was in Cape Horn ships. At any rate, his story was accepted by those in a position to know the facts.

He was a mainland Finn, not of Scandinavian descent. He was small, slight, very dark, and handsome with regular features, a classic profile, and excellent teeth. His features were sharp and determined, and there was a fierce glow in his dark eyes. He had no gear, and wanted none. He was dressed in an old pair of blue shore-going trousers, a black shirt with white buttons, and an old coat. On his head, which was big and round, he always wore a well-battered peak cap, with the peak twisted into a semicircle. With the rakish twist to his cap and his sharp face, he looked more of an Apache than a sailor. He always carried a knife, a fine keen blade of Finnish steel, which hung in a decorated scabbard inside his breast pocket. The handle was ivory, surmounted by a carved lion's head, done in silver. I never saw him use this knife for any purpose other than sailor's work, and to eat his meals. I don't doubt he knew how to use it for other purposes, if the need arose. He spoke fluent French and English, as well as his own Finnish, good Swedish, and some Russian and German. He knew his way round most ports in Europe, and a good many in the United States as well. He was, in short, a most useful and accomplished shipmate for a surreptitious landing in the port of Nantes, in the middle of a quiet and more or less peaceful night in the early autumn of 1921.

Our object was to find employment in a sailing-ship, a deep-water sailing-ship, in commission – the *Lancing* for preference. Failing her, any sailing-ship, under any flag. Lusitania said France was the best place to look for a ship because France still had more deep-sea sailing-ships than any other nation. But we quickly discovered that not one French sailing-ship, nor any other kind of sailing-ship, in Nantes or anywhere else in France we could hear of, was in commission. Our prospects in Nantes were nil, though there were many ships there. The *Lancing* was not there. We could get no news of her. A Frenchman in the *Château D'If* said she was at Dunkirk. The Breton shipkeeper in the barque *Bossuet* said she was in America. A Russian declared she had been lost. At any rate, she was certainly not in Nantes.

Lovely big barques, ships, and four-masted barques, all high out of the water with no cargoes aboard, were moored in dejection together in tiers along a canal. Some were port-painted like the old East Indiamen; a few were already turning rapidly into heaps of rust. Stem to stern they lay together, sails unbent, running rigging sent down and stowed away, not a wisp of smoke from a galley fire, no one but a shipkeeper aboard. They were secured as if it were intended they should never be free of the land again and were to remain there for ever. The French bounty system, by means of which large fleets of sailing-ships had been kept going long after other nations had found them uneconomic (the French Government paid sailing-ships so much a mile for every mile they sailed), had been abandoned.

The system had been abused, for many ships had tried to make their voyages as long as possible regardless of where they were bound in order to collect the maximum bounty. The lovely port of Hobart saw them by the score. The most convenient port in the west winds zone for great square-riggers to touch, it had the additional advantage of being as far from France as it was possible to get without going to the Antarctic. So every deep-sea French sailing-ship, bound anywhere, cleared for Hobart for orders, though her owners required no orders and had never a scrap of cargo for Tasmania. Four-masters bound for Puget Sound and San Francisco to lift lumber or grain for Europe, coal-laden barques bound for the West Coast, full-riggers bound nowhere in particular but just sailing on the bounty in the hope of a cargo turning up, one and all sailed into the Derwent River which was a safe haven for them, and the mountains of southern Tasmania formed a noble background. Here in the ugly canal, no longer able to earn a bounty for anything, the unkempt great sailers looked lonely and forlorn.

One thing they did provide, and that was shelter. With the connivance of a Breton shipkeeper, Lusitania and I moved into the fo'c'sle of a big Bordes barque, the middle ship of a tier of three. We found seven or eight men already established there. The majority were Scandinavians of some sort or other, forced underground in a hopeless quest for work. There were one or two American Navy deserters, who had been in France some time. These were also sailing-ship sailors. In addition to the regular inhabitants, other similar characters drifted in and out, generally very late at night. We ate what we could get from ships. Ships' crews were very good to us, and we generally had at least one good meal a day. Usually we ate in the fo'c'sles of Scandinavian ships. None of us could seek any kind of work ashore, for we were all in the country illegally. Our hope was to ship in vessels which were not the concern of the French authorities. In that way neither our presence nor the manner of our coming need concern them.

It struck me as strange that a group of seafaring men should be forced to such straits, merely to seek employment. These were no bums or hooligans. They were honest men with courage enough to break laws to look for work. They asked no charity of any man or country. They were men well accustomed to reverses, and to acute hardship. They expected, and received, the help of brother seamen, whether themselves serving in ships or not. No working seaman, in those days, ever knew when he might be compelled to lead just such a life as we were then living. For this reason, if for no other, there was a fine camaraderie among working seafaring men. I found much to admire and respect in my fellow-man among such fellows. They kept themselves scrupulously clean at all times; and our surreptitious quarters were a model of tidiness. The standard of behaviour was the high one I had become accustomed to in a sailing-ship's forecastle. Among those men, courage was not a rare quality but an everyday necessity. Without it in abundance they could not live.

Not all the ships in Nantes and the canal at that time were French. Several were Norwegians. Some were British. But they were all laid up. For weeks and weeks there was not the slightest hope of a berth in a ship. Yet through all this, bitterness was unknown among our small group. The sailors looked on the whole thing as an adventure – a challenge. Getting something out of life – even that sort of life – was up to them, and they knew how to manage.

One day I heard a rumour that a sailing-ship in St Nazaire was going to sign a crew, and sail to Australia in ballast. A Norwegian sail-maker brought the news to one of our nightly conferences. He said she was a lime-juicer, a big one. She looked a good ship.

'What's her name?' I asked.

'Bell something. She's one of those Bell ships – not the heavy lift lot. The lime-juice Cape Horners.'

'Not *Bellands*?'

'*Ja, ja*. That's it. She's offering thirty bob the month, A.B., and find your own way to St Nazaire. But we could run in Australia, couldn't we, Aussie?'

'Not for me,' I said. 'Not from the *Bellands*, anyway. That's one ship I'm *not* interested in. I'm not going back in her.'

Lusitania and I did not go to St Nazaire, though some of the other men did so. I felt I could not face another period in that ship, which I had seen so desecrated. To me a four-masted barque was always something of a cathedral, and a small barque a lesser church. I hated to see them ill served.

But it was obvious there was no point in remaining any longer in Nantes or its neighbourhood. More and more sailing-ships arrived, but they were all laid up. Reports reached us of many ex German ships coming to Channel ports, to lie there in idleness while the Allies haggled as to who should have them. None was to remain in commission, as far as we could discover. We heard no news of the *Lancing* – not a word. Then one day there was a rumour that a ship or two might go into commission from the large fleet laid up at Bordeaux.

So off we went, on foot. Lusitania said it was getting time to head south anyway, for Nantes could be cold in the winter. We collected some food from a Dane in a Forenede steamer, which was well-found, and Lusitania somehow gained access to an American army dump, where there was more. For the first week we had something to eat, at any rate. We set off along the roads very cheerfully, taking care to avoid the larger towns. Sometimes we had a lift, generally in an American army vehicle driven by a Chinese. There was a large Chinese labour camp near la Rochelle, and the Chinamen were friendly and helpful. They seemed to have very much the same attitude towards life as Lusitania and his fellows. My previous experience of the Chinese was limited to haggling for vegetables with them at the Victoria market in Melbourne. The first real contact with them as human beings caused me to look on them with new eyes. They were generous souls.

I recall that walk along the coast of Biscayan France as a pleasant interlude. We were in no hurry. Time did not matter. We rarely knew the date, or cared. The alarming crises which daily arose in a lamentable world's silly affairs did not bother us (having already reduced us as far as they could, and left us undefeated). The weather continued fine; the days were long, and each worth while for its own sake. The sun rose and we washed in streams, and the birds sang and the countryside was lovely. We lived with simple things, geared down to standards of complete simplicity.

We avoided the French. Lusitania went to great pains to keep out of their way. He never touched or suffered me to touch as much as one grape in the many vineyards, though the days were hot, the roads dusty, the way long.

'They're property,' he said. 'The French love property. Leave 'em.'

This advice surprised me. How could a few grapes be missed where there were so many? Sometimes we were rather hungry. A bunch of grapes would have gone down well. But Lusitania was adamant. We touched nothing French, ever. We slept under hedges and in the shelter of hay-stacks, or barns. To roll in a blanket with the sweet smell of hedges in my nostrils and the clear stars above, after a long day's tramp, was very satisfying so long as we were not hungry.

It took us about ten days, as far as I remember, to reach Bordeaux. We did not go into the city. We brought up at a place called Bassens, down-river, where the Americans had made a great war port. Quays, warehouses, cranes, and barbed wire abounded. The barbed wire did not matter, for it was no longer guarded. The place had become a sort of jungle in which the homeless, the stranded, and the undocumented had gathered, and went about their ways. There was a dump of very large concrete drain-pipes in a corner by the Bassens wharf. We claimed one of these as our quarters. It was clean, commodious, and untenanted. We made the drain-pipe reasonably habitable, with clean sacking at both ends and some sacks to sleep on.

This sort of life was all very well and I sometimes wondered whether Lusitania, who was so adept at it, proposed to follow it indefinitely and make his way eventually towards Spain. It was now some time since I had been on the articles of a ship. The fact that I was gaining no time towards the first run of my profession – the second mate's 'ticket' – worried me very much. I had more than my share of the impatience of youth. I wanted to get on, to have my time finished with. The insecurity of life in a dockside drain-pipe near Bordeaux did not worry me as much as I suppose it ought to have done, for this beach-combing seemed then a necessary part of the seafarer's existence. But the waste of sea-time bothered me. At seventeen, the months are long.

As at Nantes, so also at Bordeaux there were plenty of sailing-ships. They were moored almost the whole way along the Bassens wharf and up to the bridge, and in the dock. Not one had as much as a sail still bent; not one had a charter, or the hope of a charter to load anything for anywhere. The British barques *Falkirk* and *Kilmallie*, the Norse full-riggers *Cate* and *Sandvigen*, the French *Marguerite Molinos*, and many more lay waiting idly. But there was no *Lancing* among them, no four-masted full-rigged ship. The *Falkirk* had a horde of apprentices standing by, doubtless getting their sea-time in, though they learned less of seafaring there than Lusitania taught me in the drain-pipe. The French full-rigger *Desaix* came in after a passage from Australia of 203 days.

'Maybe she didn't want to arrive,' said Lusitania. In any event, she did not go out again.

In all Bordeaux, out of more than a hundred square-rigged ships, only one sailing-ship was working cargo. At the Bassens wharf, not far from our drain-pipe, lay a huge bald-headed four-masted barque, flying the blue-crossed flag of Finland. Her name was *Lawhill*, her port of registry the same Marie-hamn which I had first noted on the counter of the *Mariechen* at Port Adelaide. She looked a clumsy box of a ship. She was wall-sided, and her rig was low and very square. She was one of those cargo-carriers of the 'nineties built to carry rather than to sail, and she had obviously been designed to be as economical as possible. Her lack of royals, her big square Liverpool house 'midships, her utilitarian wire rigging, her brace-winches and the like, stamped her as no *Lancing*. She was discharging grain from Australia, whence she had made a passage some six weeks better than that of the *Bellands*, despite her apparent clumsiness.

Her only crew was a handful of young boys. These became good friends of ours. We often saw her captain go ashore. He was a youngish man, very square-set, with a kindly twinkle in his deep blue eyes. The kindly twinkle in a shipmaster's eyes meant nothing to Lusitania or to me. But the *Lawhill*'s boys told us she was probably going to remain in commission, and might sail out to Australia in ballast to look for grain. Or she might go to the Plate or beat round the Horn towards Val-paraiso. This was news. The rumour that she was to sail again became a certainty. On a tip from the boys, Lusitania and I applied to the mate forthwith for berths.

The mate gave us a cold glare.

'There'll be no blasted beachcombers signed on board here,' he said. 'Our crew is chosen by the owner and comes overland from Mariehamn.'

Well, this was a blow.

CHAPTER NINE

THE PLEASANT *LAWHILL*

'WHAT do we do now?' I asked Lusitania, as we ate our meal of pancakes and peanuts in the shelter of our drain-pipe home. The pancakes were provided by the boys in the *Lawhill*, and the peanuts were spilled cargo from a Brazilian steamer farther along the wharf. 'Can we get to this place Mariehamn and sign on there?'

'We can't get to Mariehamn,' my comrade declared. 'It's an island in the Gulf of Bothnia a thousand miles from here. No, we'll join the *Lawhill* here. We're not licked yet. Blast bloody mates! All bloody mates! They're a no-good bunch of slave-drivers, anyway.'

Join the *Lawhill*? How could we do that? For the moment we were certainly defeated. The few boy-seamen working in the big ship kept us informed of developments, however. We learned that the big four-master, which had been built for the jute trade in Dundee in 1892 and later sailed for years out of the east coast of the United States ports with cased oil for the Far East, was the property of a strange ship-owner who lived in a wooden house in Mariehamn. His name was Gustaf Erikson, Captain Gustaf Erikson. This was a ship-owner of whom I had never heard, though the boys said he owned several Cape Horners as well as *Lawhill*, and he had been a sailing-ship captain himself for many years. We gathered that Captain Erikson had some unusual ideas on the subject of suitable crews for his vessels. He had a firm conviction that the great majority of adult European and American seamen who had survived the recent war had been made unemployables in the process. According to the way he saw things they had been spoiled. They had been paid too much money and had had to be conceded conditions the cost of which was a charge on ships' earnings which owners could not hope to meet in normal circumstances. This sort of thing was all very well while the war was actually in progress. But now it was not, and he who geared down first was a wise man. Since it was un-economic to employ men, he used boys. In his opinion, the majority of vessels were grossly overmanned, so he cut his crews to the bare minimum. The *Lawhill*, we gathered, had already made two voyages since the end of the war with small crews, who received low wages. But they were well fed and happy. They had all been engaged in the ship's home port, where they answered an advertisement in the local Aaland newspaper. They had been selected by Captain Erikson himself.

One of the boys showed us the advertisement for new crew. It read:

CREW
Required for ships *Lawhill* and *Tjeremai*. Inquire at the Sea-men's Home, or Telefon 75.

GUSTAV ERIKSSON.

How could we telephone 75, or call on Gustav Eriksson (or Gustaf Erikson, as the name was more commonly spelled)? Even if we could, it was certain the interview would be of no use to Lusitania. I might have the chance of a berth, since the war was over when I first went to sea. I was still only seven-teen, and such wages as I had earned in my few ships had not been enough — at any rate in my own view — to spoil me. But Lusitania was very much a product of the war; it was hard on him that he should be regarded as an unemployable, merely because he *had* survived. But what could we do? Stow away? That was no use to me. I wanted to be on the ship's articles. But if the worst came to the worst we might have to stow away. It was galling to be so close to that big sailing-ship, the only ship in which we had hope of berths, yet because we had guts enough to find her for ourselves we were regarded as beachcombers and refused employment.

Meantime things were becoming rather desperate in our drain-pipe apartment. The weather was threatening to break.

On some days we went hungry. Lusitania was looking more like an Apache every day. I don't suppose I was very prepossessing myself. There had been a recent unwelcome interest in our jungle on the part of the gendarmes, who until then had left the place alone. Perhaps they were looking for someone.

Then I had an idea. I explained it carefully to Lusitania, who laughed and said he thought it was worth a trial. It was simple enough. By that time, we knew that the new crew for the *Lawhill* was already on its way to join the ship. When they arrived, I said, we would simply follow them up the gangway and pass ourselves off – if we could – as having come with them. At the worst we could only be thrown down the gangway again. We should be no worse off than we were. Of course, we realized that we had no real hope of acceptance as crew members sent from a place we had never seen; but there were disquieting rumours as to the numbers and experience of this particular crew, and I suggested to Lusitania that we might be acceptable if we offered our services at the best possible moment. This would obviously be when the officers of the ship were depressed at the prospect of sailing the *Lawhill* with insufficient crew.

With the aid of our friends in the *Lawhill*'s forecastle we followed the movements of the new crew closely as they came slowly across Europe. First they went to Stockholm, thence to Copenhagen, and on through Germany by train; thence to Belgium, Antwerp, Paris. At last the day came. 'They're coming to-day,' an eighteen-year-old able seaman named Mittler told us. 'This evening. Watch.'

We watched. Nobody came. We kept close watch until midnight. Still nobody came. But in the morning they were there. We saw them straggling along the wharf with their sea-bags and their gear. They looked like a group of youngsters migrating to the United States. They were absurdly youthful, even by my standards. They had soft, fair faces, and they were wearing high leather boots. Some were still carrying small bundles of the hard, black bread and harder sausage which had been their sustenance on the journey. There were so pitifully few of them that at first we thought they could not be the *Lawhill*'s crew. But they passed so near our drain-pipe that we could hear their conversation. They were speaking Swedish with heavy Aaland farmers' accents – Lusitania said – and they were for the *Lawhill* right enough. All ten of them.

'Well,' said Lusitania, drawing in his breath. 'Well! If *that's* the sort of crew ship-owner Erikson sends in his ships, damned if I want a job in them! Suicide, it'll be – bloody suicide!'

'Come on!' I said. 'Let's have a go. We can't be worse off.'

I was dubious myself about the wisdom of shipping in so undermanned a vessel. Some quick mental arithmetic indicated that it must be intended to send that big four-masted barque on a long voyage, perhaps for years, with a crew of less than twenty hands. We knew how many were aboard. We counted the party joining. It seemed almost criminal.

But I did not then know the Aaland Finns. Lusitania was a mainlander, if that strange young man was a Finn at all.

When they reached the foot of the gangway we tagged on, both in our shirts, looking, we hoped, like sailors already belonging to the ship. Our jackets were handy for putting on when we got aboard.

'Let's give a hand with the sea-bag mate,' said my companion, speaking in Swedish to a heavy-limbed, tired boy. 'And let's have a piece of that bread. Long time since I had any of this real stuff!'

The youth looked at Lusitania like a grateful dog.

We trudged up the gangway and followed the party aft. Two large seafaring men, easily recognized by us as the master and mate of the vessel, were standing by the break of the poop. They were anxiously examining a sheaf of papers, and they looked like a pair of very worried men. They did not look at us. The conversation was all in Swedish and was lost on me, though I had been taking lessons in the drain-pipe for some time. It was obvious that they were as horrified as we were at the wretched number of inexperienced lads they had been sent as crew.

So far so good, anyway. We were aboard, and the stage was fast setting for an appropriate moment to offer our services.

The officers left the deck and went into the saloon in the poop. An order was given which presumably meant that the party was to follow them. I noticed, then, that the high leather boots many were wearing had curiously built-up pointed toes.

'For skis,' Lusitania whispered, noticing my curiosity.

Skis? Skis aboard a four-masted barque? I was bewildered, but I marched along with the rest. We had our jackets on now, and filed with the others into the companion that led to the saloon. But skis? What sort of a ship *was* this? I looked round half-expecting to see boys on roller-skates on the main deck, and a toboggan slide along the mainyard. It looked big enough to support one.

Nobody was carrying skis, however, as one by one the boys of the new crew stepped up to the saloon table, put down little black books, signed some papers, received little brown books, and marched out again. I noticed with alarm that the little black books were passports.We had no such things. There was a stranger seated at the saloon table, and he was having a good look at those passports.

One by one, the youths signed the *Lawhill*'s articles. I was close enough to read their names and ages – 'Harald Johansson, 17 years, Saltvik, Aaland, Able Seaman. Clarens Andersen, 15 years, Jomala, Aaland, Ordinary Seaman. Birga Johansson, 16 years, Kulla, Aaland, Deckboy. Runnar Mattsson, 16 years, Eckerø, Aaland, Deckboy,' and so on. A parade of youth indeed. I had no objection whatever to boys in crews, but boys as crew – that was a different thing.

Now it was my turn. The depressed faces of the master and mate did not look up. I put down my small sheaf of paper discharges from my trio of square-rigged ships.

Then they looked up.

The mate began to bluster, in Swedish first, and then in English. He was not welcoming me in either language.

'Did you come from Mariehamn? Has the owner sent you?' And so forth.

'No, sir,' I said, when he gave me a chance. 'I have not come from Mariehamn. But I came with those men and I want a place aboard if there is one for me.' I thought it unnecessary to mention that I had come with the 'men' only from as far as the wharf alongside the ship.

The mate began to bluster again.

'Just a moment,' said the captain, who was a considerably younger man and much more pleasantly featured. 'You say you want to ship here? This is a Finnish ship, on Finnish articles. Do you know where the ship is bound, what we pay? Are you a sailing-ship man? What is your nationality?'

I replied that the answer to the first question was yes, decidedly. As for nationality, I was an Australian. I had served already in three square-rigged ships, and my papers were before him. As for the other questions, I would take the ship as I found her.

'Hummm,' mused the captain, looking at me with a scrutinizing glance and then at my certificates of discharge, which he read very carefully. 'Well,' he went on at last, 'we are going to Australia, in ballast – Port Lincoln for orders. We will load wheat for the Channel for orders. We pay 450 Finnmarks a month, A.B. That's about – no, less than – two English pounds. We sign articles for two years, 60 south to 75 north, go anywhere. Pay off anywhere in Europe. Are you sure you won't want to leave in Australia? Or run away?'

The main thing that struck me in all this was that he had not as much as mentioned the status of ordinary seaman. By accepted British standards I had not then served sufficient sea time for able seaman's rating. Nor was I a grown man. I would gladly have accepted a berth as ordinary seaman. To be rated able seaman was an advancement I had never expected.

I explained that I was trying to serve four years in deep-sea sailing-ships before sitting for my British second mate's certificate. Since I was unable to find a British sailing-ship in commission, I had no doubt that I should be very happy to stay in the *Lawhill*. By that time I had forgotten my misgivings about the insufficient crew.

The captain gave me another searching glance, and said something to the mate in Swedish.

'All right, then,' he said. 'You can sign on here. A.B.'

'Passport?' snapped the stranger at the table, who until then had held his peace. 'Vere it is, no?'

'No,' I said.

'No?'

'No.'

'*No? No* passport? Vat you in France doink, hey? Vere you comink from? 'Ow you get 'ere, no?'

How long this sort of conversation might have lasted I don't know, but I explained that I had paid off a British ship at St Nazaire, and that I was in France seeking a ship. I had no passport. I had not previously been asked for one when I signed in a ship. As far as I knew, sailors did not require a passport. According to the official, everybody should have a passport. Everybody, even babes in arms. The official knew quite well that I should have been shipped out of France; I thought it unnecessary to mention that I had. After a great deal of argument he finally consented at least to my being signed on, though he was far from satisfied that my papers were either adequate or proof of identity.

I signed on.

After all the trouble over my perfectly straightforward set of documents there was no trouble at all over Lusitania, who had none. Perhaps the passport official thought that, papers or no papers, that strange young man was well out of France. At any rate, he was signed on as able seaman, too. I don't doubt the afterguard were pleased enough to find two extra hands come up the gangway from nowhere, with their Mariehamn contingent. To get that big ship to Australia with her small crew was not going to be a picnic for them, or anyone.

I was extremely pleased to be on a ship's articles again, to be working as a crew member, getting in some time towards that far-off certificate. The poor pay didn't matter. What mattered was the good spirit of the ship. She had a very contented ship's company, and I was glad to belong. Beachcombing might be a necessary part of the sailor's existence when times were bad, but I had never bargained to become a vagabond.

I found the Aaland islanders pleasant young fellows, with whom it was easy to get on. Few spoke any English, but Lusitania continued to be an excellent friend and mentor. I was the only non-Finn in the ship. This did not worry me or anyone else. All the boys who formed the crew were also serving their time before going up for their officers' certificates. English was a compulsory subject in the examination, and for this reason they seemed pleased to be able to begin learning that very necessary seamen's tongue. I was welcome because I was another hand, and because they could learn some English from me. More than that, I liked the innate sense of real democracy, the insistence on genuine fair dealing, which I always found to be part of the Scandinavian character, at any rate among seafaring men.

In many ways the *Lawhill* was an unusual sailing-ship. In the first place, she had her topgallant masts stepped *abaft* her topmasts instead of on the fore part, as was the case in every other ship I had seen. Her lower masts and topmasts were hollow steel columns, from keelson to topmast head, and her tall jigger mast was one long steel pole. She had exceptionally strong standing rigging, and was obviously a ship which could be driven hard. Though she had been intended only as a wind-blown jute warehouse, her people said she had a long tradition of good passages and sailed very well despite her rather clumsy appearance. Her peculiar rig offended my youthful eye. Even at seventeen, I was an arch conservative on the subject of square-rigged ships. To me even the absence of royals was an eyesore, though I had seen many stump t'gall'nt ships. The bald-headed rig was common enough in the last days of the square-rigger. Just as sailors of an older generation thought no ship looked really trim if she had double tops'ls and a spike bowsprit instead of the classic single tops'ls and long, rigged-out jib-boom, I found the innovations in the *Lawhill*'s austere

rig distasteful to my æsthetic sense. But they were very
sensible innovations indeed, as I was to learn as soon as she
came outside.

The food was good and there was full and plenty. In many
ways the big four-master reminded me of the little *James
Craig*, under Murdo' Murchison. Both ships gained, I think,
from having no odd persons aboard – no half-decks, no apprentices. What had been the half-deck in the *Lawhill*'s lime-juice
days was now a sail-locker, and the thirty-four bunks in her
'midships section were occupied by sixteen youths. The cook
and steward really took pains over their work. The cook was a
young man, too, and he was alleged actually to study such
things as diet, in books. To me this was an unheard-of thing.
True, one day something upset him and he ran amok with an
axe. But he did not murder anyone. I never did discover what
upset him, since he raved in Finnish, a mellifluous, rolling
tongue not in much use aboard Aaland ships. I tried to find out
from Lusitania, but he would not say. I have an idea it was
because Erkki, the cook, had found Lusitania dispensing an
undue proportion of his food to a group of jungle-dwellers on
the quay.

The *Lawhill*'s Australian grain was quickly sucked out of her,
and she was ballasted for the run towards Australia. Dumps of
earth and builders' refuse were built up in the squares of the
main and mizzen hatches, and considerable care was taken to
see that nothing in these earth-mounds could move, even if the
ship began to leap like a Grand National steeplechaser. The
sides and tops of the ballast mounds were carefully trimmed,
and secured with hatches and pieces of timber so that not as
much as a shovelful of dirt could begin to run. We must have
stowed about 1,400 or 1,500 tons of the stuff down below, all
told. As in most sailing-ships, the *Lawhill*'s hold was one
enormous cargo-space without bulkheads or subdivision of
any kind. A mere 1,500 tons of ballast looked nothing in that
great cavern.

No time was wasted. In working hours we worked hard, and

we were frequently called out in our free time as well when stores came down late or some fool steamer, hurrying past, carried away some of our moorings. The masts and yards were painted down, the braces and the brace-winches overhauled, and everything made shipshape. By the time the last of the wheat was being discharged the ballast was all aboard and secured, for the unloading had been contrived so that the last 700 tons or so went out through the hatches not being used for ballast. I studied this kind of thing carefully, for a ballast voyage was something new to me. By the time our discharge was completed the sails were aloft and we were ready for sea. Within a few hours a tug was alongside and we were towing down the Gironde on our way towards the sea. There were no delays. No one was drunk. There were no riotous scenes of revelry. The cargo was out and the ballast in. The ship was stored for a year and the sails were aloft and the gear all in order. We were ready. We sailed.

It was so new to me that I found the very idea bewildering. What, no days wasted at anchorage? No delays? What if the wind were unfavourable? We were setting out from the lee-ward corner of the Bay of Biscay. I felt sure we should anchor a while at the mouth of the Gironde.

While we were at Bordeaux we were expecting more sailors to arrive from Mariehamn, daily, to complete our manning. None ever did arrive. New mates and a new steward came. When we slipped from the wharf and towed down the river Lusitania was nowhere to be found. He had said he would desert if we shipped no more crew and had been strongly urging me to go with him. We might, he said, find the *Lancing* yet; in any case, it was better to face life in a drain-pipe than to drown in an undermanned ship at sea. There were times when I seriously considered joining him, for it seemed a fool-hardy thing to try to manage that huge four-masted barque with a half-crew of boys. But I decided to remain. After all, the captain and his mates were obviously experienced and competent men, whatever their crew might be. It was not credible that they would deliberately sail out to suicide. If they thought their boys could handle that great ship, I was prepared to stay with them and see how they managed it. After all, the experience might be interesting and valuable.

But not to Lusitania. He was gone. With him, unfortunately, was our only other real able seaman, the only other sailor in the forecastle who had had a rounded experience of the sea. I never saw Lusitania again. I missed him. He was a good fellow.

We were left, then, with seven able seamen, of whom the oldest was twenty, three were seventeen, and none save myself (still a very ordinary seaman by any standards other than the *Lawhill*'s) had experience of any other deep-sea sailing-ship. Besides the A.B.s there were two ordinary seamen who had been one previous voyage, and seven deckboys. With the bos'n (who was also the sail-maker), carpenter, steward, cook, three mates, and master, we were twenty-four hands all told. We had a crew almost as large in the *Rothesay Bay*. What was I letting myself in for?

I very quickly found out. I was embarked upon the smartest piece of deep-sea sailing it has been my good fortune to enjoy. I was setting out as an almost unwilling participant in a feat of ship-handling under sail which was stimulating, instructive, and of lifelong value. I was about to be a privileged sharer in the sailing of a happy great ship from France to South Australia in seventy-four days.

But I knew none of those things as the *Lawhill* towed down the long Gironde and, to my great astonishment, continued out to sea. We went straight out, almost like a steamer, though there was little wind, and what there was came from ahead.

We had the six tops'ls on her before the tug left, and some fore-and-afters to help with the steering. Quickly sail was piled on sail, and the morning sunshine found us slipping gently along under every stitch we had – twenty-three sails – with as little fuss as if we had been an onion ketch bound for La Rochelle instead of a deep-water four-poster, outward bound towards Australia. Whew! So this is a Finnish ship, I thought. Murdo' Murchison of the *Craig* and his brother Finlay of the

Wathara would have liked this, to say nothing of Tom Proctor of the lovely *White Pine*, old Learmont of the *Bengairn*, and the shade of Jackie Shimmins. And every other sailing-ship master worth his salt anywhere.

The thing which surprised me most on that day of surprises was the unexpected simplicity with which the boy-crew and their young officers got that big ship under sail. Our ski-booted deck-boys from Mariehamn might have been new-comers to a four-masted barque, but they were sailors – every man-jack of them. I learned later that they all had many summers of experience in Aaland's firewood galeasses, hard-bitten little two-masters which carried wood to the market at Stockholm. Several had been in Baltic barquentines. All had been accustomed to boats and boat-work from earliest boy-hood, for they were raised on island farms where boats were as necessary as ploughs. Captain Erikson knew his countrymen.

The wind freshened, and drew farther ahead. It was a dead muzzler. Now we will put back, I thought: there isn't room to beat this great sea-bruiser, wearing her round at the end of each necessarily short board. To wear the usual big square-rigger in ballast is an operation calling for plenty of sea-room, and that we had not. But as the wind sang and the ship plunged into life there was not the slightest sign of putting back to any anchorage. The yards were swung for'ard until all the tacks were inboard, and the ship snored along full-and-by with the wind about seven points on the starboard bow. Still it headed her, working steadily to the west, forcing us to sail towards the coast of Spain.

'Ready about!'

The order, in clear English, rang out from the poop. Main-sail and crojack were hauled up in their gear; blocks of jib-sheets and stays'ls were put over stays to run clear when the fore-and-afters were shifted over; the lighter braces were coiled down on the deck, clear for running. Hands went to stations with a little quick marshalling from the mates. The carpenter and one A.B. went to the forecastle head with the mate generally supervising for'ard. The second mate took the main braces, the third the mizzen, and kept a hand by to shift over the spanker. An able seaman was at the wheel. The ship was allowed to sail a little free of the wind, smashing along. What, I thought, they aren't going to *tack* her, surely? Without a crew? And with brace-winches? Sprays were breaking over the huge wall of the weather side.

'Lee-o! Down helm!'

Tack her? That's just precisely what they were doing. Into the wind she came, as if she loved it, like a gigantic yacht – no trace of the clumsy windbag now. Into the wind she came, all aback without losing headway. Head to wind – 'Mainsail haul!' and the main and mizzen yards flew round like clock-work while the ship continued to throw herself across the face of the wind. Brace-whips slackened, the drums of the brace-winches paid out and took in the sleek oiled wires faultlessly. These were obviously the ideal machinery for going about. An able seaman accustomed to this sort of thing (however unused he might be to seamanship outside his youthful experience) stood by the winch-brakes; others took in the slack of the t'gallant braces, hand over hand. In two minutes she was round, headyards and everything, and the boys were getting the mains'l back on her, tautening the stays'l sheets, adjusting the trim of the yards that these might present the best aero-foil possible to the head wind. The headyards came round with-out difficulty, with main and mizzen already filling on the other tack. The *Lawhill* gathered way and was snoring along on a course free from danger. Still the wind freshened. Still her master held on to all sail, though the ballasted ship lay over until one had to put a foot upon the wheel-axle to keep one's balance there.

But the wind still headed. 'Ready about!' again – aye, ready about. Again perfect ship-handling, as the coordination of wil-ling boys and able afterguard put the ship through her paces. We *were* going to beat her out; and beat her out we did. We had time for meals, but there was no watch below that first day. One watch could not put the ship about. Any heavy job required all hands. But all hands worked willingly, some of the new boys galloping from job to job with such zeal that it was dangerous to get in their way. They took pride in getting things done as quickly as possible, and they seemed to get the hang of the ship with astonishing ease. The good leavening of fellows from the previous voyage was a great help, but I came to the conclusion that there was nothing wrong with boys, provided there was a nucleus among them who knew their business, they had good preparatory training (such as their Baltic sailers had provided), and they were well led and well handled. Boys were the best crew one could find. The manner in which the ship was handled and the happy spirit of all aboard were revelations to me. Here were no bleary-eyed drunkards setting out forlornly. No tremulous fool kept his ship at an expensive tow-rope's end until she was fifty miles from land. Here no discontents, mindful of their hunger and their ease, soldiered on sailors' jobs! *This* was sailing – sailing as it was meant to be – sailing in which all hands could feel the importance of their own skilled labour, their own strength, and the delights of the achievements of their own well-directed energies. Here each was a happy part of an harmonious whole. Good Lord, I'd almost forgotten that the feeling could exist, since we'd beat the responsive little *Craig* out of the Bay of Islands. This was the real thing once again, and it was a privilege to be there.

As she set out, so she continued. Sailing-day was hard and our crew was small, but every effort was made to lighten labour. The watches were carefully selected to give fair halves of our brawn and brain to each. There was no slightest sign of hazing. As if He were pleased with our efforts and our ship, the Lord sent a light fair wind on the second morning, and the *Lawhill* passed on her way out of the Bay of Biscay, picked up a northerly air off the coast of Portugal, and ran down towards the north-east trades. The old man (who was remarkably young) walked cheerfully on the sunny poop and the mates went out of their way to devise means for lightening the boys' necessarily heavy labours. Watches and wheel-turns were contrived to allow the longest break possible below and the least possible degree of hardship. In my previous ships, wheel-turns were always two hours. Here they were an hour and a half by day, an hour by night. The four on–four off system was discarded by day in favour of a long morning watch, and a long afternoon watch, so that every day we had either the whole morning or the whole afternoon to ourselves. I found this an excellent idea, for it meant that we could have a fair rest, and the short wheel-turns were a delight.

On deck and in the rigging, too, some master-mind among sailing-ship sailors had been at work. The *Lawhill* was a masterpiece of labour-saving devices on deck and aloft. Unorthodox arrangements of downhauls, clewlines, and buntlines had been contrived so that her sails really could be hauled snug up to the yards from the deck. In theory this was so in all square-riggers, but in fact it was not, and the *Lawhill*'s innovations should have been enforced in all ships. Her peculiar masting gave clear access to both t'gall'nts, which could be handled with considerably greater ease and safety than in the more normally rigged vessel. Her wheelhouse was a delight. Her 'midships accommodation was warm and dry. Her brace-winches worked perfectly. Every yard carried double jackstays, which meant that not only could the sails be more promptly secured and with much less trouble, but there was double the usual grip for the boys aloft. There was a threefold chain purchase on the mizzen tops'l which meant that even one of our small watches could hoist the heavy yard. Every lead in her was clear, and chafe was at a minimum.

In short, the *Lawhill* was that rarity among sailing-ships – a ship in which an alert and highly competent mind had really set systematically about the business of simplifying the immense task of handling her canvas and gear, without any regard for the orthodox and the old.

For these improvements the credit was no Finn's. They were the work of Brace-winch Jarvis, of Tayport, in Fife, the inventor of the brace-winch (for which he received little reward), the master of the *Earl Dalhousie* and the *Duntrune*, and of the

Lawhill, for many years in the Anglo-American company's case-oil trade. When I joined that ship it was ten years and more since Captain Jarvis had walked her poop, but the spirit of that able and ingenious man was everywhere about her. To him, too, a crew of youth was nothing strange, for he had sailed the *Earl Dalhousie* from San Pedro to Iquique with twelve in crew, whereof the majority were apprentices, aged sixteen. It took him sixty-three days and he was compelled to do it, for he could get no crew in San Pedro. It was the same remarkable Jarvis who brought the *Duntrune* home, with no headgear and stove-in bows, after colliding with an iceberg in the far south somewhere near Cape Horn. Brace-winch Jarvis would have designed the perfect square-rigged ship if any financier had ever had courage enough to stand behind him. But he was both before his time and behind it too; he sailed great ships when ship-owners were convinced that sail was done and the free wind at sea could go to waste for ever, and the clippermen had laughed at him as an idealist with unworkable ideas. His ideas were wholly sound. It was his ambition to perfect a sailing-ship in which the work could be done in safety from the deck. He could have succeeded in this, given the chance. But he was pensioned off ashore. Years after I sailed in the *Lawhill* I met the grand old man, by the Shore Road which runs round the Brooklyn foreshore round New York's harbour, and I thanked him for what he had done with *Lawhill*'s rigging to help our small crew sail her in safety about the world.

It seemed to me, too, that this Aalander in command was in the Jarvis tradition. He was a worthy successor of the old Scots ship-master. He got the best out of ship and crew.

The north-east trades were light, and we were nearly four weeks out before we reached the Line. Here we'll be stopped, I thought; but the big ship was worked out of the doldrums belt and in the south-east trade within four days. Maximum use was made of every catspaw, even though each might help the ship only a hundred cables. The young Aalanders, none of whom had been troubled by seasickness, felt the oppressive heat badly during our few days of calm. They had spent the whole of their lives until then north of 60; but they became acclimatized very well on the whole.

The south-east trades were good, and the *Lawhill* galloped on. Forty-one days out from Bordeaux we sighted Tristan da Cunha, on a stormy day of wild west wind. Within a week we were past the longitude of the Cape of Good Hope, forty-eight days from Bordeaux. The west winds were good and we raced towards Australia before the favouring gales. The best sails in the ship were bent, and often there were two of us to hold her at the wheel. The wind howled in the rigging, and sometimes in the great seas she rolled so that I feared she might fall over. But the ballast stood. Not a shovelful moved.

Three weeks from the Cape we were off Spencer's Gulf, but the wind fell light then and we were delayed a while. We had seen ice, and the road had been rough and hard on the boys. The *Lawhill* was driven hard despite the smallness of crew; but her master knew what he was doing. We blew out no sails. We had no accidents.

On the evening of the seventy-fourth day the lights of Port Lincoln were before us. I was feeling very pleased. After taking five months between Melbourne and St Nazaire, the two and a half months' run back again was child's play. I liked the big *Lawhill* and was well accepted aboard. The captain had told me that he would pay me Australian wages for the run back to Europe. This was extremely good of him, for I had signed the same articles as the rest.

After nightfall, all hands on deck, we approached the anchorage off Port Lincoln with a slowly freshening fair wind. The night was black and threatening. We were taking the sail off her easily, to bring her up under the upper tops'ls only. The lower tops'ls were clewed up. Five of us were aloft getting a handsome stow on the fore lower tops'l. The mate was on the forecastle head with the carpenter, standing by to let go. The few lights of Port Lincoln looked welcoming, after we had seen nothing for seventy-four days.

Suddenly there was a shout from for'ard. How dark was the sea before the bows.

'I believe we sail ashore!' It was the mate's voice, with a note of urgency. Immediately there was a roar of cable as he let go.

And immediately, too, the forefoot of the big ship came up on the beach, as she hit Australia a gentle thump which quivered the masts and all the rigging. Caught off balance, working with two hands, I was pitched from the yard and hurtled to the deck. I was so surprised that I had no time to be frightened. One moment I was working away, full of pleasurable thoughts. Next moment, the rigging was flying past me, and a tar-covered wire hit me a grazing clout. I felt myself strike other rigging. Then the deck. It seemed to me, in a last instant of consciousness, that the deck was surprisingly soft.

It was not the deck that was soft. It was I.

CHAPTER TEN

FORE-AND-AFT INTERLUDE

THE approach from the sea towards Port Lincoln is impeded by a low point of land. Off this a small spherical buoy was supposed to be lighted. On the night we were coming in the light was out. So we finished our seventy-four-day run with the bowsprit overhanging a farmyard, and the farmer's dogs barked at us from the beach. A night of great effort followed to get the ship afloat again, before there was any question of ruinous salvage. The wind freshened, as it always does when there is trouble, and the work of carrying out anchors was laborious to the small crew, already tried by the long run in the Roaring Forties. By the morning, however, the *Lawhill* was afloat. She had grounded very lightly, only with her forefoot. She was hauled off with her own kedges and a bower. It might have been a great deal worse. The ship suffered no damage and a tow to the roadstead was arranged for a hundred pounds, which was cheap. I was the only casualty.

I was lucky not to be dead. I was carted along the deck on a piece of canvas and put in a bunk in the charthouse, while the more important business of refloating the ship was attended to. The second mate patched me up. In the morning the port doctor came. By the grace of God and the profusion of the *Lawhill*'s rigging I had not been badly injured. I had no broken bones – only a wrenched pelvis, some internal injuries, and a nasty jab in the left thigh where I had fallen on a ringbolt. I have fitful memories of that long night, of waking in some dulled pain and hearing the wind in the rigging and the cries of the sailors, my shipmates, as they went about their work. I was past caring what happened to the ship or, for the moment, to me. Yet I was well aware that this was a major calamity.

Since the early days when I had first climbed over the futtock shrouds of a full-rigged ship alongside in the River Yarra,

I don't think I had given a thought to the possibility of falling from aloft. Falls were most unusual. I never saw another at sea. The apparent danger of working aloft was so completely accepted by nerveless youth that it ceased to exist. It was something of a shock to find the danger real after all. I wondered whether I should ever be able to work aloft again. According to the doctor, it might be some time before I could walk. I had one hope and one hope only, as far as I could see, and that was to be properly restored to health before the *Lawhill* had her orders and was loaded for the homeward passage. Then I could stay with her and finish my time. Another round voyage ought to do it.

It was a slim hope. For a while, as the *Lawhill* lay off Port Lincoln in the roadstead and no orders came, there seemed a chance of pulling it off. But my hurts healed slowly. I lay on my back a long time, staring at the tell-tale compass which was slung in gimbals below the deckhead above me (for this was the master's bad-weather bunk) and I had plenty of leisure to listen to the wind in the rigging. The mate and second mate looked after me, and did it very well. They were a fine pair of young fellows, and brought me books which they were at pains to acquire from the other vessels at Port Lincoln – the four-masted barque *Garthpool*, and the barques *Inverclyde* and *Bonnevaine*. The *Garthpool* and the *Inverclyde* were loading grain for Europe, but the *Bonnevaine* was scouting for a cargo just as we were.

When we had been in the roads three weeks, orders came that the ship was to move round to Port Adelaide and load wheat there in bags for a destination either in France or the United Kingdom. She sailed at once, and beat round to the Semaphore in four days. Once there, a tug whisked her to the loading berth up the river. There was an unseemly haste to get her cargo stowed and to have her off. Meantime I could sit up, but I could not walk. I could not stay in the good *Lawhill* and there was no other ship I could go in. What could I do? For the time being nothing – not until I could walk again. Then we would see. To be a physical wreck at eighteen, while the last of the Cape Horn sailing-ships died on their keels all round me, and to be unable to sail in any of them, was galling. Yet I was not quite a wreck.

My mail included letters from old shipmates giving their news of ships. Johnny and Sharkey had helped 'run' the *Oaklands* up to Norway after all, and had then returned to ship as A.B.s in the *Omega* for her coal-haul towards Callao. She was going the Panama way, said Johnny, and had a fair prospect of arriving. I wondered what would happen to Johnny and Sharkey when the *Omega* reached Callao, if she ever did. Tom Germein was in the *Kirkudbrightshire*, but expected to be stranded in England. Sid Higgins, a fellow Melburnian from Captain Suffern's school, had shipped in the *Hougomont* and was on the beach in London. He wrote that the only way he could find to get a ship again was to work a passage as steward in an immigrant ship bound for Australia, and if he had to be a steward, he would never go to sea again. Dave Freeman, from the *Rothesay Bay*, wrote that he had been compelled to go in steam. Ginger MacNamara had been wrecked in the Fiji Islands.

Worst of all, Captain Suffern was dead. My brother Frank wrote that it was useless to come to Melbourne, for there were no ships there. Almost nothing was left crossing yards in the Tasman Sea, except a couple of tops'l schooners. Even the Tasmanian barquentines had gone. The barquentine *Southern Cross* and the small barque *Manurewa* were posted missing, each with some of Captain Suffern's boys aboard. Not a single sailing-ship flying either the British or the American flag had been in Melbourne that year. The prospects for finding another ship anywhere, even when I was fit to go in one, were bleak. How could I stay in sail? How, indeed, was I to remain at sea at all?

The captain of the *Lawhill*, who was a cheerful man with an endless delight in the life under sail, sometimes used to come in the charthouse and yarn with me. Nothing depressed him, except the wait for cargo. He was optimistic about the future for sailing-ships, and grinned at the accounts of depression and woe which were prevalent among his brother shipmasters. He used to explain to me how such ships as the *Lawhill* were made to pay their way, and how it was that she could continue to sail when most other sailing-ships were laid up. He said there would always be grain for ships which geared down their economies low enough to afford to carry it. That was the secret. Steamers wanted delivery of too much cargo alongside each day: without at least 500 tons a day they could not accept a charter. With a sailing-ship in which the capital investment was very low and the crew all boys, a wait of six weeks to load her cargo in a cheap port such as those round South Australia's Spencer Gulf would not matter, though he would not tell the charterers that.

I listened to these economic details, fascinated. The captain yarned with me, I suppose, because I was a good listener. Like all sailing-ship masters, he was a very lonely man.

A few days before the *Lawhill* was to sail towards Falmouth for orders, I was paid off. I could just walk. I felt groggy and far from strong, but I could stand on my feet. I took my wretched pay at the shipping office. It was barely sufficient to pay my railway fare back to Melbourne. There was no question of workmen's compensation. The matter was not raised. I could walk. I went. My shipmates took my sea-bag and put it in the compartment. I sank into a corner seat and stayed there until the train had come to Melbourne. The jolting of the train was painful and I did not care to move.

In the morning, there was Spencer Street again, the same untidy sprawl of sun-swept station, and my heart sank within me. Home! Home again from the sea. Frank was there. He was in a schooner, he said apologetically. He noticed my limp.

'What's the matter?' he said. 'Fall? Or knocked down by the sea? No, you couldn't be knocked down by the sea – not on a ballast run.'

'I fell,' I said. 'Not a word to the others, now.'

'All right.'

How I could hope that my mother would fail to notice that I could scarcely drag myself about, I don't know. But I knew she was working with a clothing firm in Flinders Lane, and I was well aware that she had plenty of worries without being bothered also with mine. I felt a failure to be coming home at all, without my time in, without even a ship. The younger children were still small and were away at school all day. Frank said there was plenty of depression in Melbourne and the outlook for seafaring men was poor. I hoped my thigh would mend soon so that I could get some kind of work, until I was fit again to work aloft. My mother did not come home until late in the evening, and was off again before seven in the mornings.

It was useless to seek work afloat. I found a job in an iron foundry instead. The assortment of factories not far from Collett Street included a steel spring works. It was a collection of galvanized iron sheds and furnaces, and in the sheds were devices for twisting hot metal into springs. The weather was dreadfully hot, for it was Melbourne's summer. Work in iron foundries was not popular, and I had little trouble getting a job. My work was to manipulate a machine which twisted the lighter springs, and though I was on my feet all day I did not have to move round much. The work was ghastly, like all factory jobs. But it was a job. It paid reasonably well. The foundry was manned by a large number of men whose spirit was not that of the sailing-ship sailor, and could scarcely be expected to be. Yet there was dignity about the heavy labour, too.

At the foundry I toughened up for the sea again. But there was no sea. There were no ships, only steamers.

I kept a vigilant eye on the comings and goings in the river and at Williamstown. Once there was a bald-headed four-masted schooner lying in the Yarra. She had a motor and her lines were abominable. She was a scow-shaped thing with a stern like a box; but I had heard she was short of an able seaman, and I thought she might be a good ship for me, temporarily, since there would be little going aloft in her. So I swallowed my pride and hid my disgust of her and went aboard. Her name was *Kermandie*.

'Is there a job aboard for an A.B.?' I asked a sour man in an old felt hat, who was driving a motor-winch. He was the mate.

'No,' he said, though I knew there was. As I walked ashore I heard him say, 'We don't want no bloody Square'eads 'ere.'

Bloody Squarehead! In my own home town! I looked at him and his ugly barge in amazement. For the moment I felt inclined to go back and hit him, for his crass narrow-mindedness and complacent stupidity. But what was the use? I suppose I must have picked up something of a strange accent after my months in Europe and in the *Lawhill*. I wandered disconsolately along the Yarra wharves, and my reflections on life in the city of Melbourne were not pleasant.

In the Little Dock, at the foot of Spencer Street, I heard there was a job in the ketch *Hawk*. She was a wretched little wooden thing over half a century old, and even the Tasmanian deadbeats who had previously manned her could stand the parsimony of her skipper-owner no longer, and fled. I looked at this *Hawk*. She was a vessel which normally I would never have glanced at twice. A man in a slouch cap was working at her pumps, and a thin stream of the muddy Yarra trickled across her decks.

I was given the job in the *Hawk*. Indeed, I think I was given two men's jobs, if not three. I turned to on the pump straightaway, and the man in the slouch cap went ashore to the pub on the Flinders Street corner.

Though I thought I had toughened up in the iron foundry, life in the wretched *Hawk* was almost more than I could bear. We towed down the river to a berth at Yarraville and filled her with bags of superphosphates for Launceston, in Tasmania. Stowing her 100-odd tons of cargo was a full day's work, but when that was done we filled her decks with cased benzine. When the decks were full and the reek of fumes was pronounced, we lashed our firebox atop the cargo, and a fire was lit in it to boil some tea. This calm proceeding gave me a bit of a shock, and I understood at once why several of these Tasmanian traders were on the missing list. It did not seem to occur to my shipmates – the mate, a Tasmanian nondescript, and a cripple – that this was highly dangerous.

'How the hell else can we git our tea?' said the mate, who thought I was mad when I suggested it would be better to do without.

This firebox consisted of a primitive sort of range in a wooden box, and was the only means of preparing food. In addition to the firebox, our single boat was also lashed on the benzine. The poor state of this wooden boat scarcely mattered, for it was carefully stowed where an outbreak of fire would be sure to get it first. I wondered whether I was being wise shipping in the *Hawk*, but reflected that after all she had been sailing a long time. It was reasonable to hope that she might survive a few more voyages. She had once been a fine little vessel, but by 1922 she had fallen on evil days.

As soon as our cargo was secured, the boat lashed down, and our tea drunk, we towed down the Yarra to an anchorage off Williamstown to sail with the turn off the tide. We were bound in the first instance towards the Tamar River. If we got so far, we were to load sawn Tasmanian hardwood for the return passage to Melbourne.

We sailed at midnight, for the master-owner of the *Hawk* believed in wasting no wind. In the morning we passed through the maelstrom of Melbourne Heads. The motion of the little ketch was violent in the Rip, and almost as bad when she reached the tumbling waters of Bass Strait outside. Wind and sea got up as the day grew older, and before long she was trying to turn somersaults. Everyone was seasick from the reek of benzine fumes, and her cargo began to shift. The fumes were so bad that even the mate hesitated to light the firebox fire. The *Hawk* was leaking badly; her sails were rotten; the miserable hutch of a forecastle streamed with water; there was no thought of a proper meal. Compared with her, the *Lawhill* carried the crew of a liner, and the living standards of the *Bellands* were those of a luxury hotel.

She sailed all right, or would have done if her sails had held together. A bit of a squall blew the mainsail out, and we had to put about and run back for Port Phillip Bay to repair the damage. It was with a mighty sense of relief that we entered

smooth water in the bay again and came to anchor off a sea-
side resort called Sorrento.

Sail repairs and restowage of the benzine cases went on at
once. In big lime-juice ships the slogan might be hunger and
ease; here it was hunger without the ease. We worked hard,
ate little, and got what rest we could in our cramped and sodden quarters. Next morning we were off again, and rolled and
stumbled through the Rip which boils at Melbourne Heads,
and beat about Bass Straits. The wind and sea got up again,
quickly, but this time we were too far outside, and did not go
back. Again the fumes sickened everyone; again there was no
food, no rest. There was no such thing as a daylight watch
below in the *Hawk*, while I was there. After a while it was
necessary to get the main gaff tops'l in (she had none on the
mizzen); I discovered I was the only one who could go aloft. I
had not been aloft since the fall in the *Lawhill*, months earlier,
and the fight with that gaff tops'l stands out in my memory as
one of the worst experiences I ever had in the rigging of a
sailing-ship. The *Hawk* was only 70 tons and that tops'l was
not the eighth part of any sail in a deep-sea ship. But in the
big ships there was company; one did not fight alone. There
were fellow-spirits with whom one had much in common;
there was a commodious deck, with a great rigging plentifully
supplied with ratlines, and foot-ropes along all the yards, and
shrouds and stays to cling to, and a whole maze of running
rigging. The bare masts of the *Hawk* writhed murderously as
the little vessel jumped and rolled. The lean, whipping mainmast seemed the wand of a murderer, as the wet malignant
bulk of the tops'l thundered at me and wrapped around me.
The rain beat upon me and the squall screamed; the canvas
tore again and again from my hold. Now I was flung in against
the wet, sticky pine by an unpredictable lurch of the ship (for
she flung herself about with no ordered rhythm); now far out
over the sea as she leapt to wind'ard, and the play of the pine
spar was frightening. I streamed with sweat and rain, and I
could feel the hot blood pouring down my leg. Good God! I
thought – a sailor's life! Those boys in the *Lawhill began* in

this kind of thing, with the ice of the Baltic thrown in for good measure. No wonder they were superb young sailors who laughed at the difficulties of sailing a comfortable deep-water ship! Had I begun in a thing like the *Hawk*, I doubted very much whether I would ever have continued. Nor was there much solace in the thought that she made short passages and the worse discomforts would soon be past. So also would they soon begin again.

The wheel of the ketch was a small brassbound thing, like a yacht's. It was not high enough for a grown youth to stand at, and steer. It was necessary to crouch to see the compass, and by night the constant strain told heavily on the back of the neck. Turns at the wheel were four hours. Watches were come on and stay on. Meals were provided by barracuda, for which a line trailed day and night. Where there should have been a plentiful supply of fresh food (whereof a cheap abundance was to be had in the public markets of both Melbourne and Launceston), we had only bad potatoes and poor salt beef, which was kept in a harness cask on the tiny poop as if she were a Cape Horner.

We reached the Tamar after two days, and by the grace of God it had not been possible to light a fire on the way over. The wind was down the river, and we beat up fifteen miles. How lovely was this Tasmanian stream! The sun shone, and up-river the day was peaceful. It was grand to see the loveliness of Tasmania once again, and though it took all night to warp the wretched ketch to the berth assigned her (for there is a great rise and fall in the Tamar River) and I was sore and tired, I was delighted to lift up my eyes from the deck of the *Hawk* towards those wooded hills.

At eight in the morning we turned to again, after a few hours' sleep, and got the benzine off. I worked with a will at this, for I was glad to see it go. Man-handling the heavy bags of superphosphates was, however, a different matter. With my broken *Lawhill* wounds, it was almost too much for me. The master was kind enough to suggest that if I could find someone to take my place I could pay off in Launceston. Pay off! With what? I had three pounds coming to me. How could I get a job? No, no, I would not pay off. There were no sailing-ships in Tasmanian ports, save a few more ketches of the *Hawk* variety. It was of no use to change the *Hawk* for another vessel which might be even worse.

We loaded sawn hardwood, in due course, for the passage back to Melbourne, for there was plenty of timber offering. These ketches managed a hard living by shipping parcels of planks from outports at freight rates which even the most un-economically run coastal steamer could not approach. The steamer insisted on picking up her cargo at central points. The sailer would go anywhere.

We loaded with dispatch and sailed back to Melbourne. Again the wind was from the west, and the *Hawk* danced and skipped across Bass Straits. Without the benzine she was a happier ship, but she was still an infernally hard one. There was little excuse for her poor food, and for the constant state of damp in the quarters.

We made another passage and came into Melbourne a few days before Christmas. The thin-lipped young master, whose temper had not improved upon further acquaintance, told us there would be a bonus if we worked hard and discharged the cargo before the holiday. This we did, and he gave us five shillings each, and paid us off. Our jobs, he said, would be there for us after the holidays. As for mine, he could keep it: for I had decided that even a steamer was better to finish my time in than the *Hawk*. I left the decrepit ketch without regrets, except that I had been fool enough to go in her. After that experience I looked more closely at the picturesque little ships in the Spencer Street Dock, with a clearer eye for their defects and their dangers.

But what next? A steamer, did I say? Was I prepared for *that* sacrilege?

Well, it looked like being a steamer or nothing. How did one get a berth in steam? A Britisher was useless, for she would only strand me again in the United Kingdom. I did not care for another share of beachcombing. As for sailing-ships, my *Law-hill* wounds were still not thoroughly healed and service in the *Hawk* had done them no good. I was not fit for Cape Horn ships. It *had* to be steam. I had no money to stay ashore, nor had I inclination. I thought that a voyage in a steamer would provide not only a berth; it would give me an insight into the probable career I should have when I became an officer. Though it was only three years or so since I first went to sea, already it was obvious that I could never hope to rise to command in an Australian or a British deep-sea sailing-ship. There were no Australians left at all, and very few Britishers. If I did not ship in a steamer it seemed that I might not get my four years' sea-time in at all.

The first thing I had to do, if I were to ship in steam, was to join the Australian seamen's union, for no one other than union members could be employed in Australian steamers. When I went to the union office my father's Labour background smoothed all difficulties, and within a week or two I had the offer of a ship by simply sitting in the office a few hours a day and keeping my mouth shut. The union had the bloody mates where it wanted them, the secretary told me: they had to come to the office for their men, and accept anyone who was offered. That union office showed me an altogether new spirit towards ships and the sea, and it was a spirit in which I found little to admire. The secretary's job, which he did with vigour and determination, was to raise hell in ships. He seemed to have power enough to tie up all the shipping on the Australian coast, and the Commonwealth Government's line besides. I was offered a berth as able seaman in the Commonwealth Government's new cargo steamer *Erriba*, lying in Hobson's Bay, for a round voyage to Europe with grain. I accepted it.

The *Erriba* was a tramp of about 6,000 tons which had been built in Australia as part of the war programme for merchant shipping. Being completed too late to be of use in the war or even to profit from the high freights offering immediately afterwards, she had been laid up some time in the bay. She was about to make her maiden voyage. She looked a clumsy lump to me, as she rode high at her anchors with her hull and upper works painted war-time grey. She was provided with what seemed to me an enormous crew – forty-two hands all told, who included three watchkeeping officers on deck, a bos'n, seven able seamen, nine firemen, three trimmers, three greasers and a donkeyman below, stewards, cooks, and mess-boys. Her cargo capacity was little in excess of the *Lawhill*'s, and I wondered how she could be made to pay. Perhaps in the Commonwealth Line that didn't matter. The crew lived aft, which was a new thing to me, and the life was comfortable and organized. The food was excellent and abundant, and our quarters were spacious and reasonably airy. Bedding was supplied, and the ship's articles stipulated that our linen must be changed once weekly at least, and laundered at ship's expense. Overtime was generous and fairly easily earned. We were to be given additional leave in port for each week spent at sea, or receive extra pay at overtime rates, as we chose. The ship was on the three-watch system at sea, and an eight-hour day in port. There were separate forecastles and mess-rooms for the sailors and firemen, and a messboy was appointed to look after each.

We loaded grain in sacks at Port Lincoln for Las Palmas for orders, and went by way of the Cape of Good Hope with a call at Albany. I was appointed to the 8 to 12 watch, which meant that I was on duty from 8 AM until noon, and again from 8 PM until midnight. The rest of the day was mine. I felt like a passenger who helped with the lookouts and steering and now and again did two hours menial labour on deck. Most of my watch was taken up with wheel turns and lookouts. A week of this was longer than a month of the *Lawhill*'s watches. The principal occupation off-watch was sleeping, or joining the poker school in the firemen's mess-room. I read a lot and studied my dull tomes to learn what a second mate should know. The *Erriba*'s officers kept their watches on the bridge and, apart from the mate, did little else. The mate was about the decks all day.

As the steamer pushed her way across the southern Indian Ocean in the face of the weather, I wondered a great deal about the sea profession. We were three weeks from the Cape to Las Palmas — three weeks of steady sunny weather and effortless progress, with good meals, good watches, too much leisure. Those three weeks seemed longer than any three months at sea in a sailing-ship, even the hungry *Bellands*. The monotony of the steamer's repetitive jobs, the absence of all real interest in the accomplishment of the voyage (for that was in the hands of the black gang down below), made the profession merely another form of labouring. An able seaman was a helmsman, a keeper of lookouts, a reader of the patent log, a petty mechanic to jostle with the cargo-gear, a washer of paint and scraper of winches. At the best he was a quartermaster; at the worst an unskilled labourer whose employment happened to be in a ship at sea. I observed the three mates very closely, and except that their lives (barring the chief mate's) were even lazier, they did not seem any better off than the seamen. There was some real dignity of work in tending the fires and keeping the engines going; but a deck officer was a bit of a navigator, a watchkeeper, a compiler of the log, a senior lookout, flat-footing on the bridge. He was not concerned even with the administration of the crew — dared not be concerned, for fear of offending the seamen's union. The second and third mates had scarcely any dealings with the crew, except to pass necessary orders to helmsmen and lookouts. The mate, who had the general responsibility for the ship's maintenance, passed his orders through the bos'n, who filtered them as he saw fit and passed them on in accordance with the principles of the seamen's union. He was a member of the union, too, and stood in some fear of being brought to account if he did anything to offend his fellow-members. We chipped rust, washed paint, cleaned out boats, cleaned winches, oiled wires, steered, looked out, slept, and ate. Day followed day, and it was all aimless. What use was it to be an officer in such a ship, or any steamer? For sheer boredom, the second and third mates' jobs aboard that tramp must have been hard to equal, and the mate was even more frustrated.

As for the master, he seemed a pleasant man and kindly disposed. He did a little navigation and exercised himself upon the bridge as he saw fit. He was available at the end of a speaking-tube day and night, in his apartment immediately below the navigating bridge. What he did in there all day and all night I don't know. Perhaps he read a lot, or had some hobby. When we approached a port, pilots took over the ship-handling, when it would have been interesting, and tugs helped to berth the ship. In port, agents of the Line did the ship's business. To some degree the master administered the crew; but even in that it struck me that his main function, and chief responsibility, was to see there was no trouble with the union which could spread to other ships. The chief engineer sat about, and took life very pleasantly. He was a 'guarantee' chief. Since this was the *Erriba*'s first voyage he was sent with her by the builders to ensure that the engines were all right. They were right enough, and his cheerful acceptance of the holiday was sufficient guarantee of that. What else he guaranteed I don't know.

We lay several days at Las Palmas, but there were no orders. We then went on to Falmouth, where the German four-masted barque *Magdalene Vinnen* took my eye, until I noticed that she was auxiliary. In due course we took our grain to Newcastle-on-Tyne. By the time we were ready to discharge, the wheat had been in the hold for nearly seventy days. The *Lawhill* could have done nearly as well with half the crew and a fifth the costs, and the *Preussen* and *Potosi* would have done even better. I scouted ashore for news of the *Lancing*, but there was none, except that she was reported to be for sale to the scrappers. There was not a single deep-sea sailing-ship in a Yorkshire port.

One day in Newcastle, while the *Erriba* was alongside discharging her grain, the crew was called upon to shift ship during the hour set aside for the midday meal. The men refused. The mate came personally to their quarters and almost begged them to turn to, explaining that our berth was required for another vessel already in mid-stream. We had only to move along the wharf, about the ship's length. It was a trifling operation. They would be paid overtime. But they refused. When one refused they all felt they must do likewise, or lose their standing with the union. Under our agreement we could not be compelled to work overtime in port, or accept disturbance of a meal hour. So the refusal was not mutiny. It was merely insisting on our 'rights'. The mate could fume as much as he liked, which in fact was not much, for he knew where he stood. The steamer waiting for the berth could barge about in mid-stream, and the pilot curse. The order of the port could be disrupted, while our mariners reclined in their bunks until the proper time for turning to.

This was a new sort of seafaring to me. I had been brought up to put the ship first. I wondered about the men who were sabotaging the people's ships. My shipmates boasted, now and again, of their methods of 'job control', and the ease with which they could hold up ships for trifling reasons, or no reason at all. Most of our crew were older men who had certainly known some oppression by the ship-owners in former days; but now there was oppression by the workers. The net result of my shipmates' attitude was to make it impossible for the Government's steamships to survive in a competitive world. If the union members had been out to kill the Line, they could not have gone about the job more thoroughly than they did; yet this Line was the people's and its destruction was the devoutest wish of the other ship-owners. Its success was – or should have been – one of the stoutest planks in the Labour platform. The Line was a great idea and ought to have developed into a great Australian asset. To say the least, it is a poor country which cannot provide ships for the carriage of its own produce, and seamen to man the ships. If the function of a crew be not properly and at all times to serve the ship – and that before all other considerations – then they are frauds and have no purpose in the ship at all. If officers are powerless and useless, then so also will the ships they serve become. That sailors should have reasonable conditions and just rewards, all fair-minded men will agree. But to lose sight of their duties in a great profession is to lose their place as honourable sea-faring men. Without a clear basis of recognized duties as well as a fierce charter of their 'rights', crews must be worthless in steamers or in sailing-ships. If they are worthless in sailing-ships, they die. If they are worthless in steamships, then the ships must die. My countrymen would learn this, sooner or later. I hoped it would be sooner.

Indeed, my countrymen had very little to do with the matter, for there were few of them in the *Erriba*. Nearly all the crew were seamen from the United Kingdom, who had managed to join the Australian Seamen's Union.

The *Erriba*, her grain discharged at last, loaded coal in Cardiff for a place called Djibouti, in French Somaliland, and sailed there via Suez. At Djibouti the crew caused trouble because the weather was very warm. I noted the loveliness of the local dhows.

There was no further charter for the ship, and she returned to Melbourne. With overtime, my pay came to over a hundred pounds. I had my time in now, and the money to finance a course ashore for second mate's ticket. My *Lawhill* wounds still bothered me and continued to worry me for years, but I was all right. However, the prospects of becoming a watch-keeping officer in such a vessel as the *Erriba* did not appeal to me. It was obvious that I could no longer achieve my ambition of becoming a master in deep-sea sail. I did not care for what I had seen of steamers under my own flag, and I did not contemplate a life's service under any other. There was no appeal for me in a career of watchkeeping on some dull steamer's bridge, exercising my mind from time to time with a little pilotage or navigation, with no real part in the running of the ship or crew, and with nothing to look forward to but the indefinite continuance of such conditions for many years with, at last, a dull command. Not for me! Perhaps I could best serve the Cape Horn sailing-ship if I moved ashore.

I decided to leave the sea and go to Hobart in Tasmania and begin life afresh.

CHAPTER ELEVEN

A TASMANIAN NEWSPAPER OFFICE

Just how I was going to make my way in Tasmania, I didn't know. Here I was, nineteen years old, with nothing to my credit but four years of wasted time trying to qualify for a profession which I no longer considered worth following. I was well aware that in order to have any chance of making my way ashore I must be somewhere beyond the range of Cape Horn ships. None of these sailed to Hobart. I should not be tempted back to the sea from there. The city was small, the island beautiful, the people pleasant, the climate delightful. According to my friends in Melbourne, it was foolish to go to Tasmania. Things in the 'Speck', they said, were very bad. It was better to be in the larger centres on the mainland.

I went to Hobart as a passenger by Bass Strait ferry and train from Launceston, and I found a cheap boarding-house on Campbell Street, near the water-front. There I looked carefully about me, and liked what I saw. There was something of a trade slump, but this was better than France. I spoke the language and I should get on. If I could get out of a drain-pipe in the Bordeaux docks, I could graduate from a boarding-house by the Hobart water-front.

The first necessity was a job, any job. The pessimists said there were no jobs. You could prospect for osmiridium if you could get someone to stake you, and you knew osmiridium when you saw it. I didn't. You could grow apples, if you had plenty of capital to throw down the drain. I hadn't. You could work the busy season loading ships on the water-front, if you would subscribe to the union's restrictive practices. I wouldn't. You could find a job if you looked for one, and would take anything. I did. I must say that I have never yet met a sailing-ship sailor who had much difficulty finding work ashore, if he really wanted it, or who failed to make his way when he came ashore.

I found a job simply by walking round Hobart with my eyes open, and noticing a great deal of construction at a new plant at a place called Risdon, on the banks of the River Derwent. The plant was a huge one for the extraction of zinc by electrolysis, and about that I knew nothing. But I did know something about rigging, and there was obviously plenty of that to be done. At the first time of asking, I was hired as a rigger's assistant, and was on the pay-roll with money enough to pay my way.

I enjoyed the work at Risdon. There were towers to be erected, and large scaffolding, and other jobs where skill with rope and wire was needed. When this work came to an end and I was laid off, I picked up a casual job at a jam factory, for the fruit season was in full swing. Meantime I was looking about for some field of employment in which I could really feel I was using my abilities, such as they were, to the full, with a fair prospect of getting on. These stop-gap jobs were all very well, but I had no intention of becoming a dead-end labourer in Tasmania, or anywhere else. The jam factory was on the waterfront, and I still had an interest in ships – all ships. No deep-sea sailing-ships came in, but I met an old shipmate serving in the ketch *Aristides*, who told me of the fast four-masted barque *Marlborough Hill* which was loading grain at Port Adelaide for Europe, and looking for men. She was a Finn, like the *Luwhill*, but she was offering Australian wages. Aye, I said, and the beach in Europe. But she was a famous ship and one in which I should like to serve. I thought a lot about the *Marlborough Hill*.

While I was in a quandary as to what to do, my friend from the *Aristides* and I chanced to be waiting outside the Hobart town-hall one Sunday afternoon, waiting for the doors to open for a musical concert, when a small car drove up to the newspaper office opposite, and a smart young man got out. He was well dressed and appeared prosperous. My shipmate knew him, and they exchanged greetings. The smart young man let himself into a side-door of the newspaper building, and I wondered what he could be doing there.

'Why, that's Jack Williams, from Devonport,' my friend told me. 'He's a newspaper reporter – you know, a journalist. He works for the *Mercury* here. I expect he's gone in there to write up his report of something or other from last night, in time for tomorrow's paper.'

A newspaper reporter? Why, this was just the thing for me! Until then I had never thought of journalism as a profession I could enter. The Labour journals for which my father wrote paid nothing, and dealt only in propaganda. I had not realized that young men were employed to report news. From the appearance of Mr Williams the profession must be a profitable one. The possession of an automobile was itself a mark of affluence. No sailor, I knew, could afford such a thing in Australia. It came to me almost with the suddenness of a bomb-burst that newspaper reporting was just the thing that I could do.

It was all very well to decide that I intended to become a journalist, but how could I set about it? The only possible approach, I thought, was the direct one. I had no influence and no Tasmanian friends. The thing to do, I thought, was to prepare a note requesting an interview, and take the note along to the newspaper office myself. So upon the Monday morning I took an hour's leave from the jam factory and presented myself at the front office of the *Mercury*, with a request to see the editor. I did not know that editors of morning newspapers were rarely in their offices in the morning. My note was sent to the manager, who must have been a kindly man. At any rate, a message that a sailor was outside who wished to become a journalist was sufficient to open his door. It was my great good fortune that I had hit upon one of those men who would themselves have loved to lead just the life I had been leading, to whom the great sailing-ship was almost as compellingly attractive as it was to me. Tasmania abounded in ship-loving citizens, for its maritime history was recent, great, and stirring. I don't doubt that the *Mercury*'s manager would have gone off in a Cape Horner, if he could. He received me pleasantly, and I was soon at my ease.

I should like, I said, to become a newspaper reporter. What were my qualifications? Well, I had done fairly well at school and had matriculated, with a scholarship; I had served several years in deep-sea sailing-ships, and had wandered over some part of the world; I thought I could at least make a job of a column in the *Mercury* headed 'Shipping Intelligence', which was neither very accurate about ships nor particularly intelligent; I liked writing concise accounts of things. Well, he said, not very gratified by my remark about his shipping column, the young junior who writes that covers the Hobart magistrate's court, fire-stations, and hospitals as well, and does a turn of telephone duty in the evenings, taking down in shorthand news phoned in by district correspondents. How should I get on with all that? His reporter's knowledge of shipping might be deficient in some points, but he had served four years as a cadet and junior reporter, and had been a copy-holder in the readers' room for a year before that. He could write shorthand and use a typewriter. He knew the *Mercury*'s style, and its sources of information.

The manager went on to point out that in order to become a reporter at all, it was necessary to serve a three-years' cadet-ship; and to be selected as a cadet one must first serve at least twelve months in the readers' room to learn something of the ropes. There were already four youths in that room waiting for the chance to become cadet reporters and some had been waiting two years. There was also a list of young gentlemen, well recommended by their schools, who were waiting to enter the reading room.

The manager said I could come back that evening to discuss the matter with the head reader, if I wished, and if I would send in the journals I had kept aboard my various ships, he would read them with interest. I should have to learn to write shorthand at least 120 words a minute, and be prepared to reach licensed shorthand writers' standard, for the *Mercury* took its verbatim reports seriously and provided the State Parliament with its records. I should also be required to learn how to use a typewriter, at my own expense. If I was prepared to do all these things, and to spend at least a year in the proof-reading room, my name might be added to the waiting list.

When I called on the head reader that evening I learned that the prospects were even slimmer than the manager had suggested. A copy-holder, I gathered, was a youth who read aloud from the reporters' manuscript or typescript while a proof-reader corrected the proofs, in order to ensure that what was printed was, at any rate, what had been written down. To begin with, I should earn no more than 25s or 30s a week, and my board in Campbell Street cost more than that. There were far more applicants than there were vacancies. The *Mercury* was a comfortable office and, once employed there, people rarely left. Sometimes the more enterprising spirits did migrate to Melbourne or Sydney, where, he said, there was a steady demand for *Mercury*-trained journalists. I gathered that, to stand a chance of reaching even the first low rung of the ladder to a real newspaper job, I should have to wait either until a member of the editorial or reading staffs died, or some young man decided to try his fortune in one of the mainland capitals.

The head reader took down my name and temporary address, and advised me to keep the job I had until a vacancy occurred in the *Mercury*. But I could keep my job only as long as the fruit season lasted, and that was ending. Weeks passed. I heard nothing from the newspaper office. A month passed. I wrote. The head reader acknowledged the letter. No vacancies yet, he said. Two months passed. I was without a job. At dawn I was outside the *Mercury* office reading the front page which was posted there, to see if there were any jobs I could go after, and I began to wonder whether that was as close as I would ever get to that or any other newspaper office. I hawked insurance for a very short spell. That was no job for me. Meanwhile I had enrolled myself at a local business college, learning shorthand and typewriting at night with a group of merry Tasmanian girls whose studies were not always confined to the curriculum of the business school. I read avidly and studied anything I could get hold of which had any bearing on the newspaper life.

Three months passed. I was back at the zinc works doing more rigging. This lasted only a week or two, and I was laid off again. Still there was no vacancy at the *Mercury*. I began to wander about the water-front more frequently and to take a keen interest in the old *Alma Doepel*, a tops'l schooner which was the only vessel hailing from the port which still crossed yards. One of the coal hulks at the Hobart wharves was the barque *Otago*. I knew this was the square-rigger which Joseph Conrad had once commanded. Even as a blackened hulk, her loveliness of line was a delight. Her bowsprit had been shorn away, and she was cut down to her lower masts. Some of the yards which once spread her lovely sails now stood up-ended in her holds, to carry cargo gear. An ugly galvanized iron house stood on the fore-deck to cover a donkey-boiler which provided steam for her friction winches. No one lived aboard, and her decks were covered with coal-dust, and neglected. She still carried her original wheel and all the fittings on the poop. Apart from the grime, the absence of rigging, and the removal of the binnacle, her poop was much as Conrad must have known it. Sometimes she felt the urge of the sea at her plebeian berth, and tugged at her moorings. I loved to go aboard and walk the tiny poop in the very early mornings while the sunrise brought serene beauty to all of Derwentside. What a lovely command she must have been! No wonder Conrad was proud of her, and took her through Torres Straits. She was small, even smaller than the *James Craig*. But she was a little beauty, and must have been as responsive as a well-bred horse. There was still a fine air of the deep sea about old Hobart in the 1920s, though all the blue-gum clippers were long gone and the slipway where many of them were built was overgrown with grass. It was a good place for the *Otago* to rest her bones. I don't know whether Conrad himself ever visited Hobart. If he did, I think he must have approved of the place, though the only employment it could find for his sweet iron barque was to hawk dirty coal to steamers.

Patience, patience – how difficult a quality to maintain when one is nineteen. I began to think I should never be offered the promised job at the newspaper office. I began to long again for the restless sea, that queller of turbulence with its own wild spirit. Had there been any *Otago*s or *James Craig*s in commission I should never have remained ashore in Hobart. But the *Marlborough Hill* had sailed, woefully short-handed, and there was a coal strike again in New South Wales to hold up the handful of Cape Horners still in Newcastle.

I graduated from the business college, without distinction. I could write shorthand fast enough, and produce rough type-script without serious injury to a strong typewriter.

At last, when I had almost given up hope, I was summoned one morning to the manager's office and informed that I could begin as a copy-holder that same night. And because he knew I should have to live on my pay and was not in the position of the youngsters normally beginning in the readers' room, my pay would be two pounds a week as a start. This was generous. I still had something of my savings from the *Erriba* and from the zinc works rigging job. I didn't like the idea of grubbing along for the next four years or so on a few pounds; but we should see. The main thing was to begin. I should find ways to make good, in due course. No young man more determined to succeed in the newspaper profession – or to make good gener-ally – ever mounted those old stairs.

The work was night-work, and far from difficult. I read aloud from scraps of paper while a harassed reader checked the wet and sticky proofs, now and then cursing and jabbing at them with a large pen, making queer hieroglyphs in the margin. I began at six in the evening and finished when the last proof went to the composing room, which was generally be-tween one and two next morning. At least I was supposed to finish then. Generally, I hung round the office until the paper had gone to press, for having at last gained a foothold inside I was loath to leave again, even to sleep. I wanted to learn as much as possible as quickly as I could, and I was determined that somehow or other, I would develop into a qualified re-porter in less than four years. I liked the work, and I liked the spirit of the office, but I very quickly lost my belief in the in-

fallibility of the press, and never regained it. I discovered that
daily newspapers weren't written: they were flung together, in
a great hurry, from a mass of cabled puzzles and a host of
typed reports from the ends of the earth. The nightly set-up in
that pleasant office was somehow not unlike the teamwork of
a square-rigged ship. The able seamen were the reporters.
The petty officers were the cable editors and the rewrite men,
who made what sense they could from the flimsy cables and
telegrams which brought overseas and Commonwealth news.
Above these were the watchkeeping officers, the chief sub-
editors, of whom one worked by day and the other by night.
They had charge of the decks, under the master who was the
editor, and like the master of a ship, rarely if ever interfered,
and was not often seen. The bos'n was the chief-of-staff, who
ran the reporters. There was an associate editor who acted as
a sort of leader-writer and political expert: he had no counter-
part in a sailing-ship. Neither had a lowly copy-holder: I was
not even a deckboy and I was certainly not a passenger.

I settled into the copy-holder's routine easily, and looked
for new worlds to conquer. There were none. I seemed destined to remain a copy-holder for years. The three youths
ahead of me for promotion to cadet-reporter were smart young
fellows, and the whole editorial staff was radiant with health.
Promotion from the readers' room was ordinarily by seniority
alone; I was up against a brick wall. Months passed. I became
a reader of revise proofs, a corrector of corrected proofs which
had been sent back to the composing room for their offending
lines to be reset. This was child's play. A proof-reader had to
have his wits about him and soon acquired a thorough knowledge of not only the paper's style but the names and titles,
and so forth, of the citizens and bodies whose doings were
recorded in the *Mercury*'s news. I could see why young reporters were required to begin as readers. There was no better
training ground. The trouble as far as I was concerned was that
the training went on too long.

In due course, I had a turn at day-reading, and to keep me
out of mischief was given the additional job of racing editor

of the *Mercury*'s associated weekly newspaper. The original racing editor, who had long been dead, had used the name of Tam o' Shanter. So Tam o' Shanter I became. It was my business to dish up to the readers once weekly a page or two about local horse-racing and to predict for them lists of the nags most likely to win and to gain places in the next Saturday's racing. I was expected to go to all the race meetings in southern Tasmania, where there were more than enough, and to follow the racing intelligently when I got there. But on the course I could hide behind my anonymity; if my tips were terrible no one could assault me.

As for that, I suppose my tips were as good as most. A broken-down jockey sent in notes from the track, and was supposed to provide the inside knowledge. I often wondered why, if he knew so much about the horses which would probably win, he did not profit by the knowledge himself. His real job was hedging, not tipping. He gave every horse a chance, and hated to name winners. I had to do that. I did it by the simple process of taking a list of the horses and, closing my eyes, stabbing at the list with a pin. Sometimes I varied the process by selecting a trotter or a hurdler with a sailing-ship's name, or some other name which seemed attractive. This got me into trouble once, for in complete ignorance I tipped a dark horse to win just the race it had been planned for him to win, and the owner and trainer were furious at the 'leak'.

The chief reader on the day watches was a delightful old gentleman whose real interest – and calling – was conducting a brass band. This he did with such regularity and devotion that he had not enough sleep, and he was accustomed, therefore, to take a nap in the office. His grey head would nod, his eyes close, his pencil drop, and there he was, as peacefully asleep as a baby. While he slept I hurriedly transformed myself into the horsey Tam, and pored over the peculiar notes of my ex-jockey accomplice, wrestling with the business of so forecasting the events of the next Saturday's racing that, no matter what horses won, I had given a fair chance to the lot of them. A Tasmanian confrère named Clive Turnbull, a youth who was made for better things, got on with the reading, which was rarely arduous.

This sort of thing was all very well, but, as far as I could see, it might continue for years. No old reporters died, and no young ones showed the least desire to migrate to the bright lights of Melbourne. The barque *Otago* knew me well; and again I was very interested in the *Alma Doepel*.

One day I saw a familiar figure on the water-front. It was old Jackie Shimmins, ex-mate of the *Rothesay Bay*. He had been forced to give up the sea, he said, for it no longer held any attractions for a young man. (He was over eighty.) So he had married a comely widow and settled down in Tasmania. He looked tolerably prosperous and fit for another twenty years. I heard from other sources that his widow had four daughters, and old Jackie led them all a hell of a life by insisting upon getting up at every change in the weather and going outside to see that all was secure, and by turning out the 'hands' sharp at six every morning. As the hands were young females over twenty years old, they found the old man a bit hard to put up with. He died, I heard, within a year; and there was a general sigh of relief at his departure.

I had become extremely restless and almost despaired of ever getting on, for the pace of things ashore was painfully slow and most of the shore-siders seemed so damned content and complacent about everything, when one day a little fleet of strange vessels put into Storm Bay and steamed up to Hobart's wharves. There were five of them. They were small, lithe steamers, with high flared bows and lovely lines. Their high mainmasts carried lookout barrels and in the bows of each was a small stubby gun. Some of them had come from Norway, some from Seattle. The flag they flew was Norwegian and the tough-looking men aboard spoke a language I could not understand, for seamen's Norwegian did not differ very much from Swedish. After them, keeping a rendezvous, came a large steamer, her decks a clutter of boilers and curious gear and boats. She was unlike any other steamer I had seen. There was considerable secrecy about the ships and their purpose, but the water-front gossip was that they were modern whalers, bound upon an expedition to a new, great whaling ground somewhere in the ice of the Antarctic.

I quickly confirmed the gossip from the men themselves. I learned that the large steamer, the name of which was *Sir James Clark Ross*, was short of men and wished to recruit at Hobart. Roald Amundsen had reported that Tasmanians were good seafaring people and had a living tradition of whaling. I was not a Tasmanian except by choice, but I presented myself forthwith to the captain of the whaling-ship, and was signed on at the Norwegian Consulate as a whaler's labourer, at a wage of four pounds a month and a share in the oil which amounted to about a farthing a barrel. It struck me that this expedition ought to be the making of an extremely interesting story, and I was just the fellow to go after it. This was Opportunity, knocking loudly, and I was in. The proof-reading and Tam o' Shanter could go to the devil.

CHAPTER TWELVE

TO THE ANTARCTIC FOR WHALES

On November 30th, 1923, I sailed from Hobart in the whale factory-ship *Sir James Clark Ross*, bound in the first instance towards Macquarie Island and thence towards the pack-ice and the Ross Sea. Beyond that, whatever harbour we might be able to find, either in the face of the Great Ice Barrier or along the coast of South Victoria Land, there to carry on the business of catching whales with the small ships, and converting their blubber and flesh into oil aboard the big one. This was the first modern whaling expedition into the Ross Sea, which previously had been visited only by scientists and explorers. Until then, no ordinary citizen or seafaring man had had the opportunity to visit the Antarctic, and most of the accounts of it had been written by scientists and expedition leaders. This was my chance to present what picture I could for the newspaper readers at least of Tasmania and perhaps also of Australia. Before the expedition sailed, I made an arrangement with the *Mercury* to let me have a cheap camera and some films; and the newspaper, besides giving me an authority to send press messages in Australia and New Zealand, promised me my job back when I returned with no loss of place on the roster for promotion, and ten pounds if I turned in a good story. This was good enough, though I had no intention of returning to proof-reading.

There was a keen maritime interest about the old Hobart journal, and both the night and the day chief subs were enthusiastic supporters of my enterprise. I suspect they would gladly have gone themselves, had they been younger. The *Sir James Clark Ross* and her five chasers remained at Hobart only three days, and there was no time for any competitor to come from the mainland, if the idea occurred to them. When it was known in Hobart that the ships were for the Antarctic, there were many pessimists who said it was foolish to go there in steel ships. Hobart had seen something of Antarctic exploration, and all other ships had been wooden sealers or specially built vessels which could withstand pressure in the ice. Some even of those had been lost. The *Sir James Clark Ross* was nothing but an old cargo vessel from the Brocklebank Line which had been sold cheaply to the port of Sandefjord in Norway, and converted for whaling. Her only protection against ice was some greenheart sheathing at the bows, and if she was ever nipped in the ice she would fold up like a large tin can. As for the catchers, some of the old sea-dogs predicted they would roll over long before we reached the ice-rim, and they had no protection whatever.

I paid no attention to the pessimists. One thing I had already learned from my brief newspaper experience was to get at facts quickly, and the facts of this expedition seemed all right to me. It was led by the outstanding figure in modern whaling, a Norseman named Captain Carl Anton Larsen, who had already pioneered the whaling industry in South Georgia in the Atlantic, and had taken a considerable part in whaling from bases in the South Shetland Islands in the Weddell Sea, to the south of Cape Horn. The mere fact that the fleet was Norwegian was guarantee enough of its seaworthiness. The Norsemen were good sailors, and not fools. They would take no undue risks. In both shipping and whaling, they knew what they were doing. As for hazards, they would help the story.

There were hazards enough, God knows, and the life was infernally comfortless. The factory-ship was not run in accordance with the precepts of the Australian seamen's union, and life aboard was tough. She had a large crew of some 150 men, but there was more than enough work for all of us. I soon discovered that the function of a whaler's labourer was to labour, hard, twelve hours a day. To us the fact that the *Sir James Clark Ross* was a ship was incidental. She was a factory first, and the effort required to make her function was prodigious. We lived in a large cabin which was part of an additional forecastle built into the ship beneath the usual accommodation, in the fore 'tween-decks. This place was called the penguin rookery. It was steam-heated, but sometimes the system broke down. It provided a bunk each to sleep in and a mess table to eat at, and that was all. The ship carried a good supply of cold-weather clothing, which was available at reasonable prices. The food was nourishing and abundant, especially on the grounds. There were twelve Tasmanians, all told, and the Norsemen accepted them pleasantly. Our particular work was assisting to clear up the 'tween-decks and to clear up some tanks in the lower hold, making ready for the oil. The decks of the factory-ship were a working platform, the 'tween-decks housed the blubber boilers and the necessary machinery for converting blubber into more or less purified oil, and the lower hold was divided into tanks to store the oil. When we joined the ship most of these tanks were full of Welsh coal. We had to clear out the coal and scrub down the tanks. We did this for twelve hours every day, Sundays included, and trimmed the coal to the ship's bunkers. On the grounds, we also coaled the five whale-chasers and stored them. We also helped on deck, dragging blubber about and so forth; but our principal job was clearing out tanks and attending to the wants of the chasers.

As well as my ship and factory duties, I exercised whatever newsgathering talent I might have, to learn all I could of the expedition, the ships, their people, and modern whaling generally. As far as I knew, only Norwegians and Japanese did any whaling, and the Japanese were confined to their home waters. The last Yankee whaler had been lost some years previously, though a few open boats still went after the odd humpback or sperm from shore stations at Norfolk Island, the coast of New South Wales, and the Shetland Islands. It was obvious that our fleet intended to kill a lot of whales and must do so to pay its way, for the modern methods, although efficient, were very costly. The old sailing whalers could wander leisurely about the face of the waters, here, there, and everywhere, with never a ton of bunkers to buy, and only a small crew to pay off in the end. With their small open boats they could hunt whales singly, almost to the last whale. They had not been able to sail through pack-ice, and they had not dared hunt the giant blue and fin whales of the Antarctic and Arctic waters, because these sank when they died, and could not be raised again except by immense effort. The effort was beyond the resources of a vessel blown by the wind. The stubby guns high in the bows of our little steamers threw steel harpoons into the bodies of any whales they could approach. Once struck, the explosive head of the harpoon burst in the whale's vitals and, as soon as he died — which, I gathered, was not always as shortly after his frightful wounding as might be expected — his carcass was hove to the surface by means of a powerful steam winch. Then a sharp nozzle blew a little compressed air into him to keep him afloat; he was flagged so that he could be seen, and cast adrift while the chaser hunted more whales. They tried to take at least two or three a day, which they then towed to the factory-ship where the blubber was stripped from them. The factory hoped to treat not less than ten whales a day, throughout a season lasting three months or more. It was obvious that we were going to need a lot of whales.

It seemed equally obvious, for some time, that we weren't going to get any. To be successful, the factory-ship required a harbour somewhere convenient to the whales' feeding-ground. Amundsen and others had reported that whales fed in the Ross Sea, and Captain Larsen himself had seen them in the Weddell Sea. But how about a harbour? Amundsen had required a mere temporary base ashore, from which to begin his great run towards the Pole: the *Sir James Clark Ross*, however, would need a safe harbour for some months. We steamed towards the pack ice by way of Macquarie Island, where there were neither whales nor harbour. There was nothing there but an open roads, and the ruins of the shacks in which old Captain Hatch had boiled down penguins. A couple of shaggy horses, very aged and benevolent, wandered down to the kelp at the water's edge to meet us and stare at us pleasantly, and penguins and sea-elephants abounded. The horses were probably survivors of the Hatch establishment. We said hallo to them and passed on towards the Balleny Islands, but the Balleny Islands were hidden behind miles of impenetrable pack. The success of the expedition depended wholly upon being able to force a way through the pack-ice into the open waters of the Ross Sea beyond, and this was impossible unless the summer sun rotted the ice sufficiently to allow us to break a way through without risk of knocking holes in the ship's thin hull. There was no sun, and the ice was like armour. For days and days we floundered in the ice, with the five chasers in tow astern, taking an awful hammering. Once we were jammed in so badly that all hands had to take to the ice and saw the fleet free by hand. Penguins came from far and near to stare at the strange sight and offer advice, which went unheeded. The penguins seemed considerably astonished at our proceedings. They were cheerful little birds, and very human. A little Norwegian dog scared them for a while, until they realized that the dog was a very foolish animal and paid no more attention to it. When they were in a hurry (which was not often) the penguins got down on their downy bellies and skidded along, like small boys having fun on a toboggan.

On December 20th, 1923, we entered the open waters of the Ross Sea, and sighted not a single whale. If a fleet of steamers had difficulty in negotiating the pack, it was too much for creatures which had only their own soft backs to break it, and must come up for air every twenty minutes or so.

We steamed down to the Bay of Whales, which Amundsen had recommended. The Bay was full of hard ice, frozen fast, and we could not get in. There was no harbour there and would not be until the ice drifted out. But the ice seemed secure in there for ever. Meanwhile, one of the chasers was missing. She could easily have hit a small berg; the tiniest growler of a berg would be enough to sink any of the chasers. The weather, which had been good while we steamed towards the Bay, now broke. A gale sprang up from nowhere and screamed at us. When that subsided there was fog, and the little chasers clung closely round us, bleating on their sirens. The lost chaser had not arrived. We made a depot and left a bottle with instructions, on the safest place we could find, and steamed off to find some other harbour. There was no harbour anywhere – not along the coast of Victoria Land, not along the whole Barrier face, not in McMurdo Sound. We could not approach either the Sound or the few possibly useful indentations on the coast, because heavy ice filled them all. Whales began to trickle in, and we saw a spout or two, but they were very thin. They had come a long way, and had not yet had time to fatten on the minute sea-creatures which were their food, and which abounded in the Ross Sea. Some whales were killed, and the greasy business of cutting them in began. Yankee whalers used to cut in their whales from staging rigged outboard, from which skilled men used blubber spades on the carcass lying afloat beneath them. The method in the Norwegian ship was to secure the carcasses alongside and hoist out small flat-bottomed boats from which men worked with long knives, cutting off the blubber in strips which were hauled aboard with the ship's cargo gear, which consisted of all the usual derricks, winches, wires, and blocks. This was all very well in a harbour, but it would not work in anything of a sea. In the open sea it was quite useless. The men could not work. The surging of the whale carcass, the roll of the ship, the jumping about of the small boat, the sudden incalculable strains on the cargo gear, combined to make the work slow and dangerous. There were accidents when wires carried away and strips of fresh blubber fell on the unfortunates in the boats, pitching them into the sea. The men who did the skilled work of stripping blubber were known as flensers. Their work was flensing whales. They were a tough gang of large bewhiskered men, skilful at their trade and usually silent. But they were not silent at this sort of thing. It was hopeless. We *had* to find a harbour

The whole Barrier face, that mirage of savage beauty, mocked at us, and there was no harbour. Whales began to stream in. Still no harbour. Ice filled the Bay of Whales and all McMurdo Sound. When the weather was calm the flensers could carry on, and the bloody business of whale butchery reeked about our decks. The smell of rotting whales sickened me at first, but after a day or two I became accustomed to it. Even on a calm day, the weather was quite unpredictable. Not just squalls, but whole gales could arise suddenly, without any warning, and shriek through the rigging as if screaming with ironic laughter at the whole enterprise, while dangerous icebergs littered the sea. Some of the older men, well accustomed to hardships as they were, began to mutter savagely. As week followed week and the take of oil mounted imperceptibly, they knew the season would be a failure. They began to say they had been misled, that they would have done better to have gone out to the land stations at South Georgia or with one of the South Shetlands expeditions, as had been their custom. There was an ugly spirit for a while. Everyone in the enterprise (except the purser and a couple of scientists) was on a 'lay', and the bad season meant poor pay.

As the summer sun shone fitfully and worked on the old ice afloat in the sea at the Barrier face, we found a split in the ice-wall which, dreadful as it was, sufficed as a poor harbour. It was frigid and precarious. The place was called Discovery Inlet, after the barque *Discovery*, which found it. It was to the west'ard of the Bay of Whales. The least sounding we could get was 280 fathoms, but it was the best anchorage offering. We steamed in, and put down an anchor on 750 fathoms of heavy wire. This could hold us only in good weather, which was rare. Steam had to be kept up, and the utmost vigilance maintained lest the ship be blown out to sea, or smashed into the Barrier face. This barrier was a thousand-mile cliff of ice, like a fantastic elongation of the Dover cliffs all frozen and pitted with caves. Our Discovery Inlet was like the interior of an ice-box in a frozen hell more eternally damned than any hell of fire and brimstone. We lay there for months, and the grim business of converting blubber, flesh, and bone into oil went on. Frequently the whales froze as they lay belly-up in the water alongside, before they could be flensed. When this happened the blubber could be cut only with axes. Even the blades of our steam saws (which were meant for bones) could not handle it, and broke. Pieces of the

Barrier face were continuously breaking adrift, as the colossal glacier, whose edge they were, pushed them from the polar plateau and the summer sun slightly warmed the water. Some of these pieces of ice were as large as small islands, and these floated slowly off to become icebergs in the Southern Ocean. Sometimes whole miles of the Barrier crumbled away without warning, and tumbled into the sea, a lovely cascade of shining blue-green ice which shimmered and scintillated as it fell, but set up the devil of a sea and made the flensers leap for their lives. Sometimes blizzards got up suddenly and hurled frozen snow horizontally in our faces, and the decks were a shambles of blubber, grease, and frozen blood. Steam from the blubber boilers covered everything with ice. The whole ship looked frequently as if she had been carved out of the ice, too, and would remain down there for ever, solidified into a dreadful berg.

Life in the factory-ship under these conditions was bad enough, but in the little chasers it was hellish. Their decks were completely exposed, and the harpooner's gun stood right out in the open. They frequently came in from their hunting excursions covered with thick ice and, with their bunkers empty, in considerable danger of turning over. Yet they remained a minimum of time beside the factory-ship and steamed off again on the chase as soon as their immediate wants were supplied. Once one of them came in with her masts gone, her lookout barrel crushed, her bridge damaged, and her funnel awry. She had actually got in under the face of the Barrier in a fog and brushed her masts off beneath the 100-foot wall of ice. Yet the chasers always went out again. They never gave up while there was a chance of taking whales. They were magnificent little vessels, designed if not for these conditions, at any rate for the worst imaginable, until we had the ill fortune to pioneer modern whaling in the Ross Sea in a bad ice season. Their captains were their own harpooners, and each chaser carried only four men on deck. The only warm place aboard was the galley. Even the engineer and the fireman went about their duties below in fur-lined coats and caps.

Bad visibility was the worst enemy. Sometimes the big ship, with perhaps a couple of chasers alongside and nine or ten whales waiting to be flensed, would be swept from her precarious anchorage and blown about the inlet. It was impossible to see where she was drifting. Periods of poor visibility were not confined to calms. Frost-smoke from the freezing sea would fill the air; or snow would blow almost horizontally. Captain Larsen and his ice-pilot Gjertsen (who had been with Amundsen) would keep the bridge and watch anxiously until the weather cleared, which might take days. At such times, no one could work overboard. Sometimes great fields of ice, drifting down from the head of the inlet, would sweep past us, grinding away all the whales alongside and taking them out to sea.

In most of this sort of thing we had to work barehanded, for gloves were dangerous where there were so many keen knives. The flensers and the blubber-cutters kept the frostbite off by dipping their hands in the warm whales' blood. Sometimes the whales became putrid and, first distending like barrage balloons, would explode with a dreadful mess of mile-long innards and a stench which penetrated even our defences. When there was nothing else to be done there were always ten thousand more tons of Welsh coal to be moved. Inside the inlet, the coal-dust froze solidly to the tank ceilings and nothing would remove it. We tried to scrape it off, but it was almost impossible. We tried to steam it, but the steam froze, too, and only gummed the dust more securely to the ship's steel side.

Yet sometimes there were tolerable days when the beauty of the wild Antarctic was almost overwhelming – the pure white and pale blue ice of the Barrier, a stone's throw from the ship across the water brown with plankton; great pieces of old pack-ice and cold blue slabs of new, drifting slowly past the ship on the wind, with skua gulls on some, watching the whale carcass with keen eyes, or comical Adelie penguins strutting to and fro shouting about the futility of our enterprise (for they knew better than to work); the great ship's decks a picture of man's courageous industry among Nature's wastes. But there was nothing beautiful about those utilitarian blubber-filled decks. Generally we had a dozen or so whale carcasses alongside, not because the hunt was good, but because the inadequate gear caused bottle-necks. Some would be fresh, recently killed whales with the bluish blubber speckled with white, and with enormous bent harpoons still protruding from their sides. When a whale was taken, the fleshy part of its flukes was cut off to facilitate the passing of the towing chain, and notches were cut on the stub of tail, to indicate how many harpoons were inside. I saw some with five, many with three. The harpoons were recovered during flensing, and straightened in the ship's smithy for re-issue to the chasers. The fore-deck, which was the blubber deck, would be a mass of chunks of blubber looking like slabs of pork fat, and round the deck a hundred men toiled cutting blubber, feeding it to slicing machines whence endless chains like those of a bucket-dredge scooped the rashers and fed them to the square steel boilers. A couple of scientists measured the embryo of a well-formed whale some twenty feet long, lying pathetically on its back in a welter of its mother's and its cousins' blood. Steam gushed from countless pipes; the chain-drive of the blubber-hauling machinery clanked; and the men, oil-skinned and heavy-booted, hacked with their flensers' knives at tons of creamy blubber suspended from the ship's cargo gear. Ice matted their thick beards, and was in the corners of their eyes.

In all this, for month after month, I did my share of the work, and photographed, and took notes. I sent off all the news which Captain Larsen would permit, and this was not much, for he suppressed all our misfortunes. While the ship lay in Discovery Inlet it was frequently impossible to keep wireless touch with New Zealand's powerful station at Awarua – the only station through which we could communicate – and though I received several requests for news, I could do very little to satisfy them. The editors could restrain their impatience, which was a good sign anyway. I photographed every aspect of modern whaling, and was permitted to make short runs in the chasers to photograph there. I had not used a camera before, or even thought of owning one, but the *Mercury*'s photographer had given me a lesson, and the thing was simple enough. I could not develop aboard. The films were kept in a biscuit tin until I returned to Tasmania.

I was happy in the Ross Sea. Indeed, I was extremely happy. I found the Great Ice Barrier and the whole life of the expedition fascinating, and never got over my sense of privilege in being there. The seascape was often lovely and the ice had beauties I had never imagined it could possess. When the nights began to come they brought also sunsets and dawns, and some of these were magnificent. We saw them all, for our working day was now fourteen hours, sometimes sixteen. The overtime rate was eightpence an hour. We lived on whale-steaks, which were excellent, but we did not grow fat. The penguins were of absorbing interest. The whole thing was a grand adventure for me, and I revelled in it. It was a great break for a young man of twenty on his first assignment.

The weather never did improve. The ice conditions never became good. Our difficulties were never dispersed. They could not be overcome without a complete transformation of the factory-ship's gear, for it was obvious that the idea of flensing outboard could not be entertained. New methods were essential if whaling was to succeed in the Ross Sea. Whales would have to be hauled bodily aboard, and the only way that could be done was by cutting a slipway into the stern of the vessel. Welsh coal as fuel for Antarctic whale-ships would have to give way to fuel-oil, or the ships must be re-engined with Diesels.

This was all very well, but it would mean the expenditure of considerable capital. It was common knowledge for'ard that the ship must take at least 20,000 barrels of oil to clear current costs, without providing any dividend for the shareholders. By the end of February we had not taken 15,000, and the new ice was beginning to form in Discovery Inlet. Moreover, as the older men pointed out, the success of this pioneering enterprise depended upon subsequent good seasons, and to hope to pay at all, the *Sir James Clark Ross* must retain a monopoly in Ross Sea whaling at least for the first few years. Captain Larsen had attended to this when he received permission from the British to take his fleet south, for the Ross Sea and its hinterland were entitled the 'Ross Dependency' and attached to New Zealand. A charter had been granted which gave the *Ross* a five years' monopoly of whaling in territorial waters there. With a slipway aft, however, factory-ships would be independent of territorial waters, for they could keep the sea. By developing the necessary new methods Captain Larsen would also lose his monopoly, and from our experience it seemed there was no superfluity of whales for other expeditions.

This was only one of the difficulties. Meantime morale declined, though the Norsemen were not moaners. Captain Larsen hated to give up. He clung to our precarious ice-hole in Discovery Inlet. Early in March the chaser captains reported that the whales were heading north and were very scarce. We stayed. In the second week of March a ship's officer questioned each man, seeking a majority agreement to continue the enterprise at Norwegian Bay in North-west Australia, when the new ice forced us away from the Antarctic. The idea was to fill some tanks with humpback whale-oil from Australian waters, but the men would not hear of it. They had signed articles for a whaling voyage to the Ross Sea only, for the one season. They could not be compelled to go elsewhere. What bothered them was that if the ship went off to North Australia, she could not return to Sandefjord in time for them to ship with the South Georgia or South Shetlands fleets for the following season, and they would lose two seasons instead of one.

Some of the chaser captains refused to look for whales, going outside the inlet and hiding there out of sight. They declared that there were no more whales in the area and, if the expedition delayed its sailing much longer, we should all be jammed in the ice. This was true. The weather had always been bad and now it was steadily worsening. Sometimes the mirages in the inlet were almost frighteningly fantastic. The place began to get on the people's nerves. The smaller penguins had all gone. The whales had gone. The seals were gone, and even the few birds. The whole lifeless, threatening waste was like a continual nightmare, and the whale-ships' men daily became more savage and morose. We had killed little more than 200 whales, instead of the hoped for 1,000, and we had a wretched 17,000 barrels of whale oil in the tanks of the lower hold.

The winter's ice began to form. It was time to go. In mid-March we sailed, and the Barrier face gyrated in queer mirage astern of us. As soon as we were outside, the temperature appeared to rise at least fifteen degrees, and Captain Larsen spoke of whaling again inside the pack, or outside, or at Campbell Island and the Antipodes on our way towards New Zealand. But the weather continued bad, and there was no longer any pack to keep the Southern Ocean's rollers out of the Ross Sea. It was futile to think of whaling in that great seaway.

'This place will be the greatest whaling-ground in all the world,' Captain Larsen said as we steamed north. 'I will return in December with new gear.'

When they heard this the flensers laughed.

We steamed across the belt of furious storms between the Antarctic Circle and the South Island of New Zealand, while the chasers were all but overwhelmed, and even the great factory-ship, light as she was, wallowed and rolled. There were many anxious countings of the five lookout barrels to check that all our small fleet was still with us. We came to Campbell Island, but not to the Antipodes. There was a first-class harbour at Campbell Island and the fleet remained there ten days, while the chasers scoured the surrounding seas for blue whales. There were no whales. Where they had gone from the Ross Sea we did not know, but it was certainly nowhere in the area of Campbell Island. The island supported several thousand sheep and a large colony of royal albatrosses. Five men looked after the sheep, and these thought at first they were watching the arrival of a pirate fleet when they saw our lean, armed chasers slipping quietly into their lonely harbour. They thought the chasers were pirate ships, and the *Ross* a victim they were bringing in to strip.

From Campbell Island, fascinating place, we steamed to Stewart Island, where the chasers were de-commissioned to await the following season, for Captain Larsen was determined to come down again. The factory-ship went on to Port Chalmers, and the Tasmanians were paid off. My share of the take, plus wages and prodigious overtime, came to twenty-eight pounds, which was about sufficient to get me back to Hobart. But I had sent off a good account by cable to Australia, and before we had been two days in New Zealand I saw my story cabled back again and headlined in the local press.

I knew, then, that my enterprise had succeeded, and I hoped as I crossed the Tasman Sea towards Sydney in a passenger steamer that now I should get my chance as a cadet reporter, and should not have to go back to the reading-room.

CHAPTER THIRTEEN

COULD I WRITE A BOOK?

BACK in Hobart, I learned that my cabled news had been sold round the world, and the editor informed me that I should be appointed at once to the staff as a junior reporter and not require to serve any part of the customary three years' cadetship. This was an excellent dividend. One of the *Mercury*'s young men had at last brought himself to depart for the mainland, and there were rumours that an evening newspaper was to be launched in opposition to the morning. This was leading to some increase in staff, which was my good fortune. My fifteen articles about the whaling voyage were syndicated throughout Australia and New Zealand, and brought in a couple of hundred pounds. I was twenty years old; the year, mid-1924.

I found the work of a junior reporter a delight and a relaxation after proof-reading and seafaring. I threw myself heart and soul into this new profession. All I had to do was to go where the news editor sent me, and record in a minimum of clear and accurate prose what I had heard or seen. What a calling to be paid for! All the scheduled happenings for each day were listed in a large book, called the assignment book, and each evening about six o'clock the news editor — a Yorkshireman named Ussher — entered opposite each item the name of the reporter responsible for 'covering' it upon the morrow. Regular assignments such as police courts and hospitals and so forth were arranged in 'rounds', or 'beats', and juniors were appointed to keep an eye on them regularly. There were always meetings, functions of various sorts, deputations to Government ministers, sports contests, and prominent persons arriving in the state who were considered worth an interview. There were obituaries to be prepared, libraries of cuttings to be kept up, events to be foreseen, country functions to be attended when they were big enough to be worth while. The *Mercury* did not normally send its reporters far afield, but kept staff men at strategic points throughout Tasmania. It sent Tasmanian news to a chain of mainland newspapers, and in turn received a digest of mainland news from them. It was a small newspaper, I suppose, but it was a state newspaper, and in its service there was excellent experience.

Within less than six months, with that two hundred pounds behind me, I was married and trying to settle down. I married a girl on the *Mercury* staff. She was a blonde. I liked blondes and never looked at a brunette or a redhead in those days. I suppose I still had some remnants of my childish admiration for the little Norwegian girl in the ship *Asmund*, who had so favourably impressed me from the poop of her father's full-rigged ship years before. In the absence of Norwegians, a Tasmanian blonde would do very well. We set up house in a little place on Macquarie Street, opposite All Saints' Church, almost in the shadow of Mount Wellington, and it was my plan to establish myself ashore. No more sea! Square-rigged ships were finished, though I still hankered after them.

Meantime, the *Sir James Clark Ross* had been to Rotterdam, discharged her whale-oil, refitted extensively at Sandefjord, and sailed again for the Ross Sea to make a second voyage. The veteran Carl Anton Larsen was still in command. While I was on a brief honeymoon, news came that he had died as the ship broke through the Ross Sea ice, and I was hurriedly recalled to the office to prepare his obituary. Brave old man, he died as the first whale of the second season was taken, on the eve of a voyage as successful as any known until then in whaling. The second voyage of the *Sir James Clark Ross* vindicated him, and the shareholders forgot that they had abused him. His body was brought back to Norway and lies in the graveyard at Sandefjord. His plans for pelagic Antarctic whaling with factory-ships hauling the whale bodily aboard through slipways, cut into their sterns, led in a year or two to the building of 20,000-tonners with flensing-decks as large as parks and colossal gear capable of handling the largest whales. Just as he had foreseen, the success of this new method brought to nothing his own plans for safeguarding his enterprise. The open sea was all men's; a licence to whale in territorial waters was useless in an ocean where there were no territorial waters, and the Ross Sea was open to the world. The first true pelagic whaler in the Ross Sea, indeed, was not one belonging to Captain Larsen's company, but the *N. T. Nielsen-Alonso*, belonging to Melsom's of Larvik, who had tried the slipway method in a ship of theirs named *Lancing* off the coast of Africa.

Lancing? Lancing, did I say? Was this news of my four-masted full-rigged ship at last? Unfortunately it was not. At any rate, it concerned no sailing-ship still in existence. Messrs Melsom had in fact owned the fast full-rigger, but she had been broken up, and the vessel with the whale slipway was a converted steamer which had been given the same name for good fortune.

My younger brother Frank sailed in the *Nielsen-Alonso* and kept an eye on the story for me. Frank had already sailed in Scandinavian vessels for the same reason as myself. He had been forced to, to get square-rigged experience. He spoke Norwegian well and was with the whale-ship two seasons. By that time I was enmeshed in the round of council meetings, parliaments, murders, and so on which made up the newspaper life. I was promoted general reporter inside a year, and senior in two years. As such I was paid in a week more than the master of the *Lawhill* received in a month. Yet I sometimes envied Frank in his whaler, and envied him even more when, fed up with whale butchery, he shipped in the *Hougomont*. The *Hougomont* paid him four pounds a month and kept him months at sea. She had been sold to the ship-owner Erikson, in the Aaland Islands, and now and again I heard of this old shipmaster building up his fleet with yet further purchases of well-known ships, most of which he put in the Australian grain trade. From the news desk in far-off Hobart, which was just about as far from Mariehamn as it was possible to get, I followed his career as well as I could. But at the time I paid no particular attention to it.

My articles on the whaling voyage had done so well in Australia that the *Mercury* reissued them in a sort of book form. The title of this work was *To the Frozen South*, and it was, I suppose, my first book. It was not really a book. It was simply a bound reprint of the articles and their illustrations, from the same type and the same blocks. Its circulation was limited to Australia, and I don't think it went very far there. But its publication had one result I did not foresee. A Hobart lawyer who chanced to be going to England at the time the booklet was issued took a copy with him. I did not know this lawyer, except by repute, and was not in touch with him. But he took it upon himself to try to sell my book to the literary agents in London. Since the subject was a new one, he did not have to hawk the thing very far before he found an agent who was interested enough to undertake to find a publisher on both sides of the Atlantic, if the writer could extend the material to some 100,000 words from the 60,000 already written, and add further photographs.

I knew nothing about all this. At the time I had far too great a respect for the book world to imagine that anything I had written or ever would write was worth real book-covers. I had no idea that such persons as literary agents existed. I had the utmost respect for publishers and authors and regarded them as belonging to the same mysterious, infallible world which I had once imagined to produce newspapers. I had never seen an author or a publisher. There were, apparently, few of either breed in Australia. None went to sea. None lived in Collett Street, except my father. He wrote only poetry and political articles, and was buried long before a slim volume of his verse appeared in a paper binding.

The lawyer returned to Hobart. He was a foxy rascal. I don't doubt that he saw some easy money in me. A trip to England was an expensive undertaking from Tasmania, and he wanted some of his outlay back. At any rate, when he had been back a day or two he sent for me and asked me if I thought I could write a book. No, I said, I thought not. Well, he said, he could perhaps get a book published for me if I would undertake to add some 30,000 or 40,000 words to my whaling articles and let him have a full collection of my photographs from the expedition. But first I should have to grant him an option over all my rights and title in the accounts I had written or should write about the whaling voyage, and my photographs. This, he assured me, was a mere formality. He would then, he said, use his best endeavours to have a volume by me published in the United Kingdom and the United States, and he would conduct all the negotiations for this at his own expense.

Unaware that the venture would cost him nothing but a few postage stamps, I signed the contract which the foxy one had ready. I have the iniquitous thing in front of me now, a quarter of a century later. It seems incredible that anyone should prepare such a document in the twentieth century, and still less credible that anyone should sign it. But I signed it with alacrity, imagining only that this philanthropist was going to make an author of me and have my name in golden letters on the binding of a book – a real book. I would have signed anything. What I actually did sign was a contract giving away all rights in any book I might produce about the whaling voyage, and for this I was to receive half the book's earnings, less expenses. For his astuteness in approaching the London agent, the lawyer contented himself with a mere 50 per cent of my book earnings.

When my reporting was finished that day, I went straight home and sat down at the typewriter. Within a day or two I had finished the book, as if the printer's devil had been at my elbow screaming for the copy. I had acquired the habit of working quickly – too quickly – from the newspaper training. I had no idea then of the ghastly permanence of the published book, no nightmare – as I should have had – of the hastily written thing following me through the years, haunting me, sneering at me. *So you rushed me through the typewriter in a couple of days, did you? Clever fellow! And how do you like reading me now? Can't stand it? No wonder. If you only learned not to do the like again, perhaps it won't be so bad. But did you? DID YOU?*

No, I foresaw no nightmares. To me the printed word – my printed words – were something which recorded the day's happenings on the morrow, and on the morrow afterwards were dead. I had no vision of myself adding a volume to the long, long shelves of real books. My book was called *Whaling in the Frozen South.* It was published both in London and America, and translations followed. It sold well, and was kindly reviewed. The lawyer must have felt very pleased with himself. I was pleased enough with my name in gilt lettering on a thing which looked like a book; but I dared not read it. My esteem for the publishing world somehow declined when I knew that my own hastily prepared stuff was considered fit to join it, and I found myself looking at the flood of books with new eyes, wondering just how many which passed across our reviewing desks came to be written.

Before the whaling book was published abroad, my friend the lawyer took a new partner into his old-established firm. This partner had not been very long in the business before he sent for me. He looked like a villain straight out of a Dickens novel. He was a pale-faced, nervous wretch with cold blue eyes, and I though of him immediately as Mr Scrooge. Mr Scrooge had been having fun reading the firm's contracts, which included the one with me. His eyes must have glinted when he read that. For Mr Scrooge noticed that the contracts sent from London and America included an option clause. If I produced further books at any time the publishers of the whaling book wished at least to have the first refusal of them. Noting this with satisfaction, Mr Scrooge then read carefully through the criminal verbiage I had signed. A fellow who would sign that would doubtless sign anything. So he prepared further contracts wherein I was to be bound to the firm not only for the whaling book, but for any other books I might produce, for ever. From all these books I was to receive one hundred pounds out of their earnings; after that Scrooge and Co were to have the lot.

I had paid little attention to the option clause, since I had no plans for writing further books. An Antarctic expedition did not call at the port of Hobart every day, with no one to write its story. So I had no great interest in Mr Scrooge's contracts, especially when he pointed out that whether I signed them or not I was legally bound to submit my next two books through him, in accordance with the terms of the option clause which, he said, his partner had negotiated. He said his partner had gone to very great trouble on my behalf. (I did not know the real facts until I met the literary agent himself in London some years later.) It had cost him a lot of money. As a very young man, I should be eternally grateful to the firm for the interest they were taking in me, and the least I could do was to sign this mild agreement. I signed. At the time I had received nothing from them. There was a hint that I never should receive anything if I didn't sign. As I was not going to write any more books, it could scarcely matter much. As for all the rights I was blithely signing away, I had no idea what rights existed in literary property. There were no literary agents in Tasmania, or Australia, and I had not heard of the Society of Authors.

Outside, the sun shone in narrow Elizabeth Street where the two-decker street-cars trundled cheerfully along, and at the foot of the street the waters of the Derwent river sparkled. The publishing worlds of New York and London seemed so remote as almost to belong to another planet. In sunny, pleasant Tasmania is was difficult to believe in Mr Shyster Scrooge, setting up office in the heart of Hobart, and pushing sealed messes of crafty verbiage across dusty tables at me. I had heard of reprehensible solicitors whose souls were lost in their quest for coin, but I did not expect to have any dealings with them. It was a pity I did not take my copies of those contracts to another lawyer. Almost any other lawyer in the town would have brought them to the immediate notice of the local branch of the Law Society, which would have known how to deal with the solicitor who prepared them.

As I walked along the sunny street I noticed the flags flying from the signal station informing all interested that a vessel from overseas was coming into port. Thinking the signal heralded the arrival of some Cunarder or Clan liner to lift local fruit or wool, I paid little attention. It was a shock to see, as I came in view of the harbour, a big full-rigged ship under sail making towards the wharves. She was hove-to, waiting for her pilot. I hurried down, interested in more than the news aspect of this unexpected arrival. The year was 1925; I had been married less than twelve months; I thought I was done with the sea. And here came this full-rigged ship. The sun shone on her high, white sails, and she was a picture of beauty as she came creaming along. Her hull was silver-grey; I saw the flag she flew was German. Her name was *Hamburg*; she was one of the Frenchmen from the Canal de la Martinière, sold to the Germans as a schoolship. She looked to me very like one of the vessels in which Lusitania and I sought temporary refuge in Nantes, not so many years before. As she came closer I saw that this was she indeed. Her pillared white sails stirred me far more deeply than I thought they could, and I found myself turning over in my mind wild schemes for a return to the sea, the real sea of Cape Horn sailing-ships and square sails. Return to the sea? How? For the moment, at any rate, that could be no more than an idea. But I began again to take a great interest in the old *Otago*, which still lay at the Hobart wharves, a lowly coal hulk. What a pity she had not been kept up as the lovely barque she was, to serve as a schoolship for Tasmanian boys and preserve the traditions of the sea in that grand island. Tasmania, I thought, ought to be the Down East of Australia, like the Norway of Europe or the Devon and Cornwall of old England. Here was a place with glorious maritime traditions, which had built and sailed Cape Horners fit to rank with the great clippers; which had sent its fleet schooners and its brigs throughout the islands of the South Seas; which had kept its old barques whaling and sealing in southern waters after even the hardy Yankees had been driven from the trade. Yet now all those traditions were going to waste. There was no attempt to develop the seamanship latent in Tasmanian

It took all hands to make fast the mainsail of the *Parma*. There were not many of them

It was blowing a full gale, and the seas smashed over the deeply loaded grain-racer. A maindeck view aboard the *Parma* near Cape Horn

She rolled her lee rail under – a view looking along the leeside of the grain-racer *Grace Harwar*

Our 'engines' were the sails in sight above us, and the wind is free. But sails are expensive, and must be looked after. Here a lower topsail is being changed on the *Parma*

Our *Parma* paid for herself on her first Australian voyage. A view showing her under all sail, photographed from one of her boats on a quiet day

I sailed in Arab dhows in the Red Sea and down the coast of East Africa. A typical Kuwait *boom*

youth, for powered vessels did not appeal to them. Here, I thought, was the real hope of the Commonwealth Government's Line, which still straggled on. This was the place which ought to have a sailing schoolship. But for the time being I kept my ideas to myself.

I managed to get some ocean sailing while the *Hamburg* was at Hobart. It was as part crew in a yawl on a race round Bruni Island, under the command of a well-known Tasmanian yachtsman named Owen Tinning. My respect for Yachtsman Tinning and all his cheerful fraternity increased greatly during that race, for the yawl was thirty-five feet long, behaved abominably, and made me horribly seasick. I was as useful aboard as a sick cow; but the yachtsmen were all right. After that I had considerable respect for them. If there was no sailing schoolship in Tasmania, at any rate there was a strong yachting fraternity doing an excellent piece of work keeping the tradition and something of the skill of sailing alive.

I put sailing-ships out of my mind and got on with the job of being a newspaper reporter, which was employment enough. I liked the work, and I liked the staff. There was a happy spirit about the old office, and there was a real spirit of service in the newspaper, too, which appealed to me. It was an old-fashioned morning newspaper which did its best to promote an informed public opinion, according to its lights. Some real ideals animated the mature members of the staff. They had a sense of the responsibility of their calling. The editorial watchwords were 'When in doubt, leave out', and this was carried out scrupulously. The old paper was no scandal sheet and stooped to no stunts, not even when the threatened evening opposition was set up against it. This was short-lived. The *Mercury* was too well established. The evening paper made a great song about bringing the citizens Today's News Today, but the citizens liked their news in the morning in the ancient format to which they were thoroughly accustomed. Today's news the evening paper might have, but today's advertisements it had not, nor tomorrow's. So it died.

I found the newspaper work excellent education, and it gave

me a real insight into the workings of things ashore. It would have been easy to become cynical about some of them. If I found that there was something in old Jackie Shimmins' abhorrence of the shore bastards, there were many among them who were all right by any standards. What they lacked on the whole was a sense of loyalty and a feeling of true service towards the community. They gave lip service to many things, but felt no obligation to give real service towards anything save their own advancement. There was no doubt it would have done ninety per cent of them the world of good to be shipped off as deckhands in an undermanned Cape Horner. The politicians depressed me most. I was political roundsman for a year or so – the reporter responsible for covering Government and political news. I pounded the corridors of the Government offices by day, and by night, when the State Parliament was sitting, took my place in the press-box there. From there I looked down on the people's representatives with considerable wonder, while I tried to make some sense of their remarks, which were rarely brief, to discover the real motives which prompted them. It would have been very easy to become thoroughly cynical in the newspaper profession. Many journalists did.

In the Government offices one day I discovered there were state archives, and, looking into these, I found they were largely concerned with ships and the sea. Many dealt also with the doings of convicts, and some of the citizens had managed to get at these and remove a page or two down the years. There was still a certain hyper-sensitiveness about the convict period, throughout which Tasmania – then Van Diemen's Land – had been the receiving station for many brave rebels and fine men, as well as much dross. I made it my hobby to search through the maritime records of old Tasmania wherever I could find them. The *Mercury*'s own files were full of excellent material, and there were still men alive who had sailed in the blue gum clippers and Tasmanian whalers and blackbirders. There was obviously a good book in the maritime history of the island. It occurred to me that the spate of books on the sea consisted in the main of accounts at far from first-hand of events long past, and frequently inadequately reported. Old sea captains, in command of great liners in their day, had been induced to put down their reminiscences, which they did sometimes with skill, sometimes not. Compilers of sea chronicles flung books together, year after year, which were nothing but crude pieces of wordy exploitation of interest in the sea. There were some excellent books, but these were the minority.

All these writers treated the romantic Cape Horn sailing-ship as already a thing of the remote past. The handful of such ships still sailing was ignored, perhaps because they still existed, perhaps because they were nearly all Finns and Germans, with a few Swedes. The profusion of books on sailing-ships, at any rate, indicated that there was a public for such works, and I had the evidence of the American and London publishers' readiness to produce my whaling chronicle to show that they might consider, also, a work on the surviving sailing-ships. My brother Frank, still in the *Hougomont*, wrote to me of taking part in a race round the Horn towards the English Channel with a cargo of grain from South Australia. The *Hougomont*, he said, had done very well, but the *Lawhill* and the *Herzogin Cecilie* had done better. He spoke with enthusiasm about the *Herzogin Cecilie*, which was flagship of the Erikson Line.

Reflecting on these things while I surveyed the bald and curious heads of Tasmania's parliamentarians, the thought came to me that the story of these ships was one I could write. Here was an opportunity akin to that in the *Sir James Clark Ross*. My married life was not a conspicuous success, for the practice of marrying the first attractive blonde one thinks one knows, at the age of twenty, is not really to be commended. I turned more and more to work as my outlet and my hobby. My whole life was work, and I was glad to be in a profession which I could turn also into a hobby.

I had no compunction about leaving the company of the young woman who had mistakenly married me, on the poor glamour of some Antarctic whales. We had long given up the attempt to make a home, and I was a boarder in her mother's establishment on Liverpool Street. This suited me. My hours were long, and I made them longer. But I knew that this was a mere existence.

I liked the idea of the handful of surviving ships making a race of it, undermanned as they were, deep-loaded round the Horn. It was a brave gesture, wasted though it was on most of the landsmen. Not only did the idea of sailing to write appeal to me, but I was also aware that these ships, and the life aboard them, had never been properly photographed. I was no photographer, but modern methods had made this form of illustration comparatively simple, and the light at sea is usually good. The desire to sail with them was overpowering; but first I had to rid myself of the contracts with Mr Scrooge. His rights and options over my literary work and income, if any, now covered a dozen closely typed quarto sheets. Mr Scrooge was flourishing as a sort of solicitor, and had married a buxom young woman from the brewing trade. If I went back to sea in the Finnish grain-racers and wrote a book about them the entire profits throughout the world would belong to Scrooge, apart from a wretched hundred pounds. It would cost considerably more than that to go, for I should need a camera, and I should have to support my wife while I was gone.

There was one way out of the Scrooge contracts, or so it seemed to me. (The real way would have been to bring them to the notice of the Law Society.) My way was to write myself out of those option clauses, to produce two works of such indifference that no publisher would look at them. Then I could be free. If I had no literary future I was no use to Mr Scrooge.

So I sat down and wrote two novels. The first took a year. It was about a sailing-ship, and the ship fought for her head. She made me do my best for her. Left to myself, I should never have written a novel, for I knew I was no novelist. But at the age of twenty-two, since I felt I had to write the things, I got on with them as well as I was able. The writing of a novel was a long piece of reporting without any sub-editorial interference. The art of reporting consisted in getting the facts quickly, succinctly, and in as brief a space as possible. A novel suffered from no such disadvantages; indeed, it was rather a relief from the arduous daily round.

When my novel was ready it went off to London, through Mr Scrooge. To my surprise a publisher accepted it. It was the house which had produced the whaling book. Mr Scrooge was jubilant, though his enthusiasm waned considerably when the contract arrived and mentioned an advance of only fifty pounds. I was depressed, for the new contract contained a further option clause, and according to the lawyer I was bound by that for two more books. It was very discouraging, but I got on with the novels, reflecting bitterly that, once one had anything published which met with the slightest success it was impossible thereafter to produce a work too bad for print. So I tried to make the other novels as good as I could; and in due course no one would have them. The publishers had not gone bankrupt, which would not have surprised me. But the first novel did not earn its fifty pounds, and they were not interested in the others.

Meantime the sailing-ships of the world were steadily dwindling. The *Hamburg* was lost on her voyage homewards from Australia. The lime-juicers had shrunk to a wretched four, of which the ship *William Mitchell* paid a brief visit to Melbourne. I was there on leave at the time and thought of joining her, but she was a square and clumsy box with a monotonous record of poor passages to her discredit. One *Bellands* was enough; I did not want to write about a sailing warehouse. A dozen big American schooners brought lumber from the Pacific Slope to Melbourne, Port Adelaide, and Sydney, and most of them were bankrupt when they arrived and were abandoned to their crews. The four-master *Robert R. Hind*, which I had known from boyhood, brought a miserable £65 at a forced sale in Sydney. The full riggers *Chilicothe* and *Tonawanda*, in with lumber, were sold for hulks in the Islands. Even the Norwegian flag no longer flew from any ocean-going square-rigged ship.

It was 1927 – time to get on with my story of surviving

sailers if I was ever going to write it. I said nothing of my ideas to Mr Scrooge. Pallid and steely-eyed as ever, and disappointed that my latest novel had not yet found a publisher, he showed no inclination to release me from my contract as his literary property.

Early in December 1927 I was sent to Melbourne to report an inter-state conference of special interest to Tasmania. I forget what it was. As the Bass Straits ferry came in from Launceston I saw a beauty of a four-masted barque lying in the swinging basin. The now familiar blue-crossed white flag flew from her upper gaff, and I had time to see that the name on her fleet bows was *Herzogin Cecilie*. Astern of her was another lovely model of a sailing-ship, a regular old clipper though she was cut down to stump t'gall'nts. She flew the blue and gold flag of Sweden and looked to me very like the fleet *Svithiod*, which had occupied that same berth when I left the *James Craig*. The name on her counter was *Beatrice*, of Gothenburg. The big white *Herzogin Cecilie* and the lovely silver-grey *Beatrice* were as grand a pair of Cape Horners, in their own way, as had ever graced the River Yarra. I hurried from the ferry to their berth, forgetting the conference.

I boarded the Finn, which was registered in Mariehamn. Perhaps Lusitania might be aboard, or Gunnar Boman, or some other of my old shipmates from the *Lawhill*. In the big saloon aft I saw, poring over a small typewriter, the huge shoulders and square head of a man I knew.

It was Captain Ruben de Cloux, who had been master of the *Lawhill* when I joined her at Bordeaux in 1921.

CHAPTER FOURTEEN

FALMOUTH FOR ORDERS

THERE was no reason why Captain de Cloux should remember me, but he did. He seemed pleased to see someone with whom he could yarn, for he went ashore very little, only on the ship's business. We were not speaking for a moment before I found that he was very short-handed, and no one in Melbourne had sought a berth. I arranged to ship with him for the coming passage towards Europe, as able seaman, at six pounds (Australian) a month, pay off in the United Kingdom. He was, he said, to sail to Port Lincoln to load wheat as soon as he had completed discharge of his Baltic pine and taken in a little ballast, and the Swedish four-master astern of him had challenged him to a race. An association of underwriters in Stockholm was putting up a silver cup, and it was going to be a real 'go'.

I wondered I had heard nothing about this in the newspapers, for it was obviously a first-rate story. It was customary to decry the few surviving sailing-ships as cut-down, ambling hulks, poorly sailed and ill-manned, drifting about the world picking up odds and ends of Peruvian guano or Chilean nitrates, or now and again some lumber from Canada for Buenos Aires or from Oregon towards the east coast of Australia. In point of fact, the *Beatrice* was one of the few survivors (whereof there were more than a score then in commission) which had been cut down. The skysails from her fore and main and all her royals were removed in 1895 and the reduction had done her little harm, for her sail plan was still ample and nothing could upset the perfection of the Scots iron hull. She was a beauty. It was a pity her kites had gone, for her rig was somewhat squat now and the low t'gallant masts spoiled her appearance aloft. Such kites as skysails make little difference on the haul around the Horn, though her deep royals would have been useful in light airs.

As for the *Herzogin Cecilie*, she was a thoroughbred. She was a thousand tons larger than Beatrice and had a poop nearly 200 feet long, which was going to be a great asset running heavily towards the Horn. With that long poop she would run dry in any weather, for there was only a short well-deck for'ard to hold the water. *Beatrice* was the old type of sailing-ship with a long well-deck and high bulwarks. She looked as if she could be wet enough, deeply loaded with grain. The *Herzogin Cecilie*'s registered tonnage was 3,242, and she was built at Geestemunde in 1902 as schoolship for the Nord-Deutscher Lloyd Line. Her figurehead was a wood carving of the Duchess Cecilie; her rig was massive and lofty; all her masts and yards steel; she was a powerful and fleet-lined vessel which could obviously give a good account of herself.

I reported my conference, but my thoughts were with the two four-masted barques lying in the river. I had arranged to join the *Cecilie* at Port Lincoln early in the following month; for the time being I said nothing of my plans to anyone.

As far as the race was concerned, I thought the *Beatrice* had a good chance of winning. She had just been in dry dock and her underwater body was freshly cleaned and painted (a very important consideration), and her crew was ample. She had the necessary nucleus of tradesmen and petty officers, and an excellent crew of thirty sturdy cadets in their late 'teens. Her master was Captain Harald Bruce, an experienced sailing-ship man of Scots extraction whose ancestors had lived in Sweden for some centuries. Captain Bruce had seen service in the excellent ships *Bohus*, *Vinga*, and *Gullmarn*, all Australian traders under the Swedish flag, and none of them sluggards. His three mates were exceptionally capable, thoroughly experienced officers. My conference lasted a week, and I found time to visit *Beatrice* several times, as well as her Finnish rival. The chief mate of the Swede was Sam Svensson, to whom I took a great liking. If ever a sailor loved his ship, Sam Svensson loved *Beatrice*. He was a small man with fair hair, very fair skin, and mild blue eyes. But his eyes developed a steely look when he looked along the wharf towards the big *Cecilie*. There was no doubt in his mind as to who should win, though he knew the ex-German would be at a great advantage in heavy running. He knew, however, that she had not crew enough properly to manage her in real Cape Horn weather. Against *Beatrice*'s thirty boys *Cecilie* had nineteen, and no tradesmen. Her older boys acted as her tradesmen and petty officers. She had seven rated as able seamen, three ordinary seamen, three deckboys, and six first-voyage apprentices. Some of these might run away before she left Australia.

The remarkable reputation of Captain de Cloux was well known to Sam Svensson. Even in his level mind, there was a slight suspicion that de Cloux could *troller* – conjure up winds and weather he wanted. The belief among sailing-ship men that 'Russian' Finns could practise black arts was very old, and quite a real one.

'We can't fight *trolldom*,' said Sam one sunny day as we yarned together by the break of the poop. He looked pretty gloomy about it. But he was not depressed for long. There must, he said, be some other explanation for Captain de Cloux's long run of good fortune, besides the alleged possession of supernatural powers. He had done wonderfully well with the big *Lawhill*, and he had been sailing the *Herzogin Cecilie* with remarkable success for six years, though every other owner who had looked at the ship when she was on offer for Reparations account had turned her down as altogether too heavy and requiring too large a crew. Sam solaced himself by remembering de Cloux's passage of 136 days from South Australia to the Channel, and the occasion when he had allowed the *Cecilie* to go ashore on the sands off the coast of Jutland. Yet the man seemed possessed of the most extraordinary luck. The previous year he had sailed the *Cecilie* home in ninety-eight days, which was a better passage by weeks than any other vessel in the trade. As if that were not enough, his departure date had been wrongly recorded, and Lloyds credited him with a run of eighty-eight days.

'This time we'll see!' said Sam.

It was obvious that the coming 15,000-mile race from Port

Lincoln to the Lizard between these two well-matched four-masted barques ought to be as good a story as I had stumbled upon when I shipped in the *Sir James Clark Ross*. I was a little dubious about the *Cecilie* from an able seaman's point of view (especially an able seaman softened by three years ashore). She was not well manned. And she was no *Lawhill* either, well equipped with labour-saving devices. On deck she was a brute of a ship. Designed as a schoolship to train ninety boys in the German manner and to give them as much work as possible, she had deliberately been given no aids to lighten the heavy work of bracing her and handling her sails. She had the usual seven capstans for the big four-master, and she was fitted with a donkey-boiler, for raising the anchor on sailing-days. I tried her 'midships steering wheels, which stood on an exposed part of the long poop-deck which extended to forward of her mainmast. They were appallingly heavy. I looked up at the main royal yard from there, almost directly beneath it, and thought that steering by the wind was going to be no joke. (For that, the helmsman must watch the weather clew of the royal to take care that the ship does not come too near the wind, nor fall too far from it.) Some of the apprentices were tiny fellows, and there was a scarcity of grown men aboard her.

But there was Captain de Cloux, smiling. He had been handling the big ship since leaving the *Lawhill* six years before, always with boy crews. Perhaps he *could troller*. I asked him about the 136-day run, and he explained that he had no proper crew at all that passage. No crew? I asked. I thought he always went with no crew. Ah, but this time, though he'd taken all the derelicts the Consul could find, he had had to sail 15,000 miles with sixteen hands all told – more farmers than seamen. It was too few. He had tried to go the Good Hope way, for he dared not run that heavy ship so short-handed towards Cape Horn. But after beating around for twelve days in the Bight, he had had to up-helm and go for the Horn. She had been sailing almost two years at the time with no chance of entering dry-dock, as he had had to make a couple of trans-Pacific voyages when no grain charters offered for Europe. These had fouled the ship and she had no chance. Any other ship on the same voyage would have been 156 days, he said. The *Cecilie* had never let him down. He could do with a few more crew. Did I know any other young fellows in Melbourne or Tasmania with square-rigger experience who would care to come along? Unfortunately I did not. Johnny Gleeson was dead, then. He was drowned in a steamer. Tom Germein was making his way in the Canadian Australian Line. I was out of touch with the survivors from Captain Suffern's.

First, I had to work out some way in which I was free to join. There were three serious disabilities — my contracts with Mr Scrooge, my job, and my wife. As for the contracts, I thought it was high time I told Scrooge and his partners to go to the devil. When I returned to Hobart, I took the contracts to a magistrate I respected, who had recently resigned from the Bench to return to practice. He went purple in the face when he looked at them and wanted Scrooge hauled up before the Law Society there and then. This would have been a good idea, but so long as he assured me I could not be bound by the contracts I could let vengeance descend on Scrooge's head whenever it might choose to do so. Mr Scrooge was a man who must have found himself hard to live with, and he could be left to stew in his own juice. My friend the magistrate prepared letters for my publishers and the literary agent in London; I went off and tore up all my unpublished novels, and never wrote fiction again.

As for my job, I was prepared to burn my boats, though it was a pity to give up so soon what I had gained at so much pains. I knew well enough that though the *Herzogin Cecilie–Beatrice* race would interest the *Mercury*'s readers, it would not be considered worth the services of a senior reporter throughout all the months it would occupy. The *Mercury* was a local paper, and its vision did not normally extend much beyond Australia. I had to be prepared to go after the story and arrange its sale myself. Well, I thought I could do these things. I had been turning over in my mind for some time the possibility that the Mercury might send a staff man — preferably myself — to the United Kingdom and northern Europe to investigate the marketing conditions for Tasmanian exports on those markets. The chief export from southern Tasmania was apples, and everyone in the trade was doing well out of it, except the producers. I had tentatively put the idea forward to the editor when I thought of going in the *William Mitchell*, without telling him the real reason. He was strongly in favour of it, but said it would cost a thousand pounds to pay the fares and expenses of a staff man for the time necessary. A thousand pounds was a lot of money in Tasmania, more than the paper could afford.

Well, here was a way to attend to the assignment, without paying fares. The *Herzogin Cecilie* should sail mid-January and take about three months for the run to the Channel. This would bring her in excellent time for the Tasmanian apple market in England. I put it to the editor, then, that for six months' leave, my job back, and one hundred pounds towards expenses, I would get myself to England and the Continent and make a detailed survey of fruit marketing conditions for his newspaper. He jumped at the idea, as well he might. The *Mercury* was an enterprising newspaper, though unaccustomed to sending its staff men very far. This idea was too good to turn down, and it was arranged that I should make my own way to England (*how* was not mentioned) and find out just what ailed the markets there, and why the fruit-grower of an island 14,000 miles away received less than a fair price for his products. I was to go also to Antwerp, Rotterdam, Amsterdam, Bremen, Hamburg, Stockholm, and Oslo. I resolved that I would also make a call at Mariehamn, though there was no fruit market there.

My wife thought I was mad. What, give up a good job and an assured future on the *Mercury* for a wild-goose chase round Cape Horn in some frightful ship which did not even have an engine? Go back to sea? That uncertain calling of ne'er-do-wells and the unstable! She was not alone in her criticisms; but I knew what I was doing. I had faith in my ideas. The hundred pounds from the newspaper would take care of her while I was away; my six pounds a month from the ship, with the proceeds of whatever I could sell to magazines when I got to England, would keep me going. So I packed my sea-bag and departed, taking with me a cheap folding camera which I bought for thirty shillings at a local chemist's. My venture in photography aboard the whaling-ship had turned out well, and it was obvious that there was an excellent and almost untouched field in the Cape Horn sailing-ship. I have never spent thirty shillings more wisely in my life.

There was one more problem. Could I stand the life? Should I be any use aloft again, after that fall from the *Lawhill*? I no longer limped; but I had not been aloft in a big sailing-ship for half a dozen years. 1 was eighteen when I fell; now I was twenty-four.

The *Beatrice* soundly trounced the *Herzogin Cecilie* on a smart ballast run from Melbourne Heads towards Port Lincoln, beating the big Finn by half a day on a run of seventy hours during which both of them ran 60 miles in a four-hour watch, and did over 300 miles a day. This was one occasion when de Cloux's great anxiety to be gone from whatever port his ship was in did neither him nor his ship any good, for he hurried out of Melbourne with his earth ballast not properly trimmed and the *Cecilie* was a little down by the head in consequence. He dribbled out through the Heads in a near-calm, and the result was that when the *Beatrice* came out the following morning the pair of them picked up the same breeze off the Otway and raced onwards neck and neck, coming into Port Lincoln seventeen minutes apart. It was a good match, though an unsatisfactory one. It left both masters thinking they had the better vessel. When it was heard of in Sweden, another group of shipowners put up a second cup. Captain Erikson, back in Mariehamn, put up nothing.

It was January 16th before I reached Port Lincoln, and I joined the ship straight away, climbing to the main royal yard as soon as I had put my sea-bag aboard. I found I was all right.

Going aloft did not bother me, and I had no more thought about falling than I had had when a child. I was pleased about this, and even more pleased to be made very welcome aboard by Captain de Cloux and the crew. The ex-schoolship had plenty of spare accommodation, for her long poop had once housed a hundred youths instead of twenty, and there were cabins for instructors, petty officers, able seamen, and so on. She had a splendid big saloon in which de Cloux sat in very lonely state, and she could have accommodated twenty passengers without inconvenience. I was allocated a bunk in a two-berth cabin 'midships, with a leading hand named Fyhrqvist – pronounced Fearqwist – who was donkeyman, radio operator, and carpenter, as well as one of the best able seamen in the ship. Fyhrqvist was a splendid fellow, and I soon settled down. The life was tough at first and the work appallingly hard. Loading was all but completed, and the ship had to be made ready for sea. Every sail had to be dragged aloft by man-power, and bent properly with heads well stretched and all gear clear for running. Her sails were enormous and dreadfully heavy. Their bolt-ropes were wire, and the clew-iron of a course was as much as a boy could lift. All the running rigging was wire.

The woeful inadequacy of the crew was apparent even to de Cloux, and when on the last night two apprentices deserted, he was depressed. He told me he would take a dozen young Australians if any cared to come, and they could sign for the round voyage, so there would be no fear of being stranded. But this was in the days before the last of the sailing-ships were invested with a fashionable glamour, and there were no offers. The public had not heard of the grain race and the *Herzogin Cecilie* was just another ship. Within a year or two it was different. Youths from all over the world were then prepared to pay the owner five hundred dollars for the privilege of shipping in any of his vessels, and the *Cecilie* had the pick of them all.

Meanwhile, however, the fact could not be disguised that we were undermanned. The able seamen told me that in heavy weather it took four of them to steer, and trying to square her in a heavy breeze was a rupturing business. Sometimes they had to take the braces to the capstans, which was a laborious and inefficient method of trimming the yards. When there was anything to be done aloft with other than the lightest sails, all hands had to be called. Sailing the *Herzogin Cecilie* from Port Lincoln to Falmouth for orders was not going to be a picnic. Within a day or two, I had formed a poor opinion of two of her four watch-keeping mates. The chief mate went ashore in yellow kid gloves, and kept a pair of spats of the same colour for use in Europe. He dared not put them on in Australia. He yelled about the decks all day, in several languages, and harassed the good young sailors at their work. He was a huge, bullying sort of fellow, twenty-two years old. The real trouble with this young man was that he had a swollen head. He had been promoted too young. The second mate was all right, but the third looked like a cowhand. Except for our second mate, the *Beatrice* obviously had a great advantage over us in the matter of watchkeepers. But the *Beatrice* had no de Cloux.

We sailed three days after I joined. It was January 19th, 1928. *Beatrice* got under way from the anchorage off Port Lincoln at nine o'clock that morning, for she had completed loading a few hours before us. We had to clear the ship outwards that morning, and it was not until two in the afternoon that we could begin to sail. Several leading citizens saw us off and wished us well. Our orchestra, which a night or two earlier had provided music for a dance on board, played lustily as we departed, at least as long as the leading citizens were within earshot. Our orchestra consisted of two violins, a kettledrum, and a mandolin. As soon as the shore people had departed the instruments were thrown in the forecastle and the musicians galloped aloft. The wind was fresh and favourable for leaving the immediate neighbourhood of the port. Outside, it was ahead and fresh, and we had to beat. De Cloux clapped all sail on her, though the wind sang a loud note and the deeply laden ship heeled heavily over.

Throughout the afternoon and evening the wind freshened, and we saw the *Beatrice* far to wind'ard beating under a press of sail. She was snoring along, but the wind was a dead muzzler. It was blowing right into the Gulf. When night fell, with rain and squalls, we had gained a little. *Beatrice* was still in sight, beating out towards the Southern Ocean. Now it was her turn to lose the profit of her earlier sailing. As the wind persisted in the same quarter, Captain de Cloux decided on the bold course of using the Backstairs Passage. The entrance to both Spencer and St Vincent's Gulf is blocked by the large clump of Kangaroo Island, and we were trying to pass to the westward of this because there was sea-room there. There was also a way out to the eastward through which it was possible to reach the open sea. It was a narrow passage, and it could be dangerous to a big square-rigged ship. The night was dark and stormy, and we were drawing a lot of water. However, the passage was well enough lighted. It was characteristic of de Cloux, always ready to take a chance, that in the middle of that stormy night, with visibility poor and his great ship racing under a press of sail, he squared in and ran for Backstairs Passage. Up went the helm, the yards were checked in, and we raced through the night at fifteen knots. The water under the island was smooth and the big ship sailed beautifully. The danger was that we might be jammed on a lee shore after we sailed through, for the coast of the Australian mainland blocked our path if the wind headed us. It was a risky thing to do. De Cloux was banking on a land breeze from the South Australian coast-line in the morning and he knew, too, that Captain Bruce would not go that way. It was *Beatrice*'s first visit to those waters, and the Finn had the advantage there. Dawn of the first morning on that long, long race found us rolling quietly along at seven knots, heading south-east across a sunlit sea, and neither the *Beatrice* nor any other vessel, power or sail, was to be seen. Our short cut had paid.

Now began the grim business of getting the very best out of that huge ship with her boy-crew, and it was drudgery. What would we not have given for a dozen hands! We had managed to ship only one disappointed migrant to replace our deserting apprentices, and as is so often the way with failures, he was little use. The wind freshened again and the sea got up. De Cloux clung to every stitch of sail, and the yards were trimmed to every slightest variation in the breeze. Nothing but perfection in his sail-aerofoils was good enough for de Cloux. With nine hands in a watch, perfection was a hard taskmaster.

The wind drew ahead. De Cloux beat on. He intended to sail south as quickly as he could and pass to the South of Tasmania and Campbell Island, running in high latitudes towards the Horn. But the wind came ahead and we had to sail through Bass Straits. Most masters of deep-water sailing-ships dreaded approaching the land once they had safely left it. Not so de Cloux. If we could use Bass Straits with a wind which would allow us to go no other way (except towards Good Hope and that was unthinkable), then Bass Straits it was. He took short cuts among the islands, for there was deep water enough, and six days after weighing off Port Lincoln we were in the Tasman Sea. Little more three weeks later, when we had been thirty-three days at sea, we came around the Horn. It was a famous run from the south of New Zealand. We dribbled across the South Tasman Sea with calms and light airs, and fog, and variable conditions, and de Cloux looking out astern always for *Beatrice* coming. But once the west winds came, they stayed. We drove her for all she was worth — more than *we* were worth, if it comes to that. Day after day the only sails that were clewed up were those which first blew out of their bolt-ropes, and these were more than enough. The powerful four-master was designed to drive in the great seas down there, and de Cloux was nothing if not a driver. If only we had had a crew! But it was no use *trolling* for them. Our whole complement made less than a watch for that great ship under such conditions. We went short of sleep. Several of the apprentices regretted bitterly that they had lacked the guts to run away. A boy was pitched over the huge wheel by a kick of the rudder, and his shoulder wrenched. Two were ruptured trying to roll up the remnants of a wet and wind-maddened sail. The infernal mate hazed his small watch, when he could, though the second mate nursed his as much as possible. But the ship was dry and our progress was famous. Our quarters were not washed out, and the food was warm, good, and abundant. We had sailed with nine hogs, and there was fresh pork once weekly on that cold run. When a hog was slaughtered nothing was wasted.

The long poop was a godsend. I thought all Cape Horners should be built that way, instead of the well-deck deathtraps most of them were. The length of the poop kept the worst of the seas from filling the maindeck and pressing down on the ship, and this in turn meant that she could be much harder driven. She ran dry and in safety. Her massive rigging could stand anything and was asked to stand a great deal. De Cloux shifted two of the heavy steel stanchions which served the purpose of chain-plates to bear the stresses of the standing rigging. He drove the ship so hard that these actually pulled the steel side of the ship a little inboards; but nothing carried away. Nothing except sails, I should say. We blew out a round dozen of them, which could scarcely have pleased the owner if he ever knew about it. When a sail was blown out everything possible was saved, and this meant endless, dangerous work. The *Cecilie* had been extremely well found when de Cloux bought her for the Gustaf Erikson Line at Ostend in 1921 (he told me once the price was £4,000, though £11,000 was asked for the four-masted barque *Passat*); by 1928, however, many of her sails had gone. To make up for his hard driving, de Cloux was a great sailmaker. Sail-making went on constantly, for the open space beneath the poop provided a magnificent sail loft. De Cloux was the best sailmaker in the ship, probably in all the surviving sailing-ships, and it was customary for all the able seamen and everybody else who could wield a needle to lend a hand with seaming. All the sails were handsewn, every inch of them. Cutting a new sail was a work of art, and only de Cloux and the sailmaker himself put a knife to new canvas. It was de Cloux's aim to sew a complete new suit of sails every two years, and since that meant handling more than 40,000 square feet of canvas and miles of heavy wire and tarred hemp rope, it was a big job.

Throughout the whole run towards the Horn we saw no sign

of any other sailing-ship. After a while, we ceased to look for *Beatrice*. It was generally thought that she had made for the Cape of Good Hope.

One distraction we had which we had not bargained for. When the ship was a few days at sea a stowaway came up from the hold. Usually stowaways are a curse. They are almost invariably useless, for the peculiar mentality which prompts a person to steal a passage from a ship, in most circumstances, is also such as to make them more or less unemployable. They rarely have papers of any kind, or clothes. The unfortunate ship upon which they commit their crime is fined for bringing them to port, and made responsible for their return to their own country, if known. Too often no country wants to claim them, and a ship may cart their useless persons about for years. However, on that passage we should have been glad, almost, to welcome any able-bodied stowaway. But this person who burst suddenly on us was a wretched young woman, thin, straggly-haired, and seasick. She was dressed as a boy, and her angular figure aided the illusion. But she was more or less feminine. Her face was green, her nose red and long unpowdered, and the wisps of her mouse-coloured hair flicked in the wind like recalcitrant straws of a worn-out broom.

Satan's Satan! roared de Cloux, and the blustery big mate turned white and speechless. Well he might, for the woman was a rejected girl-friend of his from Port Lincoln, and he was affianced to the owner's secretary. A pretty mess it would be when she read the reports of a girl stowaway in her hero's ship! As for de Cloux, he told the girl that he would put back immediately and hand her to the police; but we held our course. A racing sailing-ship does not put back for stowaways. What a laugh the *Beatrice* would have if we threw the race away for an infernal girl. No, we stood on, though de Cloux and all hands fumed. First de Cloux thought he might get rid of her to a passing steamer, but we saw no steamers (they would not have accepted her, in any event). Then he spoke of giving her the Norwegian pram to row ashore in, as we passed an island in Bass Straits, or of making a board towards Melbourne Heads and flinging her out to the pilot cutter cruising there. Perhaps de Cloux was worried about the reception his wife would give the news when she heard it. From all accounts, Madame de Cloux was a strong-minded woman, as Cape Horn shipmasters' wives are apt to be when they are left so much to their own devices; and the old man had arranged for her to be at Falmouth to meet the ship when we came in. Meet the ship, with a girl stowaway aboard!

Our stowaway remained with us. Within a day or two, when the news got round that she had no warm clothing (and nothing, indeed, save the inappropriate rags in which she had come up from the hold) all hands ransacked their sea-bags for her, and turned in jerseys, pullovers, lengths of material for skirts, and everything they could find. De Cloux made her a pair of leather shoes, from the sail-making leather, first cutting a pair of lasts. They were good shoes. The blustery big mate made her nothing, but he kept a very wary eye on her. He was an ass of the sort who found it impossible to scorn any reasonably youthful female; at that dance of ours, a night or two before sailing, the stowaway was there. She had passed well enough in the crowd, painted and dolled up a little. The boys recalled that she was full of enthusiasm for the voyage then, and wanted to know how she could join.

'Stow away!' said the silly mate. 'Stow away – that's the thing to do.' He actually told her how it could be done.

Well, now she'd done it; and her Viking he-man mate was not pleased at all. Neither would his fiancée be when she heard about it; and hear about it she certainly would, in all possible detail. It would be idle to dilate upon the girl's complete lack of attractiveness. Why, then, suggest that she stow away? That was on the record.

The girl was put to work as cabin-boy, and she worked hard. There was plenty of room for her, and she could keep herself to herself. At this, nobody bothered her. Later, when we came to the fine weather, and she brought a large suit-case stuffed with clothes up from the hold where she had hidden it, all hands were disgusted with her. Why had she allowed us to tear up our few things for her when she had so much? We were fifty days out at the time and it was flat calm. A Swedish ordinary seaman had killed an albatross a day or two earlier. Now with the flat calm, the dead albatross, and the blasted young woman, all hands looked forward gloomily to a passage of more than a hundred days, and no longer searched the horizon astern for signs of the *Beatrice*. She must have crossed the Line long since, while we still wallowed in the South Atlantic's extensive horse latitudes.

If de Cloux could *troller*, he certainly wasn't exerting himself at that black art. We were sixty-eight days out before we came to the Line, despite the utmost endeavour to use every scrap of wind. We wallowed for weeks in the deadly variables of the horse latitudes, and had a good south-east trade only for four days. It was the most wretched luck; with good sailing breezes we could have reached the Line easily in fifty days. The *Herzogin Cecilie* might be a racehorse in a gale, but she certainly liked to stop in the sunshine and loll about in calms. We wondered what *Beatrice* was doing. It was a queer sort of race, never knowing where the other contestant was, never seeing her or hearing anything of her over a period of months. She might have been 20 miles away, or 200; or she might have gone the other way round the world.

Across the Line at last, we languished in the doldrums. I wished de Cloux would get on with some *trolling*. If this sort of thing went on, I looked like missing the apple season. But de Cloux stitched at his sails, and nursed the ship along in the catspaws and squalls. One day we spoke the Swedish *C. B. Pedersen*, a four-masted barque which had sailed from Sydney two weeks before we left Port Lincoln, and it was encouraging to sail rings round her. But she was no *Beatrice*. *Beatrice* could sail rings round her, too; and probably had done so. Our orchestra played for the *Pedersen* and we showed our stowaway to their incredulous and envious gaze, but when de Cloux offered her to them they would not take her away. They rowed across for a look; that was enough. We had a grand gam*

* Gam – a yarn between ships at sea, with exchange of visits.

with the Swedes for two days, keeping close company. They had seen nothing whatever of the *Beatrice* or any other vessel.

Working our heavy great schoolship through the doldrums was punishing work. It was a bad season on the Line; there was far too much calm, far too much shifting every sail in the ship for a dribble of wind which puffed and then was gone. These were the conditions which were most infuriating to sailing-ship men, not storms. We could do with a few storms. *Beatrice*, with her gentle hull, her clean underwater body, was far better suited to light airs than our powerful Cape Horner; we wondered that we did not see her come ghosting past us. De Cloux was sure she had gone round Good Hope, for he argued that she would not have used the Backstairs Passage, inside Kangaroo Island. She would then have missed the land breeze which gave us our start. Instead, she would have had south-easterly weather which would have encouraged her to cross the Australian Bight. The natural thing then would be to round the Leeuwin and sail across the Indian Ocean, the way we had gone in the *Bellands* in 1921. I hoped de Cloux was right.

At last the north-east trades came, and we blew along in a boil of foam once more, racing towards England. Sometimes in the early evenings, de Cloux came to the wheel when I was there, and yarned a while to keep his English in order. There was one subject to which he kept returning, and that was his plan for resuscitating a four-masted barque from the Canal de la Martinière and running her in the Australian trade. There were several good ships still there on offer very cheaply, he said. All the Frenchmen were powerful ships and some of them were beauties. He explained in detail, as if he were convincing himself, just how such a project could be organized and made to pay. I listened fascinated, for the ship was steering herself on the wind and the set of the sails took care of any slight variations in its direction. It never occurred to me to take any personal part in his plans. How could I? Though he said the prices of the surviving ships had come down and would pro-bably fall further. He thought a big French four-master could be bought for £4,000, and they were lovely ships. The idea made a pleasant topic for a trade-wind yarn. Many of the boys had dreams, too, of sailing their own ships round the world. They generally thought of pilot cutters, or Baltic traders, or perhaps a stout and seaman-like yacht. To yarn about such things while the big ship's sails, arched etchings of beauty against the starry night, brought the great ship homewards, was pleasant indeed. No one expected such perfect plans to come to anything in this imperfect world.

During the whole of the voyage I worked steadily on what was to be my book. I wrote it chapter by chapter as the voyage progressed. At first an interested audience of the fair-haired apprentices and boys would assemble in the alleyway to watch the strange sight of the ship's own personal author writing a book. But they soon tired of this, for it was far from thrilling. They had never seen a book being written before: it was soon obvious that the process was a boring one and the sight of a heavy-handed able seaman hitting a small typewriter on the edge of a bunk in a tiny cabin was without interest. I photographed all I could; and as an able seaman I was kept busy. It was a strenuous life.

We were over three months at sea when we came at last towards Falmouth Bay. On the ninety-sixth day we anchored in the roads there. *Beatrice* had not arrived!

CHAPTER FIFTEEN

BY WAY OF CAPE HORN

Beatrice had gone round the Cape after all. She was 114 days. She would have given us a good race had she gone the other way. In my opinion she ought to have won. This was an opinion shared wholeheartedly by Sam Svensson, of whom I saw a good deal when the graceful ship later came round to London to discharge.

'I'd like to see the ship that could have followed us, in our tracks.' said Sam, loyally. But that was the point. We hadn't tried. The Horn way will generally give the shorter passage from South Australia. There is too much chance of baffling conditions in the Australian Bight, light airs in the Indian Ocean, a poor rounding of the Cape. Yet the *Herzogin Cecilie* had been only ninety-eight days going that way the previous year. If *Beatrice* and she had raced together round the Cape the result would have been more interesting. Perhaps Mate Svensson was not to be blamed for his suspicion that Captain de Cloux was a *troll*, though I told him I had seen no evidence. On the contrary, during thirty of her ninety-six days, the *Cecilie* had wallowed in light airs and calms; on twenty days she had runs of less than 50 miles.

When the *Beatrice* arrived I finished my book, and all my photographs developed satisfactorily. I called the book *Falmouth for Orders*, which was a good seafaring title. It was customary for grain-laden sailing-ships to clear outwards from Australia towards Falmouth, Plymouth, or Queenstown for orders, and not for any particular port. One reason why they obtained charters was that they provided free warehousing for the grain for months, as well as transport. While they were at sea, speculators and traders sold and resold the grain, and frequently its final destination was not known until a ship arrived. Hence the need to touch at a convenient place in the

Channel for orders, which generally came down from London by telegraph. A ship might be sent anywhere between Limerick and Danzig. Most masters preferred to touch at Falmouth because they could make and sail from the roads there without expense, and because the port was convenient for most of the United Kingdom and northern Europe.

The *Herzogin Cecilie* was ordered to Cardiff to discharge. Our stowaway was still aboard, for she had no papers of identity and the immigration inspectors could not allow her to land. De Cloux hoped to be rid of her before his wife arrived: the *Beatrice* was defeated and he did not intend to prosecute her. He was a kind-hearted man and would probably not have bothered her in any event. The newspapers got hold of her and made a great fuss, photographing her in the rigging where she had never been at sea. In a day or two she found a relative somewhere in England who, intrigued by the cheap publicity, forgave her the queer manner of her coming and undertook to look after her, to the satisfaction of the immigration authorities. So she left, a few hours before Madame de Cloux was due at Cardiff; and the big mate hurried off to Mariehamn, anxious to meet his fiancée before de Cloux's reports reached the Erikson office. He must have lied well, for he was married within a month or two. As for the stowaway, I saw her later driving an elevator at Australia House, in London. She was a very fortunate young woman.

I was three months in London. It was a visit vastly different from my first, when I worked by the Peruvian barque *Omega* for my food. (The same *Omega*, I learned, was still afloat. She was a guano drogher for a company in Callao, and was still working for the same company in 1947. She carried labourers to the guano islands and brought back cargoes of guano.) I wondered how I could have missed so much of the romantic wonder of old London in 1921. To arrive at Paddington Station and mount a No 15 bus, bound for Fleet Street, and for the expenditure of a few coppers be carried on the open top deck through Oxford Street, over Oxford Circus, down the lovely quadrant of Regent Street to Piccadilly Circus, across the top of Trafalgar Square and along the crowded Strand — this was grand adventure to a young man from Tasmania, come by way of Cape Horn. This time I wasn't looking for a ship. This time I had a good idea where the next meal was coming from, and I could go into Australia House knowing I had a small credit in the branch of the Commonwealth's Savings Bank there. The first thing I did, after leaving the typescript of *Falmouth for Orders* with the literary agent who had once dealt with Mr Scrooge (he looked at me rather curiously, I thought), was to book my passage back to Tasmania. This time I was not going to be stranded. I was one of the shore-dwellers now, and I had some money.

During the whole of my stay in England I studied conditions in the overseas apple market. Agents in Tasmania had given me the addresses of their principals in London and elsewhere. I met some oily gentlemen round Covent Garden, who seemed to be doing very well out of the apple business and any other produce they could get hold of, no matter how the growers fared. Some of these gentlemen tried to put me off. They were so suspicious that I became suspicious myself, and got after them thoroughly. The New Zealand Government kept a man in London to watch the fruit markets, and he was helpful to me. As soon as I felt that I had got the bones of the story in London and the chief provincial markets, I hurried to the Continent and 'covered' that. In Hamburg I found the four-masted barques *Passat* and *Tovarisch*, a Russian, and took time off to visit them. *Passat* was a splendid Cape Horner in the German Laeisz Line, trading to Chile, and the other was a former lime-juicer turned into a Soviet training ship. The name on her bell was *Lauriston*.

From Hamburg I went to Stockholm and crossed to the Aaland Islands, though I knew well there was no apple market there. I was anxious to meet Captain Gustaf Erikson and see what sort of man he was who sent great ships to sea with crews of boys. I found Mariehamn a tourist resort for the more prosperous Swedes. It had waters which were supposed to be good for something or other. It had lots of wooden guesthouses, and fat-bottomed women flopping about in beach pyjamas. These were not Aalanders. It had a long, leafy main street which crossed a pleasant isthmus; it had good bathing beaches. But I was interested in its ships. There were several square-rigged ships lying in the harbour unemployed; and a host of small schooners, with standing gaffs, carried on a business in firewood to the Stockholm archipelago. I looked about me with interest at this pleasant little port which could still send great sailing-ships to sea and had, indeed, practically a corner in them. Of the score or so big Cape Horners then surviving, more than three out of four belonged to Mariehamn, nearly all to Captain Erikson.

I sought out Captain Erikson. He was a small man with a limp and a somewhat aggressive way of speaking. He spoke English well, as did most seafaring Aalanders. His countenance was rugged and square, and there was a determined look about the man. His eyes were a keen blue. I had gathered, before I met him, that he was considered something of a menace aboard the ships he owned, for it was his custom to have them sailed to Mariehamn to lay up under his keen eye whenever they were without employment. He had been at sea in sailing-ships himself, deep-sea and coastwise, since he was eight years old, and had been everything from cook to master. His harassed shipkeepers never knew when the little man was going to come aboard, at any hour of the day or night (there was very little night during the Aaland summer). He was as likely to turn up suddenly in the galley as the poop, and he was capable of criticizing the minutest details. His limp (the result of a fall from aloft) did not keep him out of the rigging. He had two great and opposing ambitions – one that his ships should be kept up magnificently, and the other, that no money should be spent on them. As a man who had commanded at least three Finnish Cape Horners in his time, he well knew how accounts could be kept by masters who were not above the acceptance of odd commissions. If there was a large bill for paint, he wanted to see where the paint had been used. He was indefatigable in his quest for economy, and he knew his fellow-mariners well enough to be well aware that their interests might not always be the same as his. He had built up his large fleet on three great ship-owning principles. The first of these was to buy good ships at the lowest possible price, so that there could be little or no depreciation. The second was to manage his fleet entirely himself, and therefore he had no overhead expenses. And the third was to refrain from insuring any of them, and in this way he saved the considerable cost of premiums. He was his own marine superintendent, his own surveyor, his own chief steward. His idea of a ship worth buying was one which could earn the capital invested in her within three years. He had then recently acquired the barque *Killoran* and the four-masted barques *Hougomont* and *Archibald Russell* for less than £12,000 the three, and the big barque *Winterhude* cost him something under £2,000. His total investment in twenty large sailing-ships probably did not exceed £100,000.

A moment or two's conversation was sufficient to make me realize that his affection for the big sailing-ships was a very real thing, though he might be making a handsome profit out of them. I knew it took guts to run those ships, and to carry all the risks himself. Though the capital involved might be small, it was probably all there was in Aaland. Mariehamn, I gathered, was a port that had built itself up on a tradition of acquiring old ships cheaply and running them to death. It was a good thing, I reflected, that there was such a place, for otherwise there would probably have been no Cape Horners (except the Germans) in 1928. I wondered that no one in Tasmania had thought of conducting a similar business; the southern island was infinitely better placed than this small archipelago as a haven for Cape Horn ships, and could have maintained as good a tradition of seamanship. But the Tasmanians had lost heart when the steamers forced their own clippers out of trade, and Commonwealth legislation choked their enterprise.

I tackled Ship-owner Erikson about his crews. A little on the small side, weren't they? He gave me a hard look. I gave him some facts and figures from the *Lawhill* and the *Herzogin Cecilie*. Well, he said, they had made their voyages. He would not agree that they were undermanned. Too many Aalanders ran away abroad, he said. Deserting in America and Australia was a very old custom, and he couldn't stop it. He would if he could; indeed, he was thinking of compelling parents to put up bonds when their boys signed in his ships, the money to be forfeited if they deserted. As for men, none offered themselves, and he did not want them.

'All boys with any sense should go in a big sailing-ship for a voyage or two,' he said. 'Education? Bah! The best education for life is to live, and to start to live young. In a sailing-ship they have to live. The longer they go to school the more they have to unlearn when the time comes for them to be men. The younger the boys who sail in my ships the better I like it. I will take boys from any country that has the sense to send them.'

'At a premium?' I suggested.

He admitted that he thought it fair to charge foreigners a small premium, if they were going to learn their business in his ships. But for Aalanders there was no premium. His *Herzogin Cecilie*, *Lawhill*, and *Archibald Russell* were real school-ships, and he was making arrangements to take groups of Estonian, Swedish, and German boys. The best boys could stay in the ships, and it was his custom, he said, to recruit his officers from the boys who went through his own vessels. No ship-owner had found, or was finding, more employment for Aaland's seafarers than he.

'If you say my ships are undermanned, young man,' he wound up, 'well, you get me more boys.'

At that he jumped on his bicycle and rode off to the junk-yard by the beach, where he had assembled all kinds of sailing-ships' gear brought from the ends of the earth. He bought all he could find of this sort of thing. He lived in a comfortable wooden home which was no mansion. He lived plainly, without ostentation, and he did not join the holiday-makers and the tourists at Mariehamn or anywhere. What he earned from the ships went into more ships, or back into the ships he already had. As a smaller ship became due for reclassification, he care-fully summed up the pros and cons for keeping her. Ships had to be classed whether they were insured or not, for their cargoes were insured, and they could obtain nothing to carry if the insurance rates were exorbitant. When it would pro-bably cost more to have a ship reclassed than she could earn in her declining years, he sent her to the scrappers. But he did this reluctantly, and always tried at once to replace her.

He hated to see a sailing-ship go, profitable or otherwise. In that, at any rate, he was a man after my own heart. I took a liking to the remarkable old ship-owner, though I thought he might at least have offered his masters and his officers a fair wage. Living was obviously cheap in Aaland, but it was not likely to remain so for very long if the place became a tourist attraction.

I returned to Australia by passenger vessel, travelling in a migrant ship named *Jervis Bay*, which formerly belonged to the Commonwealth Line. At Fremantle the news reached me that my articles about fruit marketing had caused a minor sensa-tion, at any rate among the growers, and the *Mercury* was issuing a reprint in book form with a foreword by the State Premier. Back in Hobart, I found myself regarded as an expert on apples in general, and the European market in particular. I was nothing of the sort, but an investigator who had gone after knowledge in the possession of others. I had neither facts nor views myself. Now I heard that I might be expected to take a seat on the fruit advisory board, and to make a lecture tour of the chief growing centres in the state. It was time to leave Tasmania. I crept back quietly to the reporters' room; but it wouldn't do. The *Mercury* was very pleased with its enterprise, and the tom-toms were beating.

I could have ridden into politics on the red skins of the island's lovely apples; I could have plugged away a few years more for the ancient *Mercury*, and have become some sort of executive. Or I could have gone to the mainland and tried fresh fields there. But the mainland had no interest for me, since I hailed from it; I wanted nothing of politics; and a long lifetime of placid toil for the *Mercury* in happy old Hobart had no real appeal − not in a world which still knew ships. I was not in Tasmania six months before I was away again. I liked Tasmania, and I still think the island state one of the most lovely places in this world. It ranks high as a place in which to live, and I hoped one day to be there again.

Early in 1929 I left the *Mercury* and shipped as able seaman in the Finnish full-rigged ship *Grace Harwar*, of the Erikson Line, my intention being to make a film of the voyage of one of those classic ships, the Cape Horn full-riggers. The *Grace Harwar* was the last in service. To judge by the look of her she might not survive for very long.

This film idea was not originally mine. It was suggested by a brother reporter named Ronald Walker, aged twenty, a young man very interested in ships and the sea. Neither he nor I knew anything about the technicalities of the cinema (we had not seen a motion-picture camera); but he suggested that my pictures from the *Herzogin Cecilie* would have been glorious if they could have come to life. The only way they could be made to do that was on the screen. It seemed to both of us that the world had place for a documentary film on the lovely sailing-ship while she still survived. Since no one else seemed disposed to make such a film, we had better get on with it. We tried to get hold of a 35-mm cine-camera in Tasmania, but there were none. However, we knew there were some in Sydney. What we needed was capital − not much. Walker raised £150 and took an insurance on his life to cover the investment. I raised a like amount from a local merchant, who loaned me the sum to write a maritime history of Tasmania. My *Falmouth for Orders* was still unpublished and had been refused by Heinemann's, whose reader had perhaps read the novel which bore my name. I needed money to support my wife. Savings did this. As for the future, the newspaper profession was a good one, and Walker and I had no doubt that we should find some sort of employment in Fleet Street when we got there.

But I had some doubts about the wisdom of shipping in such

a vessel as the *Grace Harwar*, bound round the Horn towards the Channel for orders in the middle of the southern winter. I should never have gone in such a ship, except that she was perfect photographically and, as the last full-rigger in the trade, the best ship historically for our enterprise. Many of the surviving sailing-ships were scarcely worth going in, from the photographic point of view, because of the profusion of brace-winches, halliard winches, and other gadgets, and their Liverpool houses and long poops. The *Herzogin Cecilie* was unsuitable for this reason. A long poop might be a godsend in a seaway, but on the screen it would spoil the picture. The *Garthpool* (on her last legs) had a Liverpool house, and no royals, and almost as many gadgets as the *Lawhill*. Of the fourteen big sailing-ships then in the Australian trade, only the *Grace Harwar* was perfect for our purpose. The *Hougomont* or the *Archibald Russell* might do. These were both undermanned Finns, with long maindecks, no brace-winches, and their original rigging stood intact. Our objection to brace-winches was purely pictorial; we wanted to record the age-old fight of man against the sea, and a group of men turning a brace-winch handle might be lowering a cage down a mine.

The *Grace Harwar* was a dog with a bad name. Her name was near the top of the list in my little book of ships not to sail in. She killed someone every voyage. This was no superstition, but a matter of cold fact. She was a killer and had been for years, washing sailors overboard, knocking their heads off with parted wires, dropping them out of the rigging. She was always in trouble. She had been flung ashore in a hurricane, washed out fore-and-aft off the Horn, in collision. Since the days when her master had had to bury the body of his young wife in her ballast for a trans-Pacific passage with a recalcitrant crew, the *Grace Harwar* had been a lady with a *hoodoo*. Not that I took such things too seriously; but she was certainly a ship I should prefer to avoid. There is no doubt that ships can be subject to malign influences for no reason whatever, as the differing careers of many sister-ships have shown. Built to be as nearly identical as possible, one sister will behave like a lady all her days, and the other like a devil, no matter who commands her. I had never heard the *Grace Harwar* praised.

Hoodoo or not, there were other facts about her which were disquieting. When we contemplated joining her, she had been wandering round the world for more than two years, without being cleaned in a dry-dock. Her bottom would be very dirty. She had recently delivered a cargo of Peruvian guano at Wilmington, North Carolina. Guano is a stinking cargo, full of ammonia fumes which rot ship's gear. From Wilmington, she was bound towards Spencer Gulf in ballast. She would be woefully short of gear and crew. She would be off the pitch of the Horn in the middle of winter, which meant poor light for films. She was one of Captain Erikson's smaller ships, which he was replacing with big capacity four-masted barques as quickly as he could. It was, therefore, unlikely that he proposed to spend much money on her.

Well, there she was. She was a lovely model of a cargo-carrying full-rigged ship – no clipper, but an unspoiled old-timer. She had an open wheel which would be hellish in a winter gale, and she had long, heavy hand braces. She was the best ship in the fleet, from the documentary point of view. And – this also was in her favour – she was certainly a ship in which we could both get jobs before the mast for the asking.

I explained all these things to Walker. He was a courageous young man, whose experience of ocean racing was enough for him to know what I was talking about. If I thought the *Grace Harwar* was the best ship for us, then it was all right with him. Our decision was soon made. The *Grace Harwar* it should be, with the *Hougomont* or *Archibald Russell* as second choice.

We managed to get two small standard cine-cameras from Sydney and six thousand feet of negative film. This was all we could get. The cameras cost £40 each. They were small, of German make, and could carry magazines of fifty feet only. They would be handy aloft where they would have to be used without tripods. We also bought a light meter, and some still negative. I took along the thirty-shilling Kodak which had done so well before.

This time my wife gave me an ultimatum. I could choose the sea or her. This was a choice already made. My sea-bag was packed. (It had never been unpacked.) The *Grace Harwar*, four months out on ballast passage from Wilmington, was reported to be stopping steamers in the Australian Bight asking for food. This did *not* promise well. If she were short of food even before reaching Australia, how would she be on the long voyage home? Within a day or two there were accounts in the Adelaide press of her arrival in the Gulf with a tale of woe. Her sail-maker had died in Peru. Her Captain's legs had been broken. Her crew were leaving.

It was early in March 1929. Walker and I left the *Mercury*, with the good wishes of our colleagues there, and not without regret. In Melbourne we found the four-masted barque *Ponape*, an Italian-built vessel which had once been Bell's *Bellhouse*, and was then reported as having just been sold to Gustaf Erikson for £5,500. She was in with timber from the Baltic. She was a 2,500-ton vessel: her crew consisted of two able seamen, five ordinary seamen, and seven boys. For a moment we were tempted to join her, for there was obviously room for us and she was a ship with a good reputation. But her utilitarian brace-winches and her deck full of houses settled the matter. We should be faithful to the *Harwar* lady, hungry as she was.

But my heart sank at the sight of the old full-rigger when we found her alongside the pier at Wallaroo, and Walker, tired by the long train journey, was without enthusiasm. The *Grace Harwar* appeared to be on her last legs — rust-streaked, high out of the water with the sea-growth showing heavily on her underwater hull, her crew a handful of young boys, some of her gear obviously in bad order, her Finnish ensign an old one, dirty, some of her important cordage full of the long splices which tell of worn-out rope. There was a foot-rope carried away at the quarter stirrup, on the fore topgallant yard. The two topgallant yards there came perilously close together, for one was warped. Foot-ropes which carry away will kill sailors in the best-found ships, and we were looking at a known killer. It was a Saturday afternoon when we arrived, and the sounds of drunken revelry came from her for'ard house.

We went aboard. No one questioned us. There was a party in the forecastle. Some Americans who had joined at Wilmington were now leaving, and were celebrating. A few of the *Harwar*'s crew were sprawled about. There were some boys from the Helsingfors training barque *Favell*, which was at the berth across the wharf. They were all drunk. In the old days when men manned sailing-ships, this might have been commonplace. But drunkenness among these fair-skinned, beardless boys was depressing. They had no business getting drunk. Normally, they would have had no money.

We announced our intention to join the ship, in answer to a more or less sober inquiry.

'Don' ship in this bitch!' yelled one of the Americans, who was a sailor (the rest were college boys). 'Wors' goddam son-of-a-bitch of a ship I ever been in. Hungry! Rotten gear! Stinks of guano! No goddam crew! Round the Horn in this? Not on your goddam life, boy! Not goddam likely!'

The youthful Finns looked on approvingly. We left.

'Hum,' said Walker very thoughtfully. 'You didn't say anything about drunks.'

'They won't always be drunk, poor devils,' I said. But I was worried, too.

From the time we first saw the ship a change came over young Walker. He seemed to have a premonition that she meant no good to him. From the carefree young chap he had been in Tasmania, he developed almost at once into an extremely serious young man, as if he had a weight upon his mind. I don't remember that he smiled again, from the day we joined. He remained as enthusiastic as ever about the film and the idea behind it, and he was just as keen to make himself a good sailing-ship sailor. But something of the heart had gone out of him.

Walker signed on as deckboy. I was able seaman. The master

seemed surprised we wished to come. We did not tell him of our film plans. He would learn of them when we sailed. There might be some nonsense about rights, or something, if the owner heard of it. We joined at once and took up our bunks in the forecastle, which was nothing but a low square house on the fore-deck. It was lined with bunks, in two tiers, and there was an oilskin locker at the after-end, and a rough board table in the middle. The doors fitted badly, and the deckhead leaked. The bunks were narrow, boarded shelves. The few ports leaked. There was no stove. This was going to be hellish accommodation for a Cape Horn winter's rounding. But there were some good points about the ship, as well as her photogenic quality. Her officers were thoroughly likeable and competent young men; such crew as she had consisted of very pleasant, though depressed young fellows. Her master was an extraordinary young man. He acted like a good officer with a group of men in a front-line trench, whom he well knew to be up against it. He was a quiet, pleasant-spoken man, and he looked like anything rather than the popular conception of a Cape Horn master mariner. A less likely figure to walk the poop of a notorious killer, it would be difficult to imagine. He was slight, and he stooped a little. He limped badly, for his broken legs still bothered him. The cut of his face was gentle and almost saintly, though he was no saint. His blue eyes were clear and open as a boy's. His voice was soft, and he never raised it. He was a Swedish-speaking Aalands Finn, and he had been in command of the *Grace Harwar*, then, for over four years. He looked almost as if the experience had been purifying.

We were in Australian waters for a month, for the *Grace Harwar* was in no hurry. While we were on the ballast grounds in the Gulf I worked on my maritime history of Tasmania, the notes for which I had brought with me. I worked on the forecastle table in my free time, and the young Finns, though astonished, were too mannerly to express much interest. I knew I should have little time or place for writing once the ship sailed. Walker studied angles for our film, and made photographs of the little *Favell* as she slipped away from the jetty under sail, a beautiful picture. She had been over 200 days on her previous passage between South Australia and the Channel. She looked so beautiful under her perfect sails that it was difficult to accept her as part of the world of work at all.

The middle of April had gone before we sailed. We had raked together a crew of thirteen before the mast – six able seamen, three ordinary seamen, and four boys. The 'boys' included two young railroad porters from the South Australian railways who felt the call of adventure and had not heard of the ship's bad name. Among the able seamen were Jim Evans, from Sydney, and a Frenchman named Pierre Berthoud from the *Garthpool*. Jim's last ship was the heavy *Olivebank*, a four-masted barque. Jim and Pierre were good men. So were the surviving young Finns who had been with the ship two years. The ordinary seamen were runaway apprentices from the *Favell* and *Hezogin Cecilie* who had learned, very quickly, that there were plenty of farmers in Australia ready to exploit the cheap labour they provided.

Just before we sailed, a negro was brought down the jetty under police escort, as a prohibited immigrant in Australia. He was a runaway sea-cook from the barque *Penang*, and as we were the last Erikson ship to leave Australia that season we had to take him away. He was a West Indies negro who had begun his sailing in a French logwood barque. He spoke good French, perfect Swedish, and English with an Irish accent, and he was no asset to the vessel. He settled into the forecastle and we sailed. It was April 17th, 1929.

It was September before we arrived – 138 days later. We were lucky to arrive at all. On the voyage Walker was killed, the second mate driven out of his mind, the ship sprang a serious leak, and ran out of food. We were six days from Wallaroo to the south of Tasmania, fifty-seven days to the Horn, ninety-four to the Line. We were the last ship to sail and the last in the 'race'. The whole voyage was a savage fight against the sea, in a ship which was seriously handicapped from the setting-out to the end. I understood, before very long, just why that strange young captain regarded his boy-crew as front-line soldiers, for such they were, in a ship which tried them almost beyond endurance.

Walker was killed aloft on the morning of the thirty-eighth day, at his work in the rigging. The halliards of the fore upper topgallant carried away while he was standing on the foot-rope of the lower yard, and the falling spar killed him. And so he was 'buried for aye in the sea's deep bed', as he himself had written a few weeks earlier. Death was commonplace in the ship *Grace Harwar*; but a funeral was rare. Generally she left her bodies in the sea astern of her. It was queer how Walker seemed to have a premonition of disaster from the moment he first saw the ship. One knows there is no reason in such feelings; but there it was. His was real enough. He was twenty years old, and he had not previously shown any trace of morbidity. Nor was there anything morbid about him in the ship. He was an enthusiast until the end. He was probably studying camera angles when he was killed, for the view from high aloft of the black sea breaking in phosphorescence before the bows, that moonlit morning, must have been grand. Had he not been so keen a student of the camera he might not have been killed, for he ought not to have been on the lower topgallant yard then. He had been sent there to clear a gasket which had fouled the weather sheet, as loose ends of gaskets will. That done, while the watch paused about the capstan in their work of hoisting the upper yard to let him get clear, he shouted down that all was clear. We could not see, for the moonlight was patchy and the morning black when the moon was behind cloud. The capstan was manned again, and the guano-rotted fall carried away.

After that we had a lot of easterly weather. The Cape Horn season that year was bitter. For five weeks we battled on against east and south-east gales. The struggle to get the ship across those miles and past the Horn was so bitter and all-absorbing that we forgot our other troubles. It was midwinter. The days were short, savage, sunless. The decks were full of water which swept aboard from the crests of giant combers. The forecastle was almost constantly awash. Many sails blew out. There were lesser accidents. The seas sometimes all but overwhelmed the ship, pressing her down as she rolled both rails under. Making one's way aft to relieve the wheel was a perilous adventure, but there were strong lifelines rigged up fore and aft to keep us aboard. To work aloft, struggling against some maddened sail with its guano-rotted gear carried away, was a nightmare, and we could not banish from our minds the thought that the foot-rope might be rotten, too. The two mates fought aloft with their watches on all the heavier sails; we set no kites on that part of the voyage. The captain, finding any shelter he could in the lee of a weather-cloth lashed in the mizzen rigging, kept watch alone on the poop, while a boy struggled to keep the hard-mouthed, barn-acled ship to her course. Wheel turns were hellish, and fre-quently lasted half the night. The ship ran lightless, for there was no oil to burn sidelights: even if there were, they could not be lit. The screens were washed away, and the lamps were stowed in their locker. In a hard gale off the Horn the ship sprang a leak, and after that we had to pump each watch. Before long, the stench of rotting wheat drove gases through the ventilators which blistered the paint from the bulwarks, and sent us retching to the side. The chronometer – she had only one – developed a serious irregularity, and there was no radio to receive time-signals. We ran on by dead reckoning alone, in the hands of God; and off Diego Ramirez, saw kelp and the light green of shoaling water. Nothing else. No land; no sun; no other ships; no peace.

On the seventy-third day the second mate went mad. His scream as he leapt over the side frightened us above the wind's howl. We got him back, by the grace of God and the fine sea-manship of our young captain, who saw him go. The helm was jammed down instantly and the mainyards backed. The boats were lashed down, and there were no falls rove. The lifeboats in the ship *Grace Harwar*, though seaworthy, were not taken seriously as a line of defence, and there was no boat-drill. They were lashed on the skids to prevent them from being washed overboard; time and time again the sea had stove a boat in there. Now they were wanted in a hurry. There was no panic. Falls were rove, and the boat swung out, lowered, and away with almost incredible speed. We were away in the boat before we realized how great a sea was running, or remembered that it was near the end of day. Out in the boat, falling deep in the troughs which hid the ship from view, it came into my mind that the barque *Staut* once, running her easting down, had dropped the captain's son from the mainyard-arm and sent back a boat, just like this, and neither the boy nor the boat was ever seen again, though the *Staut*'s people heard the cries of sailors following them for weeks.

There were six of us at the oars, and the mate with a steering sweep. It rained, and there was a sad crying in the wind. I watched the mate's stern, set face as he kept sharp look-out. He was about twenty-four, a quiet man, with burning blue eyes. He was much liked and respected by his watch and all of us. He kept his balance easily there, though the boat rode violently, and he kept her dry. In the day's light we found the second mate. A sea threw him up right before us, a spread-eagled figure in blue with his long hair flowing in the foam. We got him inboard with difficulty, and back to the ship. For a month afterwards he raved, and his raving worried us profoundly. For who among us might next be mad?

It his more lucid moments, the second mate blamed himself for the death of Walker, though he was in fact in no way to blame. He knew, and we all knew, that there was not wire and cordage enough in the ship to put right all that should be put right. The fall which parted that morning had been recently examined, and turned end for end. He was profoundly worried about the state of the ship's gear, about always having to send people aloft where no one knew what might carry away next, or who else might be killed. Such worries were useless; we took such precautions as we could. The foot-ropes had all been sent down and overhauled before leaving Wallaroo. Yet our second mate could not rid himself of his worries, and he had a long time to brood over them. The officers of a two-watch long voyage sailing-ship are very lonely men, and the second mate is often the loneliest. He keeps his watch alone. He eats alone, for the mate is on watch when he is below. His life is divided between his watches and a little sleep – day after day, week after week. On watch, his standard of vigilance must be extremely high, and this is difficult for twenty-four hours in every forty-eight, no matter how the watches may be divided. We saw the fear in his face every time he detailed us to lay aloft, or to go out along the bowsprit to fight a jib – fear, not for himself but us. As the ship threw her bows into the great seas with a few oil-skinned figures fighting on the steel yard there, he watched terrified that when she rose again the figures would be gone as once they had all been from the weather fore-braces of the ship *Pampa*, when he was a boy there, at the wheel. Our second mate was a man who, though young, had served Cape Horners long and hard, and his luck had not been good in them. In the *Pampa* once, in the middle of a stormy night, he saw his watchmates all rolled outboard in a furious onslaught of the sea, and he had to steer the ship on through the night away from them while they drowned in her wake astern. The watch-keeping mate had gone with them. He was left alone, unable to leave the wheel, unable to call anyone. He shouted, but no one heard. The scream of the wind in his face mocked him. The ship lurched and rolled and stumbled on, and the long brace where the watch had been hauling trailed untended over the side. It was not until the day came and some of the other watch wandered out of the forecastle, wondering why they had not been called, that they found him still at the wheel, and no one left to call them.

He had been a boy then. He was never a boy again. After that, he had been four years in the *Grace Harwar*. There was no cause for wonder that his mind snapped under the strain; his watchmates from the *Pampa* screamed at him out of the night, and the fore topgallant sail was stained with the blood no rain could wash away. While he was mad, we cut those cloths out and sewed new canvas there.

The second mate's breakdown was hard on our nerves. Perhaps because he regarded me as in a category different from most of the foremast hands, perhaps because I was Walker's friend, he was for ever sending for me, raving to me, imploring me to accept his great contrition. I had to talk to him for hour after hour, almost every day. He was confined to his cabin in the poop, and the captain and the chief mate did their best to care for him. Our captain took the second mate's watch and carried on with quiet competence. Day after day, he did his utmost to nurse the ship along, to induce her somehow to head towards England and make the best use of the wind. He never lost patience. He never failed to understand his broken second mate. The example of this quiet, soft-spoken man was a noble one; yet I wondered how much longer he could stand the *Grace Harwar*, too. As for myself, it was a good thing there was far from enough to eat in the ship that voyage. That saved many of us, I think, though it did not occur to us at the time as being in any way a good thing. We were forced to lead a monkish sort of a life, undernourished, fighting adversity with insufficient rest. A full belly is no aid to reflection. Our near-empty bellies, week after week, sharpened our minds. We were forced to find our souls, if we had no knowledge of them before. We were forced to accept in humility the help of God, or we could not have gone on. There was no escape, and there were no distractions. Yet I know I was never clearer-headed in my life. I was one of a handful of able seamen in a heavy ship, grievously undermanned. I steered. I pumped. I worked aloft. I often sewed sails all day on deck, and worked with them in the rigging half the night. I did what I could to help the second mate. I filmed and photographed, for that could not be given up, and I tried to make as good a job as Walker would have done. When the weather was good, I brought out my battered portable typewriter, and got on with my maritime history of Tasmania, for that had to be ready for press when we came in.

I think I averaged five hours of broken sleep in the twenty-four, throughout the 138 days of the passage. On a full belly, I could not have done that. Yet I would have filled my belly, had I had the chance; and I have lacked the character to recreate the circumstances since, though I was almost forced to do so once or twice in small ocean-going landing-ships during the 1939–45 War.

We tried to get some food from a steamer which we saw in the Rio lane, on the Line, but the wretched thing, seeing our hoist of flags, altered course *away*. We had scurvy aboard by then. The sail-maker was very ill, and so were several of the Finnish boys who had been longest in the ship. Our faces had thinned; eyes shone from countenances which were almost ascetic, quite different from their usual appearances. Except the nigger from the barque *Penang*. He chose this time to raise discord, and to plot against the cook. We were then pounding wheat from the hold to make a mess of flour; it was easy to stir up discord against a cook who had no viands to prepare. The nigger wanted the crew to demand the cook's deposition, and his own enrolment in that place. He wanted money, for as a deserter being deported he had no wages. He was a nuisance, a black-hearted, loud-mouth trouble-maker. But adequate steps were taken to keep him in order. The cook was not deposed.

On the hundred and twenty-first day, with the second mate back in his watch (a favour he implored from the captain, to try to keep something of his reason) and all hands weakening fast, the hands lay aft and the captain decreed that from that day until we arrived we should be on calashee watches. There should be no more working about the decks, watch and watch. We should steer, tend the sails, keep the ship pumped out and clean: no more attempt should be made to carry on with two decimated watches, with all hands turned out for every heavy job. Henceforth we should be one watch, working only when strictly necessary, getting what rest we could. The captain also said that he would make for a steamer lane again to try to get some food before the sail-maker died. We went for'ard again, and looked out for the smoke of steamers.

Three days later we spoke the fleet auxiliary *Orangeleaf*, a tanker, bound from Invergordon towards Trinidad. We had tried to signal several other steamers, but they made no answer. The *Orangeleaf* stopped, and filled the boat we sent across with fresh meat and vegetables. The fresh food saved our scurvy victims; nobody died. A day or two afterwards, near the Azores, we spoke a large Italian liner hurrying towards New York. We could see the passengers taking photographs and waving. Doubtless they thought the old full-rigger made a romantic sight. At the time we were barely able to crawl about the decks and fight our way into the rigging.

On the hundred and thirty-eighth day out we arrived off Queenstown heads, late at night, and all but stranded on the wreck of a liner which had not been there when our captain was there earlier. We saw no pilot, but he arrived in the morning, clamouring for his pilotage, and shouting that the ship must be moved farther into the harbour. We towed from Queenstown round to the Clyde to discharge, and I left at Glasgow. The six thousand feet of exposed film was in my sea-bag, and I took the first train to London.

Twenty years afterwards, having in the interval had command in a full-rigged ship myself and handled men, during the war, in circumstances equalling those in the *Grace Harwar* that voyage, I must pay a tribute to that quietly humble man who, supremely competent, always forbearing, never too greatly cast down, brought the old ship to her anchorage that voyage, under God. The captain of the *Grace Harwar* was a courageous and noble man. He never again served in a deep-sea sailing ship; I heard he lost his life when a motor-ship he commanded was bombed in the Baltic in 1943. Largely thanks to him, the second mate of the *Grace Harwar*, who was hurried home from Ireland, recovered his full sanity after a year or two ashore. I read later that he was given some award for a hazardous rescue of the crew of a fishing schooner in a North Atlantic storm.

When I was able, from Queenstown, to inform Walker's parents that he was dead, I was surprised to learn that they knew, though they could not have known. The *Grace Harwar* had no radio. A long time afterwards, his mother told me that at the moment he died, an old grandfather clock in their Hobart home suddenly began to go. It had been stopped for years. At the same instant she felt that her son – her only son – was trying to tell her something. She made a note of the precise instant. There was no mistake about it. The times were verified, corrected for difference of longitude. One hears many such stories, but this, at any rate, was authentic. Walker foresaw his death; something of him might have fled to Hobart when he died.

CHAPTER SIXTEEN

THE *PARMA* VENTURE

IF I left the *Grace Harwar* with a greatly enhanced respect for my fellow-men, I gained none in the film world in London. I was ashore two years after that voyage – time enough to learn something of the way of things in the English capital. I got a job in Fleet Street without much trouble, working for an Australian news agency in *The Times* office. I was a London roundsman (responsible for gathering news of particular Australian and New Zealand interest), and also took my turn at the cable desk, at the sending end of the cryptic puzzles which flowed out to the *Mercury* and the *Melbourne Herald* and the *Sydney Sun*, and a chain of other newspapers throughout Australia and New Zealand. I took to flying, in which I had been interested ever since two barnstormers brought an old Avro-Avian – a small, stout biplane – to a field beside the Elwick racecourse, in Tasmania, during my Tam-o'-Shanter days. Flying was a good antidote to sailing ships.

If I never became a particularly good pilot, at any rate I was a mighty careful one, as behoved a sailing-ship man. The same qualities of foresight and common sense which were essential under sail were just as necessary in the air; indeed, sailing and gliding had much in common. Then one day a seagull crashed into me, when I was slipping off some height preparatory to landing at the airport at Rochford in Essex, by the estuary of the Thames. Suddenly, I found myself coming-to, in a hazy manner, still strapped in the cockpit, and the glass on the instruments in the panel before me was broken, and pieces of it were in my face. My mouth, nose, and eyes were full of blood, and the earth was reeling drunkenly at the wingtips. What now? I thought. You damned fool! You didn't have to be here! You belong in ships. Enough nitwits are helping the world to fly! I had thought, until then, that I knew every possible kind of accident that could happen in the air; but this defeated me. I didn't know about the seagull until its body was found in the cockpit afterwards. Mechanically I turned off the gas, for a crash was inevitable, and I wanted to avoid fire. Fire in an aeroplane is not a pleasant prospect, even when semi-conscious. I tried to straighten the machine as well as I could, to fling it at the ground rather than have the earth throw itself at me. Then I crashed, and the biplane came to pieces. I was lucky not to be killed.

As for the film, it developed perfectly and some of the shots were magnificent. While far from what it might have been, if I had had more negative, it was still a fine record of the Cape Horn sailer and it could have made a splendid documentary. But I knew no one in the film world. I still had, I suppose, a considerable share of the sailor's diffidence towards the shore moguls, even after my years in journalism. I looked about me quietly for some kindred spirits who would help to cut, edit, and perhaps market the film. I never found any. Instead, I got among the boys of Wardour Street, whose ideas of making a sea film were different from mine. But I found that I had to put up with them, or there would be no film. The film was at last made into what was known as a 'feature'. This seemed to mean that in no circumstances could it be allowed to bear any avoidable relation to reality. Walker's and my photography was to be used as background for a story – any story. There was no money in a documentary, the moguls said. Even when John Masefield came to their studio and was enthusiastic about the film they lacked the sense to leave it alone. Here was one film, surely, which the public might have been allowed to see undoctored. But it was not to be. A director was let loose upon it. Actors were hired – some good, some terrible, all out of place. An excellent script-writer was called in. He was a man with whom I could have worked, but I was not allowed to; he wasn't allowed much freedom either. He was a man with a real feeling for ships and the sea; but it was the director who had the decision in everything.

I was astonished to learn how the film-men set about their work. It was my custom, from my sailing-ship experience, to apply one standard only to such work of the world as came my way – the simple, direct standard of getting on with the job and sticking at it until it was thoroughly done. You saw the job; you understood the job; you did the job. This was not the way the film-men worked, though it had been a good standard in the newspaper profession. I don't believe the film-men ever had a clear conception of what they were trying to do, at any rate with the *Grace Harwar* film. It was idle for me to say anything at the studio. I wasn't even the 'technical adviser', though experts of that ill-defined status abounded, at good pay. Once I ventured the comment that a forecastle set they had designed was more appropriate to the theatre than to a film which, however much concocted stuff was added to it, would still include enough of the real thing to make the false painfully evident. I took the director down to the London docks and aboard the *Archibald Russell*, to see a forecastle. It was a clean white house with tiers of fore-and-aft bunks, neatly arranged lockers, hooks for mugs, coats, oilskins, and so on. It was a clean and efficient domicile for Cape Horn mariners; but it was no use to that director.

'If we filmed this, the public wouldn't believe it was a sailing-ship's forecastle at all,' he said.

Good Lord, what public? Surely the public would accept the real, and might even be grateful for the opportunity. I wasted my breath. It seemed to me that the film-men were so thoroughly accustomed to dealing in the false that their minds worked in a world of falsehood, from which they could never again emerge.

I did not go to the studio again. Months afterwards I stood in a queue outside a brazen temple of films in London's West End, and when I succeeded in getting in, writhed in my seat at what I saw. What should have been a lovely and stirring record of a great phase in maritime life was no more than another piece of shadowed nonsense, and the glorious reality of the tragic old full-rigger was swamped in a thousand fathoms of counterfeit.

Nor did Walker's estate or I ever get back the £150 each,

with which we had financed the original film. Everyone else connected with it was paid, I have no doubt; our share was a pittance, after the Wardour Street men had taken their 40 per cent and the overheads had been accounted for. It was a depressing experience. I remember with abhorrence the exhibitor who, when shown the real *Grace Harwar* film – not the studio version – squirmed in his seat and had the projection stopped. He was a harsh, dark little man, of Eastern origin; and he shouted at me that his screens existed to keep such stuff *from* the public. Perhaps he spoke a greater truth than he knew.

But the film was not wholly wasted. By chance the passengers who took photographs of the old *Grace Harwar* from the Italian liner we met off the Azores included Dr Gilbert Grosvenor, the president of the National Geographic Society, of Washington. Dr Grosvenor enjoyed the sight, and dismissed the incident from his mind. Over a year afterwards, he read about my film, in a London illustrated weekly magazine. Part of his society's activities was to seek out such films and have them shown to their Washington members, in a course of winter lectures. So Dr Grosvenor tracked me down and dug me out of my Fleet Street lair. Before I knew where I was, I was booked to come across to Washington and lecture there with my films. I was astonished to find an audience of six or seven thousand, packed into a huge auditorium. The thing was a success. A lecture-agency took it up; I found myself lecturing with the film up and down the United States of America. It was an amazing experience: here was a place which could appreciate enterprise. I often spent four nights out of five in long-distance trains, hastening from university campus to lecture forum, from yacht club to museum, from geographical society to school. I simply showed the film and told the plain story of the *Grace Harwar*'s voyage, and the sailing grain trade from Australia; even in remote corners of the vast Middle West there was a real feeling for the sea and a great interest in America's own sailing traditions, from Yankee clipper days. My tour was a vast success.

In the first few weeks ashore in England I had written a book about the *Grace Harwar*'s voyage, though I had not intended to do this. *Falmouth for Orders*, I thought, ought to be sufficient account of the grain fleet; but there was a story in the old full-rigger's voyage which had to be told. The book was called *By Way of Cape Horn*. To my astonishment it quickly became a best-seller. I found myself a minor literary lion, very temporarily. I was, I read, a 'journalist who had gone to sea' and done a tolerable piece of reporting about it. Journalist who went to sea? I thought I was a sailor in the newspaper business, and thanked God for the early training in the Tasman Sea barques and the big *Lawhill*.

Riding on the backs of *Falmouth for Orders* and *By Way of Cape Horn*, my maritime history of Tasmania was offered to the public. It was called *Vanished Fleets*. From all these books and from the lecture tour, I began to collect some capital. This was an entirely new experience, and I wondered what to do with it.

In these circumstances I came upon Captain de Cloux one day in the London docks. I maintained my interest in sailing-ships and allowed no deep-waterman to come to any port in southern England without a visit from me. The barque *Plus*, an old-timer from the Laeisz Line, which flew the Finnish flag, was in with a cargo of wood from Trangsund. She was a fine old Cape Horner of the *Clan Macleod*'s type. She would have suited Murdo' Murchison for the Tasman Sea trade, for she was just the right size and she looked as if she could sail like a witch. I had heard from Aaland that Captain de Cloux had left the sea and taken to chicken-farming at his home near Godby there, not far from Mariehamn. I was surprised to find him in the *Plus*.

'Hallo, Captain,' I said. 'I thought you were chicken-farming?'

He grinned. 'I've got some shares in this ship,' he explained. 'The dam' fool who was captain before was two hundred days coming up from the Seychelles and had to put into St Helena for food, 128 days out. So I thought I would come here for a while to see how she sails, and maybe earn a little money with her. We don't want to pay to own her.'

He praised the little barque as a splendid sailer, though handicapped by her size, on the freight markets. She registered 1,100 tons – too small for long hauls, and a little on the big side for short. He was going home to Aaland with her to lay her up, for there was no further charter for her. He had hoped to go to the West Indies for logwood, but the steamers were taking the small parcels offering in that trade. She might get a charter of South Australian grain, but it was foolish to put her in that trade. Her cargo capacity was too small for her to clear a dividend, with the low freights offering. She had cleared a few hundred pounds on the wood from Trangsund, but it would cost her more to go out in ballast and fetch back Australian wheat than she would be paid for carrying it.

'But,' de Cloux said, 'that would not apply to a larger sailing-ship – a four-master, say, with a capacity for 5,000 tons.'

I pricked up my ears, remembering his schemes for acquiring a big sailing-ship. But surely there were none available now. I wondered what was coming next.

'You are still interested in going to sea in big sailing-ships?' de Cloux continued, after a pause.

I replied that I certainly was.

'Well,' he said, very slowly, 'I think there's a way. There is a big four-masted barque laid up in the Segelschiffshafen in Hamburg, and I think she could be bought very cheaply. She's every bit as good as any of those Frenchmen which used to lie in the canal at Nantes. Her name is *Parma*. She's 100 A1. She loads over 5,000 tons. I can get a crew if I can buy her. Would you like to come in?'

I certainly would. Here was an outlet for that capital! We yarned in the saloon of the old *Plus* half the night, going into ways and means for the venture. He knew, said de Cloux, that *Parma* had been offered to an English syndicate for £4,000 a year previously. The offer came to nothing because of the difficulties of running her under the British flag – mostly concerned with insurance and crew. Meantime worldwide depression had continued its downward spiralling and the value of the *Parma*, which no one wanted, had probably declined by half. Her employment was the Chilean nitrate trade, and that had stopped. As a ship, she was worth all of £12,000; but she was worth nothing if there were no employment for her. As for that, we could get a charter for grain. Depression or no depression, Europe had to eat, and grain had to be imported. Sailing-ships which could lie at anchor almost in sight of wheat-growers' farms and did not care how long it took to load were, indeed, more assured of a cargo than steamers which had to have a minimum daily delivery of 500 tons. De Cloux knew how to keep the costs down. He was running the *Plus* for less than £3 a day – the actual figure he mentioned was £2 12s. If the *Parma* cost twice that, she would still be economical, and she ought not to cost so much. She was well found. (All Laeisz ships were.) The crew which sailed *Plus* would suffice for her, with a dozen apprentices. There was no lack of them, for there was then a great surge of interest in the surviving Cape Horn ships. (My books brought many cadets to Captain Erikson.) Youths from all over the world were flocking to the Erikson ships, and paying anything up to £100 for the privilege of working. Erikson was going ahead with his fleet. De Cloux had bought the Danish *Viking* for him a year or two earlier, for £6,000. He had bought the *Melbourne* from the Germans, and was looking round for other ships to purchase. If Gustaf Erikson was not worried about the depression, neither was Ruben de Cloux. Indeed, it was the very depth of the depression which was giving us our chance.

This time we were having no trade wind yarn. Within less than a month from the day of that meeting the *Parma* was ours. The price was slightly under £2,000. The capital of our little company was £3,000, and our shareholders included a London ship-chandler whose specialized interest was the deep-water sailing ship, and a man on the Baltic Exchange, where charters were arranged. The ship-chandler would store us, on credit if needs be; the broker would get us our charter. On October 15th, 1931, we paid down a deposit of ten per cent of the purchase price to hold the *Parma* against examination in dry dock. On October 17th she was chartered to load a full cargo of wheat in sacks at any port in Spencer Gulf which could provide one, at a freight rate of thirty-one shillings a ton. We had the ship's employment assured before purchase was completed. That charter was worth, in round figures, some £8,000. This was an excellent beginning.

The *Parma* was a modern steel four-masted barque of 3,091 gross register tons, and 2,971 net, according to the Bill of Sale. She was 327·7 feet long, 46·5 feet beam, and her moulded depth was 28 feet. She was built at Port Glasgow in 1902, as the *Arrow*, and she began her career in the case-oil trade from Philadelphia and New York to the Far East, in the days before bulk installations in Japan. She had the largest unobstructed hold of any sailing-ship; like all Cape Horners, she had only a collision bulkhead, which was right forward, immediately abaft the chain locker. She was a great carrier, in excellent order, and she had been very well kept up. She was due for reclassification in 1933, and in the dry-dock we noticed that some of her bottom plates were pitted. If we were going to keep her for long, some of those plates would have to be renewed. But she was perfect as a short-term proposition. Her rigging was splendid, and she had three suits of sails. To get her into commission, all we had to do was to engage a crew, store her, reeve off the running gear, insure her, bend her sails, hire a tug to take her down the Elbe, and go. She was already ballasted, for she would not stand up empty in the dock. Captain de Cloux took command, and his good name was sufficient to have her insured for a reasonable premium on the London market. She flew the Finnish flag and was registered at Mariehamn, a good port for Cape Horners.

Our experienced crew included, as well as the officers, a sailmaker, carpenter, donkeyman, steward, cook, four able seamen, five ordinary seamen, and two young fellows from the Baltic galleasses. These were from the Aaland Islands. In addition, we shipped two excellent young German able seamen from the Laeisz Line, in Hamburg, and seven German cadets at a premium of a thousand Reichsmarks apiece. Our crew costs were under £100 a month. Our food costs, with plenty to eat, were one shilling and threepence a day for each man. New sails cost only the canvas that went into them, for we planned to buy no sails ashore. They were sewn aboard, and there were plenty of bolt-ropes. So long as we had no serious accidents we were all right.

The *Parma* towed down the Elbe early in November 1931. It was cold and grim outside, and the North Sea was at its tricks, that grey, wretched home of short seas and upset stomachs. The young apprentices stumbled and fell about the decks, for the ballasted ship leaned over heavily in the fresh head winds. We could not make for the Channel because of the adverse winds; no matter, there is more sea-room to the north of Scotland. So that way we went, upon a succession of ghastly November days when all the world was grey and wet, and cold and miserable. The first two weeks were hellish for the greenhorns. They were kept at it, for the best cure for seasickness and depression is to work them off. Giving in is a wretched prolongation, of use to nobody. There was no giving in. This may seem harsh, but it was essential. To give in is foolish and may be fatal, and the immediate grapple with the early difficulties of the voyage – of all voyages – as they arose is imperative. Our cadets were leaving comfortable homes for the first time. They were unaccustomed to the Finnish sea food, or to constant hard physical labour with short periods of broken sleep. Their faces green and their spirits depressed, they fought their way aloft to work on the high, wet yards while the black great hull of the ship crashed through the seas far beneath them. They were allowed to give nothing but their best, and our mates were experts at getting the best out of them, despite seasickness and their appalling inexperience. They did not appreciate it at the time; but later they did. That first two weeks made men of them; they were never again called upon to suffer so much.

Our *Parma*, though an enormous sailing-ship, sailed very well, and was comfortable and dry in ballast. She was sur-

prisingly light to handle. She steered well, and had a fine
whaleback wheelhouse to protect the helmsmen. Her sail plan,
though ample, was not unduly large. Her canvas was tractable
and she had a good spirit. She was a pleasant, sea-kindly ship
under de Cloux, and she was out to do her best for us. Within
two weeks she was out in the North Atlantic, free of the land.
Within three weeks she was bowling down the trades, and
there were sunshine and happiness fore and aft. There were
also, unfortunately, four stowaways, who had not as much as
a torn envelope to prove the identity of any one of them. We
rid ourselves of these by flinging them off on an island, just
before the end of the voyage. We were in Spencer Gulf after a
run of eighty-three days, and our crew by then was a highly
competent, united team, fit for anything. We were twenty-nine
hands all told, for it was no part of our plan to sail the ship
short-handed.

That first voyage we loaded 62,650 bags of wheat at a small
Spencer Gulf outport known as Port Broughton, where loading, though slow, was comparatively inexpensive. We had no
accidents on the outward run. So far, so good. On March 17th,
1932, we sailed with a quiet land breeze to waft us down the
Gulf. One hundred and three days later we anchored in Falmouth Bay. The Erikson four-master *Pamir* (which he had
bought from Laeisz for £4,500 when he learned of our purchase of *Parma*) sailed at dawn of the day we left Port
Broughton and was at Queenstown an hour or so before we anchored. We had sailed farther, and claimed the 'race'. Every
other ship was beaten by from four to forty-eight days. It was
the same old de Cloux, though *Parma* was no *Herzogin Cecilie*.
I believe if de Cloux had had the sluggard *Mozart*, he would
still have won the grain race twice in three starts.

We discharged at Cardiff, and sailed from there to Mariehamn to lay up until it was time to sail out for grain again.
Mariehamn was a cheap, safe port to rest in, and it was the
best place in the world to recruit crew. The dues charged a
big ship to lie a year there were £10. In the outer roads, it
cost nothing. Our profit on the first round voyage was £3,000 —

our whole capital returned to us, with the first cargo. Good depression! For this we had taken our lives in our hands, for the ship had broached-to and all but foundered in a great gale down by the Horn – a gale which drove the Swede *C. B. Pedersen* to Panama in distress. The *Melbourne* had been cut down by a steamer, and foundered so fast with her huge hold of grain that she sailed under without losing way. We knew what we were doing; we accepted the risks, which were considerable.

It was the end of August when we reached Mariehamn. In October the *Parma* sailed again, dry-docking at Burmeister's in Copenhagen on the way out. From Copenhagen she ran to Port Victoria for orders in ninety-six days. There was no hurry. We did not wish to lose any sails. The charter rate for grain that year was 28s 6d a ton, but since we now had no depreciation, no investment, and no overheads to worry about, and the Plimsoll marks had been moved up to give the ship an even greater carrying capacity, we were all right. She could now carry some 5,400 tons, if we wished to load her so deeply. No freight was paid on the sacks, which weighed altogether about 200 tons; but 5,200 times 28s 6d came to quite a tidy sum.

On this occasion we loaded at Port Victoria, which was nearer the open sea than Port Broughton. The bagged wheat was lightered out in small ketches and schooners, which crowded into Spencer Gulf for the wheat season. A tramp-owner had been nosing round Spencer Gulf trying to put the sailers out of business, but he soon discovered that he could not do it. He could not afford to anchor his steamers at such places as Port Broughton and Port Victoria and wait for the wheat to be lightered to them. His overheads were too high. Nor could he induce the growers to send their cargoes to larger ports for transhipment. Why should they? We were one of twenty-one sailing-ships (including the auxiliary *Magdalene Vinnen*) loading grain in the Gulf; so long as big sailing-ships could be run economically, there would be some grain for them there.

This time we sailed on March Ist. Our crew was thirty-two

hands all told. The German cadets from the previous voyage were now excellent young sailors, for nothing develops a boy more quickly than a sense of responsibility. We never had any regrets that our crew were boys, for their spirit was splendid and we had no troubles. The cadets stayed with us voyage after voyage until their time was in, and left regretfully, though as the Nazis rose to power in Germany some of our Germans turned Nazi, too, when they went home on leave, and scowled for a while at the idea of a Teuton being forced to serve in a Finnish ship. But they did not scowl for long.

Our passage from Port Victoria to Falmouth in 1932 was eighty-three days. It was one of the best runs for half a century. The *Beatrice* had long been broken up, then, and there was no faithful Sam Svensson to hint of *trolldom*. If de Cloux could *troller*, he certainly did it well on that occasion. The whole 15,000 miles was almost a soldiers' run – not a sail blown out, not a day without steerage way even in the doldrums, and only ten days with runs of less than 100 miles. We were thirty days to the Horn, fifty-six to the Line. We could not go wrong. The sea gods smiled on our *Parma* that happy voyage and upon all aboard. It was a glorious holiday. True, we had a stowaway; but he was an exceptional stowaway. He was a fine young sailor from steam-ships, who had heard so much about the classic training in sail that he was determined to stow away, to get his share of it. The days were gone when Aaland ships had to accept Consular refuse to fill their small crews. Boys and men were prepared to pay their passages from America and England down to Australia to join and pay a premium to work watch-and-watch a long voyage. There was scarcely a ship in the Erikson fleet without at least one book about her; many had two. Passengers abounded who delighted to pay ten shillings a day for their food and a bunk. In such circumstances, a plain seaman stood poor chance of a berth. Our stowaway was from the *Makura*, a steamer on the trans-Pacific run, and he hid in the hold with his sea-bag and his discharges, and all his gear. He was the only stowaway I have known who was really welcome. As a matter of fact, it was I who had told him to stow away, though I did suggest that he should choose a vessel other than the *Parma*.

From Falmouth we sailed to Hull to discharge, and thence to Mariehamn, though not to lay up. The dividend that year was a mere 70 per cent, with a substantial payment to reserves. We accepted a cargo of timber from the White Sea to London, and this paid the outward expenses to Australia. We reclassed at Copenhagen, where the ship arrived with so good a reputation that the old sea-dog who surveyed her took a very benevolent view; we renewed no plates. We knew just what metal stood in those pits; her plates were all right for a year or two yet. The renewal of pitted plates in a comparatively old steel ship can be a very expensive business. All else was in splendid order. The expense of reclassing her was negligible. We looked round for another ship to buy, and had hopes of getting hold of the Laeisz four-masters *Passat* and *Peking*. With these we could have started a sailing-ship line. But Gustaf Erikson did not want rivals in Mariehamn and bought *Passat* himself, for £6,500. *Peking* was sold to an English committee which wanted her for a stationary schoolship in the Medway. Herr Laeisz, noting our success in the grain trade, kept his other two four-masters, the more modern *Padua* and *Priwall*, and put them on the South Australian run, with considerable success.

We had to be satisfied with our *Parma*. I left her at Mariehamn in the summer of 1933; de Cloux left, when she had taken her timber cargo to London, in October of that year. She was again fixed for South Australian grain. Command was given to de Cloux's brother-in-law, I thought somewhat against his better judgement. The ship's luck changed with the change of masters. She began to have accidents, to lose boys overboard, to incur expenses which had not been foreseen and might have been avoided. She made no more famous passages. Indeed, her runs were mediocre; in 1934 even the *Mozart* and the *Grace Harwar* beat her easily. Only the small barque *Favell* had a longer passage, and she was on the reinsurance market.

Captain de Cloux's luck changed when he left the *Parma*, too. He went home to Aaland to carry on chicken-farming, he said, since there was not another sailing-ship we could buy. Within a few months he had bought a steamer. Steamers were cheap, and he thought, I suppose, that if others could make something out of them in the Baltic and North Sea trade there was no reason why he should not try it. He was still on the right side of fifty. He bought an old steamer named *Bodia* and put her in the North Sea tramping trade, mostly with timber. He took command, but there is a vast difference between deep-water sailing and piloting a powered vessel round those dangerous waters. A sailing-vessel is sailed to make the best passage she can, but a powered vessel must make good direct, economical courses. Before long, de Cloux began to have accidents, too. Perhaps he lacked the close knowledge of coastal waters which other masters had acquired through a lifetime's experience. At any rate, his *Bodia* was reported to have struck the bottom before very long. Some months later she was the subject of a salvage claim when she stranded again. Within a year or two she was a total loss, somewhere on the Norwegian coast.

It was a great pity de Cloux went into steam. He was without doubt a great deep-sea sailing-ship master, at his best when his whole energies were required for his ship and his was the driving force which made her passages. When an engine drove a floundering screw along, the same talents were not called for. Most of them then were of little value. A slight error of judgement in the highly skilled art of pilotage could have fatal results. A chance that did not quite come off, a failure – perhaps – to observe the deviation of the compass on a new course: these things could wreck the coastwise steamer. In a deep-sea sailing ship precise pilotage was an art not often needed and little exercised. In coastal steamers it was essential. I don't recall de Cloux or any other sailing-ship master I sailed with ever putting himself out very much to plot his vessel through narrow waters, with frequent accurate fixes and close watch of the surface water movement. There could have been little attempt to fix the position of the *Herzogin Cecilie* with much frequency, before she was wrecked at Salcombe in

Devon in 1936. A deep-water man may become contemptuous of coastwise work, or afraid of it.

By 1936 our *Parma* had gone. The brother-in-law had no luck. She made a run to Beira with timber from South Finland, and sailed thrice more in the grain race. In 1936, after a passage of 117 days from Port Victoria to Falmouth, she was in a minor collision with her tug in the Clyde. It was a small thing. But there was some damage to her bow. She still had those pitted plates. The cost of keeping her in commission was considered not to be worth incurring, and she was sold for scrap. The price she brought was more than we had paid for her, five years earlier.

Long before 1936, however, I had sold my shares to Captain de Cloux, and was off on another sort of sailing adventure. From my point of view the grandest thing about our *Parma* venture was the glorious chance it gave me to understudy Captain de Cloux. My previous experience was all before the mast, generally in hard-run ships. I was a puller and hauler, doing the bidding of mates. Now for the first time I had had an opportunity to learn just why all the pulling and hauling was done, to learn the art of sailing square-rigged ships under a great master who had shown, time and time again, that he could get more out of square canvas than any other man then in the trade. Captain de Cloux won the grain race from Australia more often than any other master mariner. He was a magnificent seaman, and it was a privilege to be his partner and to serve with him.

But I knew I could never rise to command in Finnish sail, for only Finnish nationals could graduate from that country's nautical academies. I could not gain any certificates there, no matter how well I mastered Swedish or how long I sailed in Finnish ships. There had not, then, been a deep-sea sailing-ship under the British flag since the *Garthpool* was run ashore on the Cape Verdes in 1929, and the state of things in the United States was no better.

I had to find some other way to achieve command, and I thought the time had come to set about doing that.

CHAPTER SEVENTEEN

MY OWN FULL-RIGGED SHIP

THERE were some features of our *Parma* venture about which I had never been happy. I had no control over what was done. I might be one of the principal owners, but we had no board and no board meetings. There was a corresponding owner ashore in the Aaland Islands, and there was de Cloux in the ship. According to de Cloux (who owned 40 per cent of the ship before I sold him back my shares at their cost), the corresponding owner was legally responsible for decisions, under Finnish law. I did not like our short-term view; I did not care for the failure to renew those pitted plates, for the ship was worth having some money spent upon her; I hated the idea of our sailors not receiving a fair wage. They were paid the wages ruling in Aaland. These were paltry. My fellow-owners said that to give more would be to spoil not only them but all the sailors in the islands. Perhaps they were right, but when I saw the hard-working bos'n come to the pay-table at Marie-hamn for a few wretched pounds after a voyage round the world, my reflections were not pleasant. True, I had often enough received a pittance from the same sort of ship; but I had not served as bos'n, nor had I thought the ships were paying 100 per cent dividends to their fortunate owners.

So I sold my shares without regret, and sought no further profit from them. I began to look about very seriously for a ship of my own. My intention was to buy a small sailing-ship, pre-ferably a brigantine, and using her as the only home I had or needed, man her with youngsters who would profit from the experience of sailing her. I wanted to do with a ship what Captain Suffern had tried to do with his Albert Park Lake establishment in Melbourne, years before, for I was a great believer in the value of experience under sail as a character builder for youth in a mechanized and maudlin age. True, sail-training was no longer necessary to gain any British certificate of sea-going competence, or preferment in the profession. But the sailing-ship still appealed to adventurous youth, and could be relied upon to develop them splendidly when they served her, whether they believed themselves destined for a sea career or not.

My own idea of a suitable vessel was a brigantine about 80 feet on the waterline, or perhaps a small barquentine. I wanted something with square rig because I thought I understood square sails, which are the best for deep-sea work. I had looked for a good brigantine around the world. I was too late. There were none, save in the Mediterranean and among the rice-ships from South-east India. I had the deep-water man's distrust of Mediterranean vessels, which to me seemed rigged for only the sunniest seas and unfit for real ocean-going. The same objection applied to the Jaffna brigs, which were designed for favourable monsoon sailing in the Burma rice trade. By 1934 there was not a brigantine left in the Baltic or all the South Seas; there was only an odd yacht of that rig in the United States and Britain. Yachts were expensive and unsuitable. Except for ocean racers, few big yachts seemed intended for serious sailing. In such vital matters as water supply, stores capacity, a decent place to work, sail-lockers, even adequate accommodation, most of them were woefully lacking. The main idea seemed to be to fill them with as many tiny cabins and chromium-plated bathrooms as possible. A chromium-plated bathroom is all very well; but the ship comes first. Without a staunch, seaworthy hull, easily driven through the water by a sensible suit of sails on a strong, low rig, neither ship nor yacht was of any use to me. I could have had the ideal brigantine designed for me, of course, and built somewhere, and indeed I seriously considered building in southern Tasmania, out of Huon pine, or from teak somewhere in China. But this would be very expensive.

As for barquentines, there were plenty of them both in the Mediterranean and in the Baltic. I thought the same objection applied to those of Mediterranean origin as to the brigantines, and most of those still sailing in the Baltic were ancient soft-wood vessels, hailing from Estonia and South Finland. They went to sea with their timber cargoes lashed to them by enormous chains so that one was not sure whether it was the hull that was floating, or the cargo. A softwood ship was no use for tropic seas even if she were otherwise fit to sail them, for the terredo worm would eat them through in no time. There were some good French fishing barquentines. I knew there had been a hundred or more of them out of Fécamp and St Malo alone, in 1924; in 1934 there still were at least thirty. But a codfish barquentine stinks to heaven and is generally a rough and homely vessel; those that came on the market were cheap, but the costs of reconditioning were bound to be heavy and might be alarming. Their timbers, too, would need good care, if they were not to go to pieces. It was my plan to sail long voyages at least to Australia, and to spend a good deal of time in eastern seas and round the South Seas islands.

I had begun to wonder whether I should ever find my ideal ship when one sunny day in June 1934, I chanced to be walking along the Langelinie in Copenhagen, down by the water-front. This was a favourite haunt of mine in that lovely seafaring capital. Off the Langelinie a most unusual sailing-ship was just getting under way. She was a tiny full-rigged ship, a veritable miniature, perfect in every detail, but almost ludicrously small to one accustomed to square-riggers of more than 3,000 tons. She was a graceful and dainty little thing, as she picked her way out of the harbour with that clean wake which tells of perfect underwater lines, and her rigging was full of boys. She was rigged with the old-fashioned single tops'ls and the long rigged-out jib-boom, which had gone out of fashion half a century and more before I went to sea. She was a little beauty, obviously designed from the golden days of deep-sea sail before the great steel sailing warehouses were thought of.

I gazed at her with admiration, but without a thought of ever buying such a vessel. Suddenly I became aware of a conversation in Danish at my elbow. A man was saying it was a pity that this ship was to be broken up, for she was due for replacement and her successor was already launched. To be broken up? My ears pricked up at that and I gazed at the ship with a completely new interest. I spoke to the Dane. Yes, he said, she was to be broken up. She had been for sale for some time, but no one had offered a bid for her. He wondered why I broke off the conversation abruptly and hurried to find a taxi-cab. It came to me suddenly that here was my ship, at last, though I had never thought of owning and sailing a single tops'l full-rigger.

I leapt into the cab and hastened to the office of a broker I knew on the Havnegade. I had come to Copenhagen at this broker's request for he had cabled me that he had a good barquentine named *Elisabeth* on offer cheaply. Knowing the fine old Marstal oak barquentine of that name, I hurried over, only to find that *Elisabeth* is a common name for Baltic sailers and the ship on offer was a softwood job built in Estonia, and already more than worn out. The best ship on the broker's books from my point of view was a schooner named *Alf*, a stout oaken vessel which had once been a brigantine, but some meddling fool had disposed of her yards and all the square sails with them. As a schooner she was not the ship for me.

As the cab hurried me along towards Hvilsom's the brokers, I turned over in my mind the opportunity which seemed to be presenting itself. This was another in the long line which, beginning with the *Sir James Clark Ross* Antarctic-bound at Hobart in 1923, had led to the *Herzogin Cecilie*, the *Grace Harwar*, and the profitable *Parma*. But what was I going to do with this minute full-rigged ship if I bought her? How could I keep her in commission? I knew I had neither capital nor income sufficient to run a ship like that indefinitely, for she would be expensive to run and it was highly unlikely that she could ever earn anything. She would be hard on her gear, and because of her rig she would need a bigger crew – much bigger – than I had ever expected to engage. There could be no fooling with a ship like that, or one would have the whole complicated structure of her rigging about one's ears in the twinkling of an eye, or sail her under.

She was the ideal schoolship. Here was a glorious opportunity to make available for others what sailing-ships and the sea had, I thought, meant for me – a full life and a happy one, and a development of character whereof I knew I was much in need and could have gained, probably in no other way. It seemed to me that all the warp and woof of my unorthodox career afloat and ashore had led to this – my sticking to sail, regardless of nationality, my books, my films. Even the late and unlamented Scrooge had his place in the pattern, for he had set my feet towards the world of publishing; and that led to capital, the investment in the *Parma*; more capital. I did not feel any glow of gratitude towards Scrooge; but I knew that I should never have imagined myself capable of handling such a vessel had it not been for the great stimulus of my experience under de Cloux. Above all, I had learned from him. Many of his mates had become masters, and most of them did well. There was, of course, the slight matter of my lack of any kind of Board of Trade certificate, but I did not let that worry me. If the far from brilliant ex-mate of the *Herzogin Cecilie* could handle a four-masted barque (as I knew he was doing), then I felt I could do at least as well as he, certificate or no certificate.

I burst in upon my friend Cahnbley at Hvilsom's and asked him if it were true the full-rigged ship was for sale. What ship? he asked, looking up slightly astonished from his catalogue of ketches and schooners. The *Georg Stage*, I said. Oh, yes, she was for sale. Probably little more than her scrap value would suffice to buy her, for there was no interest in her as a commercial proposition. She was in excellent order and had a very full inventory, but she could carry little if any cargo and might be fantastically expensive to sail. No one wanted to buy her.

'I'll buy her,' I said.

We sat down together and worked out her scrap value. It came to about £1,300. I instructed Cahnbley to make a bid on my behalf of £1,400. He did so that afternoon. It was accepted, for the committee responsible for the ship was worried lest there be no bid for her at all. The full purchase price was agreed at £1,571 0s 1d. What the penny was for I don't recall, but the £171 paid for 84 tons of pig-iron ballast, dry-docking and bottom-painting, and some extra stores which were not on her inventory.

I did not go near the ship then. There are some properties it is an insult to examine, when they have to go at prices ridiculously below their worth. The *Georg Stage* was a fairly old ship, for she was built in 1882. I knew she had been maintained in the Royal Danish naval dockyard, and she had sailed only in the summer months. She was built of Swedish iron, the most indestructible of ship materials, and she had been rigged down to her lower masts every winter. Her master for twenty years had been Captain J. B. Junker, an excellent man whose reputation I knew. These facts were enough. She was a better bargain than the *Parma*.

It was arranged that I should take delivery of the ship at the end of August, for she had to complete her summer cruise. She had eighty boys under training, and the new ship could not be ready before the following spring. I was asked to change the name, and the former owners requested permission to retain the figurehead, which was of Ship-owner Stage, for whom she was named. The following week a Polish committee arrived at Copenhagen, anxious to buy the *Georg Stage*, and they had more money to spend than I. It pays to seize opportunities.

It might pay to seize opportunities, but just how I was going to keep the ship in commission when I had her I didn't quite know. I had capital enough to make a good beginning. But she would cost at least £100 a week to run. The most sensible use for her, as a schoolship for boys, would be to cruise down to Rio or across to the West Indies in the winter months, and go coasting round the British Isles in summer, showing the flag. How did a private individual set about organizing and running a properly conducted schoolship for boys? I was, I suppose, a reasonably qualified able seaman. But I proposed to take command; and there was one thing I was determined she should never be. That was any sort of silly cooperative venture. Cooperation and the sailing-ship do not mix and cannot be blended. She would be run properly on grain-ship discipline or not at all. That ship belonged out of some English port, or Sydney, or Hobart. I could get her to any of those places, or perhaps all three. What then? I certainly could not afford to keep her in commission indefinitely as a philanthropic institution.

I could easily have made some money out of her. That is generally easy enough. No sooner was the news published that I had bought her than I was approached by promoters. But I would have none of them. Nonsense and the old *Georg Stage* had nothing in common. The promoters wished to exploit the romantic, adventurous appeal of the little ship in order to sell unnecessary products to a public grown accustomed to sales promotion by the more ordinary stunts. Well, they would get no help from me. There was a man, too, who had what he considered a great idea for sprinkling the 'tween-decks with sawdust and converting the ship into a sea-going bar-room for cruises from New York to the West Indies. This, he said, would pay handsomely. The ironic thing is that it probably would.

What really worried me, as I set about the business of organizing useful work for the ship, was that I was not sure that such a ship was wanted in either the England or Australia of the 1930s, or would find a place. I had few influential friends. An old shipmate from the *Bellands* – he in whose father's home at Golders Green Johnny Gleeson and I had once been glad to sleep – who now had a master mariner's licence in sail, opened the articles for me at Copenhagen, and had command for the North Sea crossing. I had trouble even about so simple a thing as registration. The authorities were unaccustomed to dealing with ex-foremast hands who suddenly turned up with a sailing-ship of their own, proposing to use the vessel as a schoolship. I was made to feel that I was suspect, as anyone must, I suppose, who brings a problem to officials they have not solved before. There was no precedent for my enterprise, unless they cared to go back to the days of Drake, and there was no record of the *Pelican*'s registration. I found myself rather envious of such mariners as Drake, as the days passed and my time was over-filled with finding solutions for a host of unnecessary problems. At least no one expected Drake to have a Board of Trade certificate.

I decided to make a voyage round the world, an ambling circumnavigation by way of Good Hope and the Horn, the East Indies and the South Seas; and to ship all the young fellows who cared to come and there was room for. It was my firm belief that such a voyage as this could not fail to be of incalculable benefit to any young fellow who had guts enough to go and to stay. I knew that the clean sailing-ship at sea was the ideal means of providing both time to think and food for thought. In its normal daily working throughout the making of a long passage against wind and sea, it would provide opportunities for all but clods to mould themselves into an efficient team in which they would feel necessary, and that their own skill and efforts really amounted to something worth while. This deprivation in youth of the sense of achievement, it seemed to me, was among the most destructive influences in our civilization; well, I could make my gesture to combat it. I could do the things I believed in, and I did not doubt that I could find boys enough to come along.

Yet for a while it seemed that I should not get my boys at all. About that time, and for years previously, almost since Joshua Slocum had sailed the *Spray* around the world, there had been several attempts to promote long voyages in yachts and unsuitable small sailing-ships. Such ideas were generally foolish, and at the worst might be criminal. There was no lack of gentlemen eager and able to get a few hundred pounds for themselves out of the desire of many young men to share in an adventure cruise. While I was fitting out the *Conrad* there was an old softwood schooner lying in a port on the north-east coast of England, in which a band of optimists had each invested £150, cash down, to a promoter who disappeared as soon as he had collected the money. It was then discovered that the schooner had been bought for £400 in the Baltic, beyond which she was not fit to sail. So far as I know she never did leave that English port. There were others who, though honest, had not the least idea of the problems of a long voyage under sail, and found themselves in trouble before they got out of the English Channel, or past Cape Hatteras, if they hailed from the United States. The number of such enterprises, almost always ill-conceived, was astonishing, and the publicity given to the failures was far in excess of that given to the occasional quiet fellow who went off without cooperative enthusiasts and actually succeeded in making the voyage he had planned. There were many of these, too.

At any rate, I felt that I was right. I had the feeling, too, that the Lord would not have led my feet along the Langelinie upon the only day when all circumstances were right for my acquisition of that full-rigged ship – she was there only by accident, just for an hour or two; a week later the Poles would have had her – unless it were also His will that I should do what I could with her for such youth as cared to come along. I set out with high ideals, and I never saw any evidence that they were wrong. Nor did I give them up.

I got hold of a nucleus of skilled sailing-ship men from the *Parma*, the *Penang*, and the Danish schoolships. I changed the name of the ship to *Joseph Conrad*, fitted her out at Ipswich on the Orwell in England, and on October 22nd, 1934, sailed from Harwich at the Orwell's mouth, bound in the first instance towards New York by way of the West Indies. I had twelve cadets, and the wind was south-west in the Channel, with a gale warning. I knew that I had overcome already the worst gale which could threaten that voyage, in getting the ship registered and setting out at all.

One great regret I had as I looked back towards England and the gale blew. There was a man there who should have been along – several men. It is a sad fact that those who lead full and worthwhile lives rarely find leisure to follow their inclinations; my guest cabins were all but empty, and they remained like that throughout the voyage. The name of the man I regretted leaving in England was T. E. Lawrence. He chose to be known as Shaw. Helping to sail the ship from Copenhagen to Ipswich were some friends from the literary world. One of these was Bruce Rogers, the typographer, who had then recently completed work on the book of Lawrence's translation of the *Odyssey*. B. R. was an enthusiast for sail and had already made a passage or two in the Erikson ships, between England and Mariehamn. He conceived the idea of establishing a press in the after-'tween-decks of the *Joseph Conrad*, where he and Lawrence could amuse themselves bringing out fine books throughout the voyage. It was a grand idea. Lawrence was at Plymouth at the time, working with the high-speed marine unit of the Royal Air Force. He was due to come out of the Royal Air Force in a month or two and would then, I gathered, be at something of a loose end. He had a tiny cottage somewhere in the country, but the press photographers had discovered it and stoned him out of it, throwing stones on the roof to force him out in order that they could sell pictures of him. The idea of the 'tween-decks press appealed to Lawrence. It is a pity that the idea came to nothing. He might have joined us later; but he was dead before we reached Rio.

B. R. painted the lettering at bow and stern, and on the boats and lifebelts. Later he carved a fine figurehead of Captain Conrad to adorn the bows, where once the bronze of Herr Georg Stage had stared at the cold North Sea. But he did not make a long passage.

I beat for a week in the English Channel, and that week made men of the boys aboard. The gale screamed and the short seas were fierce and boisterous. But the ship sailed well, and she beat out. I crossed the Bay and was pleased that these difficult pieces of sailing came so early in the voyage, for they were an excellent test of ship and crew. Both came through the trial splendidly. Fine little ship! She was a beauty, and seemed to delight to find the open sea before her bows — thousands of miles of it — after her half-century of Baltic waters and the North Sea. I stood down to the trades and romped across in the north-east towards the Bahamas the way Columbus sailed, and the little ship seemed to think she was on a holiday. It was great to be at sea, to watch and to guide the lovely ship as she ran upon her way, upright, graceful, sea-worthy, loyal. If only human beings could be as she was!

To walk that tiny quarter-deck between the signalling guns and the rail was a source of never-ending delight, though my major occupation then and upon all such occasions was to exercise myself mentally at coping with emergencies, for I was well aware of my limitations in command. It was my custom to imagine every possible kind of calamity or accident, and work out ways of dealing with it upon the instant. Man overboard! my inner mind would shout as I turned in my stride. What now? I would size up the situation, decide upon ways and means, work the thing out to the finest details under all possible conditions. Sudden shift of wind catches her by the lee. What now? Then I would work that one out. Jib-boom carried away. Sudden squall with eight-point jump of wind; helmsman puts the wheel the wrong way. Fore-topmast stay carried away. Main brace gone. Fore-topmast head sprung. Steering chains gone. Fire in the paint locker! There was no end to the calamities I imagined, and the exercise of working out how to cope with them was valuable and frequently of direct use, later, when just such accidents occurred. If I thought of one which defeated me, for the moment, I puzzled it out later or read it up in the seamanship manuals (if they dealt with it), or discussed it with old sailing-ship men ashore who knew the answers. After all, the *Joseph Conrad* was a small ship with a lot of rigging, and all her yards were wooden. She was a very different proposition from the huge steel ships of the Australian grain trade, which could stand up to anything. She had been designed as a ship from the great days of sail; as such, she was perhaps a little fragile for a long, hard voyage. I carried away the jib-boom before we reached Madeira, and sprung both the fore and main topgallant masts and many of the more important yards before the circumnavigation was over.

In New York I suffered an accident I had not foreseen, for I had associated only financial calamities with ports. The ship dragged ashore in a harbour gale during the first night of 1935, and it cost me £2,000 to put things to rights again. This accident had one curious result, for as soon as calamity assailed me so also did the publicity world of radio, films, and newspapers. The ship which as a sailing entity was not worth a foot of newsreel film or a mention on any broadcast was, as a seeming wreck, worth shouting about all round the world. At the time some of the shouting annoyed me greatly. It was almost completely ignorant, and frequently libellous. But the man who declared, 'Print my name: I don't care what you say, but print my name,' was on right lines. The world did not share my view that the publicity was adverse, but remembered only the ship's name and the apparent romance of her voyage.

Until the accident I had intended to round the Horn from east to west, the classic way, and to wander across the South Pacific before the trades as the pioneers had done – Cook, Byron, Carteret, Bougainville, the Hollanders Schouten and le Maire. For a square-rigged ship not bound to Australia, this was the best way to round the world, for the trades of the Pacific and the regular Indian Ocean winds would bring a ship from north of the Horn almost to Good Hope, and the south winds would waft her on from there and bring her to the Atlantic trades. But beating round the Horn might be bad. Indeed, for a little ship with a lot of rigging, high bulwarks, and a vulnerable maindeck (it was full of openings to give access to the 'tween-decks accommodation: she was all accommodation) it might be dangerous. I decided, therefore, to sail round the world the other way, from west to east – down to Rio first, then eastwards round the Cape and to the East Indies, the

South Seas, and onwards again eastwards round the Horn. This way the west winds were usable, but it might be difficult to call at many islands.

I sailed down to Rio in fifty-seven days, while the ship licked her wounds from the New York winter's grounding. From Rio to the Cape took a month, with a look at Tristan da Cunha. From the Cape to the Straits of Bali, seven weeks. I sailed through Bali Straits by night, despite the race there. I was young then. From Bali – no place for a schoolship – I went to Singapore, and then up through the South China Sea and the Sulu Sea, north-about towards Melanesia and Australia. The passage this way was difficult and trying, but I used that route for its interest, and to try to discover how the early Spanish and Portuguese sailors had made any longitude there with much the same sort of ship. Some of them had had great difficulty. I found that sailing eastwards in the North Pacific, just north of New Guinea and its islands, was tedious, but possible. It took me five months to reach the Solomons. I had not hurried. What use was it to be circumnavigating in my own vessel if I did not stop now and again to visit interesting islands? It was unlikely I should have such a chance again.

At the Solomons there was bad malaria. I made for Sydney, where the ship was welcomed with enthusiasm, but no one suggested I should base her there, to become a schoolship out of that excellent port. I was wined and dined by the great and the near-great, and so many persons wished to visit the ship that an enterprising ferry company began a service to her anchorage. She looked splendid in Sydney harbour; but there was apparently no home there for her. My funds had almost run out, and I was worried as I hove up the anchor and beat out under a press of sail. Overhead, newspaper aircraft flew, taking photographs, and launches followed us. The sun shone and an old square-rig pilot was having the day of his life putting her through her paces between the Heads. But that beautiful ship which had sailed so far was leaving Sydney for ever: not a voice was raised to detain her.

The Tasman Sea blew up its sudden gales, and I had to beat to Melbourne. We were blown about in the Tasman Sea, and the beat took me thirteen days.

I got out of Melbourne by joining the board of a gold-mining company with interests in the Louisiades, and I took their prospector and engineer with me, bound towards the island of Tagula. The prospector was alleged to know of a new alluvial gold-field somewhere on the slopes of Mount Rattlesnake, upon Tagula. After a couple of months of close contact with this gentleman I should say that the only gold he ever knew about was in his teeth, and there was precious little there. It was a queer enterprise. It meant that I must sail right into the farthest leeward corner of the blasted Coral Sea, that reef-littered zone of maritime treachery, and somehow beat out again, in the cyclone season. A Coral Sea cyclone is a West Indies hurricane by another name, not the kind of sailing breeze one would seek by choice. I had no choice. I paid all the bills in the *Joseph Conrad*. Her voyage was entirely my enterprise, and I had not as much as a first lieutenant. In Melbourne I had to take the gold-men or stay there. I took them. The prospector and his gang had not heard of the cyclone season and did not realize what they had let themselves in for. I sailed to Auckland first, to get to windward, and ran from there with a blow or two towards New Guinea. I had to enter the ship at Samarai before going to Tagula. At Samarai the gold-men left. They had had enough. Whether they ever reached their island I don't know; but I noticed that the company was wound up not very long afterwards.

From Samarai I beat a thousand miles and more to the open sea beyond Lord Howe Island. It would have been easier to sail the Torres Straits way, and circumnavigate Australia. The beat out of the Coral Sea was hot, trying, and extremely difficult. That part of the Pacific is not thoroughly surveyed, and abounds with dangers. Along the whole of my track the set and the wind were against me, trying to force the ship on the Great Barrier Reef. Reefs, islets, and even islands are unlit. The weather at that time of the year was atrocious. The tail-end of a cyclone bore down on me, and I sprung the fore-topmast head, the fore-yard, and the main topgallant mast, fighting against it lest it ham me on a reef. The reefs are precipitous, and steep-to. Visibility was frequently poor. My progress was one long, dour beat. To wind'ard! To wind'ard! Day after day, week after week: sometimes at the end of a week's hard beating I had made sixty miles.

But all the ocean world is not the Coral Sea, thank God. In due course I came to Lord Howe Island, and stood on from there through the west winds again towards Tahiti. From Samarai to Tahiti I was seventy-nine days, and came in to find that shore experts who had measured the distance with dividers on a chart and made no allowance for adverse winds had declared the ship was missing. Some wreckage had drifted ashore somewhere in New Zealand: it must be us. A distress flare was seen off the south of Tasmania: it must be us. All we had lost was a boat, washed from its davits in a wild gale: nothing else was missing.

From Tahiti to New York, round the Horn, I was 106 days. The little ship ran nobly in the great midwinter seas, though I had to heave-to four times when the sea was too great to run on. She lay quietly, hove-to, like an albatross at home upon the raging waters. Brave little ship! She did not let me down. Yet I knew when I sailed her into the port of New York at the voyage end that I could sail the ship no longer, and it seemed futile to take her back to England. I had hoped to keep the ship and to organize some further sailing for her somehow. Her boys were good and had developed splendidly, but all my capital and income were dispersed in this endeavour. With the anchor down in New York at the end of the 57,000-mile voyage, I had not a penny in the world, and liabilities of more than £3,000. Three thousand pounds! How paltry a sum that was, compared with the good it could do in that lovely ship. The voyage had cost £15,000. Well, thank God I had had the sum. It came from the sea. Now it had gone back to the sea again, which was the way things should be.

The ship was berthed in Tebo's yard at the foot of Twenty-third Street in Brooklyn, and a crowd of girl mariners played in the rigging. Meanwhile I got on with repairing the rigging, hoping against hope to keep the ship for another voyage. One day a rich young man came to the yard, looking for a diesel yacht to charter for the Miami season. He took a liking to the lovely figurehead Bruce Rogers had carved and, in tow of a broker, came aboard. He was a nice young man.

Would I sell the figurehead? Somehow the question was asked.

Not without the ship, I said, almost jokingly, though the matter was no joke.

All right: how much was the ship?

Three thousand pounds, I said, for that was the extent of my liabilities on her behalf, including the costs of paying-off and repatriating the crew.

I'll pay that, said the young man.

As easy as that. So the ship was sold. I paid off my crew and dispersed them round the world: so ended my schoolship adventure, and I wondered what its worth was. True, I had saved the ship from the break-up yards, though the Polish committee would have done that equally as well. I had sailed her round the world and had lost no life, and hurt nobody. I had kept my ideals and stood no nonsense. As a schoolship her curriculum was unorthodox, for the ship herself was the chief instructor. There could have been no better; years afterwards those boys turned out splendidly when there was a desperate call for courageous young men. As submarine commanders, fighter pilots, secret agents, Eighth Army soldiers, sub-chaser men, they did magnificently, and half of them died. Not a boy or a young man trod the *Conrad*'s decks who did not benefit by that voyage; and now I had to sell her to a rich young man who proposed to convert her into a yacht for his personal use, the kind of ship I most detested, the good ship turned harlot to be an idle piece of well-proportioned scenery at selected anchorages in the right season of the year. I had sailed round the world to deliver a 'yacht' to a Fifth Avenue millionaire, who would provide no opportunities for the training of youth, and would immediately set about putting power in the vessel, and chromium-plated bathrooms.

I hurried away to sail with the Arabs in their deep-sea dhows across the Indian Ocean, for there are no chromium bathrooms in an Arab dhow.

CHAPTER EIGHTEEN

A PLACE FOR SAIL

My sailing with the Arabs was part of a programme to occupy at least five years, by which I hoped to acquaint myself with the sailing-vessels of the world. After the *Joseph Conrad*, any other European sailing-ship would be an anticlimax; but there were still large fleets going quietly about their share of the world's sea-borne trade in the Indian Ocean and the waters of East Asia. After a year or two in dhows, I proposed to move on to India and to make at least a passage down to Mombasa with a deep-waterman from the Malabar coast, and sail a while in the Bay of Bengal with the Burma rice barques. After that my plan included a year in the Malay Archipelago with a passage in a high-pooped Makassar ketch-rigged *prau*, a teak run with a Chinese *tongkang* up some Sumatran or Borneo river, and a sail in a Balinese schooner; then to China and Japan to study junks at first hand. I should sail also in whatever sea-going canoes I could still find in the Trobriands, in a Moresby *lakatoi*, and a Maldives brig.

All this seemed to me worth while, and it was work in which I was interested. If ever I felt the need for leave from the East I could spend a month or two in a Greek *caique*, or some Syrian or Adriatic schooner, a Portuguese Grand Banker, or a West Indies sponge fisherman. A life of wandering in sailing-ships appealed to me, and I proposed to make an exhaustive survey of the types of ship and the trades I came across, and to photograph and make films as records. I could, I hoped, finance all this by writing, and an occasional lecture.

I admired the Arab mariners, though life with them was tough, even after years of Cape Horners. I sailed first in a small fast double-ender, called a *zarook*, which traded in the hot Red Sea. She was an open boat about forty feet long, with a glorious underwater body, a crew of hardy Yemenites, and an incredible thirst for the sea. She had no lights, no pumps, no charts, no compass, no decks, and no accommodation; but she had a lovely lateen sail which pulled her along magnificently among the Red Sea reefs, and her master and his sailors knew their business. Her bulwarks were built up – optimistically, I thought – with lengths of datefrond matting; her cordage was twisted by her sailors from the husks of Indian coconuts; her sails were sewn from the lightest Bombay cotton-stuff, on the sands at Mocha. She was bailed out hourly, under way, and her bilge-water stank like Hades. She was smothered with fish-oil of poor quality, and innumerable fat cockroaches overran her. But the wind and the sea accepted her gloriously as a companion fit for them, and she sailed in harmony upon a bright blue ocean which carried her lightly on its smiling breast. Her galley was a fire-pot for which there was little fuel; her food was fish from the sea, cooked in ashes, with sometimes a handful of rice or dates, and a little *ghee*. Her master was a quiet man who sailed her under God, well aware of his great debt to the Deity, and he and all the mariners prayed fervently, facing Mecca, five times daily. The master of that little dhow reminded me of the captain of the ship *Grace Harwar*. They had much the same outlook and the same competence. I suffered from malaria and from dysentery, and the *zarook* nearly killed me.

After that, when I had recovered, I made a voyage in a Kuwait deep-waterman in the trade to Zanzibar. She was a decked vessel, double-ended; she might have registered about 150 tons had she ever been measured for registration. The Arabs were opponents of the idea of submission to too thorough a method of identification for the benefit of Europeans; they knew their own vessels. The *boom* I sailed in had a different name in every major port, but to the Arabs she was known always by the name of her master. She was a good ship, and sailed splendidly. She traded with dates from Basra round the southern coasts of Arabia and to Berbera in Somaliland. With the funds from this she bought a cargo to be hawked down the coast of East Africa as far as the monsoon blew, and carried passengers by the hundred whenever any could be induced to ship in her. There was an age-old movement of the Hadhramaut Arabs down to Mombasa and Zanzibar, and she did well in this migrant trade, though she offered no proper accommodation. The passengers crowded aboard, and made the best of it on her spacious decks or in her longboat, wherever they could stow themselves and their few possessions. There were so many at one stage that their possessions hung outboard all along the rails, for there was no room left for them inboard.

I had six feet of the *nakhoda*'s bench, in the after-end of the poop, by the wheel. I had a carpet to sleep on, and the unleavened bread, strong coffee, sweet tea, and fish from the sea to live upon. The Arabs were a pleasant crew and I got on well with them, though the ship blinded me for a while, and again I suffered from malaria and dysentery, and a few other things. I lived for eight months on my six feet of bench in the open, and I photographed and made notes daily. Why anyone should wish to do such things, or how find time to do them, was beyond the sailors' comprehension, but they accepted me and were too courteous to ask questions. I learned that the loveliest of all big dhow types, the carved-stern *baggala* of the Persian Gulf, was rapidly approaching extinction, for modern haste had penetrated even the Gulf dhow-building ports, and the double-ended *boom* was both cheaper and faster to build, for it lacked all ornament, and was better in a seaway. A plan I made for saving one of the last Kuwait *baggalas* appealed to the Arab sense of adventure, and I was negotiating for the purchase of a lovely vessel of this type – the price was 4,000 Indian rupees – and doing some pearling on the Gulf banks, when the 1939–45 War burst upon the world.

That was the end of my eastern adventures. I hurried to England, writing a book about the Arab sailors on the way, and tried to join the Navy. Not without difficulty, I was at length granted a temporary commission in the Royal Naval Volunteer Reserve. In the tumult of the following years the quiet philosophy I had learned among the Arab mariners was of real value.

It took a long time to be accepted in the Navy, and even longer to feel that I was usefully employed. I was a watchkeeping officer first, in a special service vessel which never went anywhere. The almost complete immobility of this vessel – in the whole war she moved, I believe, three times – was due to two causes: the first, that when she was fitted with all the auxiliaries and so forth which were considered necessary to her special functions, her main boilers could scarcely spare steam to move her; and the second, that by the time she was ready to go anywhere there was almost nowhere left in Europe, for the time being, where she could go. I might have spent most of the war, quietly forgotten, aboard this vessel, but my strenuous efforts to get out of her resulted, in a few months, in an appointment ashore to be an instructor at a Coastal Forces training base, after an interlude minesweeping in the Channel. This work, though interesting, did not appeal to me.

Wherever I was, I used my best endeavours to break the gunners of their unfortunate habit of shooting down their own aircraft, which could ill be spared at the time. For this effrontery I was appointed to Combined Operations, that Cinderella of the services, and sent in due course to Norfolk, in Virginia. Here I found myself one of the squadron-commanders charged with the formation of squadrons of a new type of landing-craft, which might or might not be ocean-going, but were to cross the North Atlantic in midwinter to find out. These vessels were regarded, more or less, as expendable, and so were the officers in them. No escort of any kind could be spared for them, but it was hoped that the greater part of each squadron might arrive at its destination as they were required to land the Eighth Army, and others, in Sicily and Italy. They were armed with four 20-mm quick-firing cannons each. They steered like tramcars with electric power and a gadget like a carman's switch; they looked like welded steel orange-boxes, and their plates were so thin that in places they yielded at the tread of their sailors' feet, like sheets of thin plywood. They were mass-produced, like automobiles, and women welded them together at assembly points on the east coast of the United States. They were powered with eight bus engines each, in two banks of four called quads, each quad being geared to a variable pitch propeller which was adjusted electrically. To go astern, both propellers had to be adjusted to negative pitch. In charge of their intricate and expensive engine-rooms were garage hands, aged about nineteen. The little ships were full of sharp corners and protruding heavy ramps, whisker-booms, and the like, and the young gentlemen appointed to command them – few of whom had ever been to sea – used them at first as effective battering-rams. Many of them were assembled at Newark, by New York's harbour, and the ferries there soon learned to give them a wide berth.

The same young gentlemen, benefiting from their lack of sea experience and knowing not, perhaps, what they did, took the ships gaily over the North Atlantic which at the time was full of hostile submarines, any one of which could have sat upon the surface and sunk a whole squadron by gunfire with the greatest of ease, and little if any risk to itself. But the U-boats, probably alarmed at the strange profiles of the landing-craft and never imagining their real purpose, left us alone. I was glad of this, for the only 'gun' of any calibre in my squadron was made from a piece of a Norfolk telegraph pole. There was a nasty moment not far from the Azores, when an Admiralty signal informed me that a pack of submarines was shadowing my group, probably planning to attack. What do I do now? I wondered. It was dusk – a cold, miserable dusk, with the sea running lumpy, and high. It looked a cold place to drown in. I had twenty-four ships, a few depth-charges, some smoke-floats, and five officers of experience. If I knew where the U-boats were I would turn towards them with my little fleet; but I didn't know. I thought quickly. If I scattered (one of the few things a convoy could do when attacked) I would certainly disperse my squadron to the four winds and God alone knew where some of them might get to. More than that, I should then be advertising to the enemy that we were afraid of him. I could not turn towards him when I did not know where he was; the only thing to do was to stand on and disregard him. This we did, and there was no attack.

Months afterwards, we learned that the U-boats were afraid of us, thinking the landing-craft some new sort of scourge developed in America against them, for about that time there was alarm among some U-boat officers at their increasing rate of loss. The whisker-booms and the ramp outhaul wires at the bows of some of the ships increased the enemy's concern, for he feared that these were some new type of listening device to detect his presence. I saw nothing. If I had not received the Admiralty signal I never would have known the U-boats were there.

The queer little ships – they were called LCI(L) – proved themselves to be splendid sea-boats. Even successful attempts to carve them in two through collisions among themselves in the blacked-out nights did them no lasting harm. I have seen more than one of them cruising along at a good ten knots, with its hull flapping open like a piece of drifting seaweed, and the sea washing in and out of a fractured troop-space.

The manner in which these vessels played their part in the amphibious war must be told in another book, when the time is right for the writing of it. In their own way, they were good little ships, and they did splendidly in all the operations from Sicily onwards, at Reggio, Salerno, Anzio, in the Adriatic, and Normandy. When the bridgeheads were secure in France, my squadron was re-formed at once to go to the Far East, and we steamed from Plymouth to Bombay in thirty-five days. Thence to the Arakan coast and on for the landings at Rangoon, where the sight of a native sailing-vessel wandering placidly down an arm of the Irrawaddy was a startling glimpse of beauty on a murky morning. Later we found ourselves at Singapore, to help reopen the port; thence to Java and Sumatra, far up the Siak River; and on to Indo-China, and Siam. Both in Indo-China and Java there were still queer wars which were none of our business.

By early 1946, having run them hard for the preceding three years, I was required to return my LCI to the US Navy at Subic Bay in the Philippines, just north of Manila. Engine spares and maintenance had always been our greatest problems. By that time half the ships were working on not more than three of their eight engines and the whole lot were more or less decrepit. The original hope had been that they might last for one landing, perhaps two. But they were lend-lease ships, or had been. Mr Roosevelt was dead, and Washington had decreed that lend-lease ships must be returned. So somehow we managed to make half the squadron fit, more or less, to tow the other half, and in the teeth of a fresh monsoon struggled on to Subic Bay. My young gentlemen by that time were fine commanders of their specialized vessels, and many of the youthful chief engineers had developed genius. Though we felt no affection for the welded metal boxes which had carried us safely so far and through so much, we had a great respect for them. Makeshift products of a tremendous war, they had done well, with their bus engines and their gear-boxes and variable-pitch screws. I looked back at them, lying half a dozen at a buoy at the naval base of Olongapo on Subic Bay. There was not one among them that had not taken part in at least five great landings, during the preceding three years. They had steamed, on an average, at least 50,000 miles, and had carried troops – 200 each lift – by the ten-thousand. We had lost many on the way, to bombs, torpedoes, mines, gunfire. If a sailor ever had command of any of them it was by chance. Yet the landsmen had done well. There was a job to be done to which the ships and the seafaring were incidental, and they did it. Brave little ships! You did a good job, and you were well enough handled. If your sea careers were brief and you knew frustration, you also knew a little glory.

In September 1946, I was demobilized from the Royal Navy, and went to live in the Cotswold hills – not from choice, though the place is lovely, but because we had found a home there. Homes were scarce and sailing-ships scarcer, through the length and breadth of a troubled world. I had seen a few Akyab barques, Jaffna brigs, Singapore *tongkangs*, and Makassar *praus* struggling back to sea after the passing of the Japanese storm. I had seen them, but I could not sail in them. For the time being, that idea had to be shelved.

In the summer of 1948, still in the Cotswolds, I survey the state of sail in a world which has gained little from its wars. Two only of my old ships still survive – the *Joseph Conrad* and the big *Lawhill*. The rich young man who bought her from me did not keep my full-rigged ship for very long. He soon handed her over to the United States Maritime Commission, which turned her back into a schoolship. She did good work throughout the recent war attached to a vast academy somewhere in Florida, where she helped to produce seamen to man the American merchant marine. Later she was to be scrapped, and was taken to the lay-up berths, but the enterprise of the Marine Historial Association of Mystic, Connecticut – that famous old home of good clipper-ships – saved her from further ignominy. Early in 1948, I was aboard her at her berth by the whale-ship *Charles W. Morgan*, in the river at Mystic. She was considerably run down, but she is now in good hands and could be made fit to sail again. I hope she is, for there are years of life in the old iron hull yet, and still plenty of useful work for her to do.

The *Lawhill* is sailing under the South African flag, trading with grain from Australia. A firm of London brokers offered her recently for a price twice that which Gustaf Erikson paid for her in the 1914–18 War. I should much like to help the fine old ship survive, but a steel hull launched in 1892 has had its day. Even the faithful *Lawhill* cannot sail on for ever, though two world wars have failed to damage her.

In August 1947, Gustaf Erikson died at his home in Mariehamn. With him died the last of commercial deep-sea sail, though a publicized handful of square-riggers may struggle on for a while. Of all his ships, only the four-masted barques *Passat* and *Viking* remained in commission under his flag when he died. In less than a year it was reported that his heir was considering selling both of these. But who would buy them? This is no time for *Parma* ventures: if the mariners of Aaland cannot continue with unsubsidized sail, then it is a question whether anyone can. Even in Mariehamn it is difficult to recruit sailing-ship crews, for the war cost seven years of training for the deep-sea ships, and the flow of good young men dried up. Not as much as a firewood ketch sails there without power. Most of the masters who survived the war went into steam, or settled ashore. The young men are disinclined to serve in the Cape Horners, when they may earn an easier living in powered vessels.

It is a pity that the Cape Horn ship must go, if all the great traditions she built up are allowed to die with her. Among man's working creations for the carriage of his goods, they alone were supremely beautiful. They were swamped in a raucous era of mechanized things, just as they might have approached their period of greatest perfection. This was not the age of the clipper-ship, though these were magnificent. Rather it could have been the age of improved *Preussen*s and *Potosi*s, big-capacity ships which sailed well, with large sail areas and comparatively small crews. These were splendid sailing-ships. Too many sailors forget just how good they were, for when the talk is of sea speeds under sail, it is nearly always the odd great run of some lightly loaded, kite-filled clipper that is lauded. The five-masted full-rigged ship *Preussen* carried more than 6,000 tons of cargo and had to beat to the westward round Cape Horn on every voyage; throughout her life (cut short in the English Channel when a stupid steamer grossly misjudged her speed and rammed her) she averaged six knots on all her voyages, short and long, outwards and homewards. The five-masted barque *Potosi* once sailed from the Line to the Lizard in sixteen days; her average passage for the 10,000-mile run from Cape Horn to the Channel over a period of ten years was fifty-four days – a thousand miles *under sail alone* every five and a half days. Many a powered convoy in the war would have been glad of such an average.

Preussen and *Potosi*, though magnificent spectacles and great pieces of sailing-ship engineering, were probably poor things aerodynamically. Something of the great tradition of these ships and their Flying 'P' sisters still survives in Hamburg. The Germans might be allowed to develop an improved type of sailing-ship, if no one else is interested — a wind-driven vessel whose sails would take advantage of all that has been learned from the wings of gliders and powered aircraft. It was the misfortune of the great Laiesz ships to come late, when the European world was already power-crazed, and when the last Yankee clipper had gone to the scrap-heap. The hurrying world was interested only in mechanical advancement, even in man, and considered progress at sea possible only in vessels which made their way despite the wind and the sea, driven by ever-mounting power down below. But the sources of power may easily go, or no longer be accessible to all who wish to draw on them.

The mechanization of all sea-borne trade, bringing with it the development of huge ships and great companies which can survive only while all the complex economic and social structure they serve and spring from is maintained with them, brings with it also a serious threat. Man is not yet so great that he has no need of the simple natural things, the gifts of God. Already the mounting difficulties in the supply of fuel-oil and the enormous increase in the costs of powered vessels are causing some owners to wonder whether they ought to reconsider their earlier decision, that the days of deep-sea sail were done. There are many trades in which the sailing-ship could still play a useful part. A civilization which has survived two world wars in a generation ought not to neglect the use of the wind as a propellant for ships at sea and discard knowledge which has been built up painfully through centuries of brave sailing.

There should still be a place for the sailing-ship in some form or other, while man must move his goods by sea and the ocean winds blow.

The voyages of the *Rothesay Bay*,
the *Bellands*, the *Lawhill* and
the *Herzogin Cecilie*

The voyages of the *Grace Harwar*,
the *Parma*, the *Joseph Conrad* and
the Arab dhows

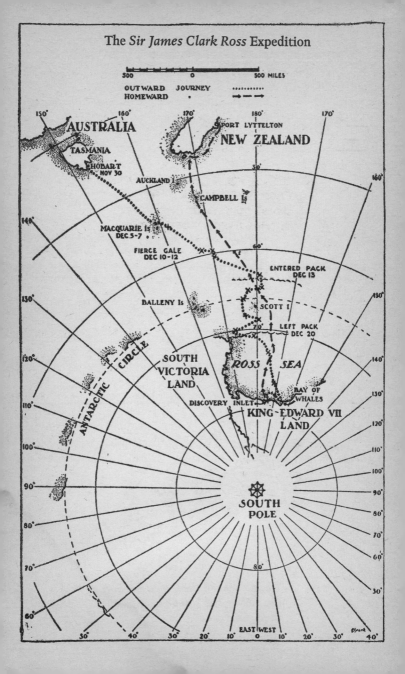

The *Sir James Clark Ross* Expedition

500 0 500 MILES

OUTWARD JOURNEY ....
HOMEWARD ←— •→

150° 160° 170° 180° 170° 160°

AUSTRALIA PORT LYTTELTON
NEW ZEALAND

TASMANIA
HOBART
NOV 30

AUCKLAND I. 50°

CAMPBELL IS

140°
MACQUARIE IS
DEC 5-7 60°

FIERCE GALE
DEC 10-12 ENTERED PACK
DEC 13

130°
BALLENY IS SCOTT I 130°

LEFT PACK
DEC 20
70°

ANTARCTIC CIRCLE
120°
SOUTH
VICTORIA
LAND **ROSS SEA** 140°

BAY OF
WHALES 130°

110° DISCOVERY INLET
**KING EDWARD VII
LAND** 120°

100° 110°

90° ✸
**SOUTH
POLE** 90°

80° 80°

70° 60°

80° 50°

60°

50° 40° 30° 20° 10° EAST WEST 10° 20° 30° 40°

If you have enjoyed this PAN Book, you may like to choose your next book from the titles listed on the following pages.

Alan Villiers

THE CRUISE OF THE CONRAD 40p

A classic in the literature of the sea by a man whose experiences under sail are unique and whose fame as a writer on ships and the sea is world-wide.

'No other story like this will ever be written' – SUNDAY TIMES

'A new chapter in the literature of the sea that will thrill all sailors and that even the dullest land-lubber will read with a stirring of the pulses' – DAILY TELEGRAPH